ON
hitler's
MOUNTAIN

WILLIAM MORROW *An Imprint of* HarperCollins *Publishers*

ON

hitler's

MOUNTAIN

OVERCOMING THE LEGACY

OF A NAZI CHILDHOOD

IRMGARD A. HUNT

Photograph Credits
From the author's personal collection: pages 10, 11, 16, 18, 24, 27, 30, 32, 43, 49, 53, 87, 88, 98, 100, 103, 110, 121, 150, 167, 172, 234, 253, 257, 260, 263, 268, 271, 273, 274; from Foto Ammon, Berchtesgaden: pages 38, 78, 246; from the National Archives, College Park, MD: pages 51, 57, 68, 80, 82, 174, 196, 209, 210, 212, 223, 240; from Archiv Christoph Links Verlag, Berlin: pages 72, 76; from Archiv der Gemeinde, Berchtesgaden: page 113; from Shubhani Sarkar: pages ii–iii, 7, 35, 95, 219.

HarperCollins books may be purchased for educational, business, or sales promotional use. For information please write: Special Markets Department, HarperCollins Publishers Inc., 10 East 53rd Street, New York, NY 10022.

FIRST EDITION

Book design by Shubhani Sarkar

Cartography by Philip Schwartzberg, Meridian Mapping, Minneapolis

Printed on acid-free paper

Library of Congress Cataloging-in-Publication Data

Hunt, Irmgard A., 1934–
    On Hitler's mountain: overcoming the legacy of a Nazi childhood / Irmgard A. Hunt.—1st ed.
        p. cm.
    ISBN 0-06-053217-3
    1. Hunt, Irmgard A., 1934—Childhood and youth.
2. World War, 1939–1945—Personal narratives, German.
3. World War, 1939–1945—Children—Germany—Berchtesgaden. 4. Children—Germany—Berchtesgaden—Biography.   I. Title.

    DD247.H86A3 2005
    943'.36—dc22   2004049959

05 06 07 08 09 DIX/RRD 10 9 8 7 6 5 4 3 2 1

TO MY CHILDREN,
PETER AND INGRID

CONTENTS

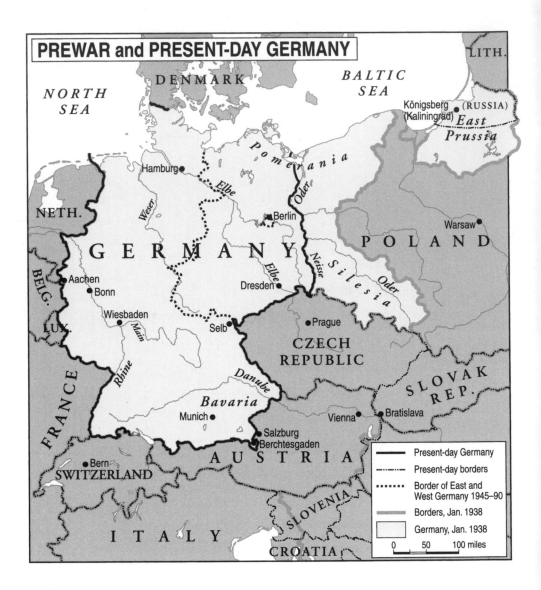

PREWAR and PRESENT-DAY GERMANY

LITH.

DENMARK

BALTIC
SEA

NORTH
SEA

Königsberg (RUSSIA)
(Kaliningrad) East
Prussia

Pomerania

Hamburg

Elbe

Oder

Berlin

Warsaw

NETH.

Weser

GERMANY

POLAND

Neisse

Silesia

BELG.

Aachen
Bonn

Elbe

Dresden

Oder

Wiesbaden

Main

Selb

Prague

LUX.

Rhine

CZECH
REPUBLIC

Danube

Bavaria

SLOVAK
REP.

FRANCE

Munich

Vienna

Bratislava

Salzburg
Berchtesgaden

AUSTRIA

Bern
SWITZERLAND

SLOVENIA

ITALY

CROATIA

Present-day Germany

Present-day borders

Border of East and
West Germany 1945–90

Borders, Jan. 1938

Germany, Jan. 1938

0   50   100 miles

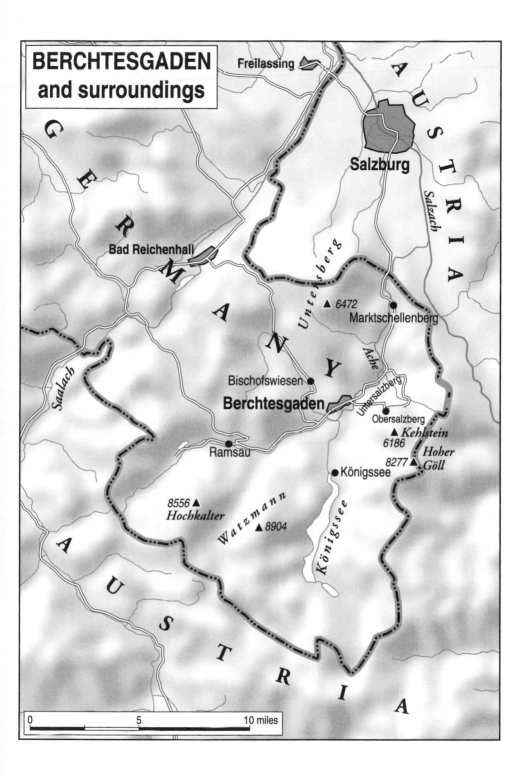

BERCHTESGADEN
and surroundings

Freilassing

AUSTRIA

Salzburg

GERMANY

Salzach

Bad Reichenhall

Untersberg

▲ 6472

Marktschellenberg

Ache

Bischofswiesen

Berchtesgaden

Untersalzberg

Obersalzberg

Saalach

▲ Kehlstein
6186

Hoher
Göll
8277 ▲

Ramsau

Königssee

8556 ▲
Hochkalter

Watzmann

▲ 8904

Königssee

AUSTRIA

0   5   10 miles

PREFACE: ON WRITING
A CHILDHOOD MEMOIR

A SENSE OF GREAT URGENCY, AFTER YEARS OF
postponement, propelled me to write this memoir. With the passing of my parents' generation many facts of everyday life under the
Nazis and the German people's feelings about the Nazi experience
are already lost forever. Firsthand accounts by the average, law-
abiding, middle-class German who helped sweep Hitler to power
and then supported him to the end are becoming a rarity. Yet the
seemingly petty details of these people's lives are actually often
symbolic and always telling. They illuminate the societal transitions from pre-Nazi, to Nazi, to post-Nazi, and from a post–World
War I to a post–World War II mind-set. In the continuing struggle
to understand the past—both personally and as a lesson from
history—these details are too important not to be recorded and
thus preserved.

Of course historians have written countless volumes docu-
menting and analyzing Hitler and the Third Reich. Biographers,
survivors, perpetrators, diarists in hiding, and novelists have presented the stories of Nazi criminals and power brokers; famous
scientists and artists who either "went along" or were killed or
forced into exile; politicians and military leaders of the era; and,
powerfully so, the victims of the Holocaust and all others who suffered the horrors of the concentration camps. Yet even now, when
enough distance from these events allows and even welcomes accounts of the Nazi era and the war from the German perspective,
little has emerged about the daily lives of German families who

considered themselves moral, honorable, and hardworking and whose adult members expected to live decent, respectable lives. It was those adults, those ordinary citizens, who most wanted to forget the past once the Nazi years were over and who preferred not to recall their participation in the Third Reich.

It was left to the next generation—my own—to seek to discover what people thought, knew, and chose to do and how it was possible for Hitler to receive their silent cooperation and often enthusiastic support. A universal answer may never be found, but perhaps an examination of just one family, mine, can provide additional understanding of what paved the way to Hitler's success and led to wholesale disaster.

I grew up in the beautiful mountains and villages of Berchtesgaden—a wide, multibranched valley located in a part of Bavaria that juts like a thumb into the Austrian Alps. I was born there in 1934, a year after my parents had voted for Hitler and he had assumed power. Hitler had chosen Obersalzberg, a hamlet above Berchtesgaden, as his home and headquarters. His presence on that mountain stamped my early years with a uniqueness that could not be claimed by other middle-class children elsewhere in Germany. The mountain loomed large over every aspect of my childhood in this highly visible and public place, in the shadow of the Eagle's Nest and near the lair of men whom the world would come to view as monsters.

How does one remember early childhood events? Once I began the task of thinking back, I realized that my childhood memories have to a great degree remained vividly and indelibly imprinted on my mind. I was a very curious, somewhat critical child, and according to my aunt, I had a precocious talent for eavesdropping and spying. For lack of entertaining or varied media offerings and other diversions, the people of Berchtesgaden, including my family and friends, thrived on local gossip, word-of-mouth news, and repeatedly told tales. The grown-ups talked and I listened, building a reservoir of recalled stories, rumors, and commentary about all that came to pass in my town during the years of Nazi rule.

Until it was quietly buried in 1945, the account of my meeting with Adolf Hitler was so much a part of our family lore that I committed every detail to memory even though I was only three and a half years old when the incident occurred. Since this is not a history but a memoir, my personal perceptions and hindsight have of course been allowed to color the happenings. Nonetheless, these impressions and perceptions that inevitably reshape memory give an accurate picture of the essence, the mood, the impact of any given event during those years.

This memoir is as much the story of my mother and my grandparents—all passed away—as it is my own. Many details from their lives and my babyhood came from Tante Emilie, ever cheerful, lucid, and full of memories at age ninety-six. During recent visits in Berchtesgaden, still home and summer home to my two sisters, I was greatly aided by long, frank conversations with them, their families, and friends whom I have known since my youth and who provided confirmations and a wealth of details. Old friends walked the old trails and the Obersalzbergstrasse with me, passing houses and cottages where we lived and played and where—unrecognizably now—the Nazi elite and the S.S. had held sway.

Thanks to my sisters and my cousins in Selb, I had access to family documents, marriage manuals, genealogical information required by the Nazis, my father's military records, letters from my Pöhlmann grandmother to her soldier husband written during World War I in the neat, steep, spiky German script that she had learned in grade school and had not practiced much since. To look at these letters was to hear the scratching of her steel pen on the lined, white pad of paper, to know from the darker script where she paused to dip her pen again into the black inkwell on the wobbly kitchen table, to sense her pauses and her hurry to finish and return to her endless chores. In addition, family photographs and documents from my mother's cupboard drawers were unearthed. They included the diary she kept during World War II, which, though terse, portrays the feelings and daily struggles of an average German woman, widowed and alone with her children, and touches on the major events of those years. The small accounting booklet she kept for eight years—1930–1937—paints a poignant picture of an utterly frugal life in which every pfennig was counted and tracked.

Throughout his years in power Hitler had remained enamored of Berchtesgaden and made some of his most momentous decisions, such as the pact with Stalin in 1939, on Obersalzberg. It was here that he received Chamberlain, Mussolini, and even the duke of Windsor and his American wife, Wallis Warfield Simpson. The conquest of Obersalzberg and the hoisting of the American flag by the 101st Airborne Division on the mountain were a fitting, symbolic ending to the war and the Third Reich.

Once the war ended and we were recovering from its anxieties and privations, we slowly began to realize to what degree the Nazis had shaped our minds and every detail of our daily lives, and the enormity of German guilt. I also began to appreciate those people, like my grandfather, who had expressed doubts, who had dared to be critical, and who, though basically powerless, had made brave attempts at resistance. They made a huge difference in my readiness to welcome the end of Hitler's reign and embrace new values despite the sadness over our many sacrifices and losses. Even then I made up my mind always to be on the lookout for the signs—however insidious and seemingly harmless—of dictatorships in the making and to resist politics that are exclusive, intolerant, or based on ideological zealotry and that demand unquestioned faith in one leader and a flag. I hope that young people everywhere learn to recognize the danger signs and join me in the mission to prevent a recurrence of one of history's most tragic chapters.

□   □

ON HITLER'S KNEE
OCTOBER 1937

A SHOUT WENT UP and the crowd pushed forward. I grabbed my mother's hand and stood frozen, waiting. Then she said, "There is

Adolf Hitler!" Indeed, here he was, outside his big rustic villa, the Berghof, walking among us and shaking hands, looking jovial and relaxed. He strode in our direction, and when he saw me, the perfect picture of a little German girl with blond braids and blue eyes, dressed for a warm fall day in a blue dirndl dress patterned with white hearts under a white pinafore, he crouched down, waved to me, and said, "Komm nur her, mein Boppele" (Come here, my little doll). Suddenly I felt scared and shy. I hid behind my mother's skirt until she coaxed me firmly to approach him. He pulled me onto his knee while his photographer prepared to take pictures. The strange man with the sharp, hypnotic eyes and dark mustache held me stiffly, not at all like my father would have, and I wanted to cry and run away. But my parents were waving at me to sit still and smile. Adolf Hitler, the great man they so admired, had singled me out, and in their eyes I was a star. As the crowd applauded, I saw my grandfather turn away and strike the air angrily with his cane.

part ONE: 1906–1934

THE PÖHLMANNS

□ □
□ □

A WEDDING
JANUARY 7, 1933

"The most beautiful girl in all of Selb is getting
married today," said the townspeople of my mother,
Albine Pöhlmann, on her wedding day in January
1933. My mother was indeed very beautiful in a very
German way inspired by the flappers of the 1920s.
She had an oval face with a small, pouting mouth, a
fine, straight nose, piercing blue eyes, and a
V-shaped hairline, a widow's peak, that she herself
called aristocratic. Her long, dark-blond hair lay in
soft, braided loops at the nape of her neck. She had
made herself a short, white chiffon dress with black
polka dots and a fashionable low waist and wore a
smart, close-fitting cap. Mutti (Mama) entered her
marriage with the conviction that a future with Max
Paul as her husband and with Hitler, who was about
to become chancellor of Germany, would be a happy
one, a life very different from that of her long-
suffering mother. Streets would become peaceful
and jobs plentiful. Saving for the future could begin
anew, and women, as housewives and mothers,
would become an important part of the new order.

□ □
□ □

1 ROOTS OF DISCONTENT

IN 1933, THE YEAR THEY GOT MARRIED, BOTH MY parents voted for Hitler in the election that confirmed him as German chancellor and completed his grab for power. In trying to grasp what made my mother and father put their faith in Adolf Hitler and make some sense of the events of my own childhood, I needed to recapture their early years. They had both grown up during the hunger-filled years of World War I, the defeat of Germany, and the economically devastating 1920s, a very different world from the one they expected to live in after their marriage at the beginning of the Hitler regime.

Throughout my childhood, instead of reading a fairy tale at bedtime, my mother would tell me of her youth during those difficult years. These stories, together with my father's more occasional recollections and later those of my mother's childhood friend Emilie, formed my earliest pictures of my parents' lives before I came to be.

Mutti's first nine years passed in a warrenlike apartment building in the city of Wiesbaden on the river Rhine, where her parents had settled when they were first married in 1910. "My mother was twelve years older than my father," she somewhat grudgingly admitted, giving me to understand that one would normally expect a man to be older than his wife. The two had fallen in love around 1907 when her father passed through Wiesbaden during his *Wanderschaft*. Albin Pöhlmann, my grandfather, was a journeyman carpenter. Like the journeymen of every trade, he was required to complete a *Wanderschaft*—three years of traveling

My grandfather, Albin Pöhlmann *(second from right)*, when he was a journeyman carpenter, and the carpenter master *(second from left)* in Mainz.

throughout Germany working with different masters of their trade before submitting a masterpiece to the guild and receiving the title of master, which would allow him to train apprentices and open a business.

When Albin Pöhlmann arrived in Wiesbaden he was a tall, lanky young man, with a narrow mustache and bright blue eyes. He wore his journeyman's cap at a dashing angle and slung his knapsack, with a tin water cup dangling on the outside and an extra set of clothes inside, carelessly over his shoulder. He counted on luck and the grapevine of road companions to find work and sustenance. His *Wanderschaft* had begun months before in his hometown of Selb, a small factory town in Franconia; following a lead, he had landed in Wiesbaden, the elegant and ancient spa city known from Roman times for its healing waters. Orchards and vineyards surrounded the city, and jagged, crumbling ruins of castles dotted the banks up and down the mighty Rhine River—hence its full name: Wiesbaden am Rhein.

Albin knew that the freedom and adventure of his travels were

but an interlude before set-
tling down, starting his own
carpentry business, and looking for a thrifty wife. He must
have found the black-haired,
petite Luise Damm to be just
right; they became engaged,
and he moved on, intending to
marry her the moment he
completed his journey two
years hence.

I have trouble imagining
my stern, unsmiling grandmother as the attractive young
woman she must have been
when my grandfather pro-
posed to her. She was certainly
unusual, a single woman in
her thirties who as a very young

Wedding picture of my grandparents, Albin
Pöhlmann and Luise Damm, Wiesbaden,
1910.

girl had left her spiteful stepparents to make her own way in the
city. She knew all the best families in town, for she ironed their
fancy silk dresses, their lace underwear, and their damask table and
bed linens to perfection. She immediately fancied Albin, the handsome journeyman cabinetmaker, who seemed ambitious and in-
dustrious, who was high-spirited, who made her laugh and took
her dancing. She could see herself as the future master carpenter's
wife, a member of the respectable middle class, with a household
to run and her husband's business to be proud of. With peace in the
land they had a reasonable expectation of a prosperous future in
spite of their difference in age and divergent backgrounds. Hard
work, thrift, and a God-fearing life would assure it. It has always
saddened me to look at my grandparents' wedding picture, to see
them looking so dead serious, but I put it down to the fashion of the
times, not to a premonition they had of their future.

The Pöhlmann family in Selb, meanwhile, was alarmed at the

thought of their twenty-four-year-old son's rash decision to marry this much older woman whom they had never met. But there was a bigger problem than my grandmother's age, a deep, dark family secret that I didn't learn until I was a teenager—namely, that my mother, little Albine, was already two years old when her parents' wedding took place. According to my great-aunt in Wiesbaden, after the engagement and Albin's departure to continue his *Wanderschaft,* Luise found herself pregnant. She was too proud to tell him, afraid of hindering his progress, but she called the little girl Albine in his memory. When her fiancé returned two years later to make good on his promise of marriage, he found her with the little girl and quickly made her an honest woman. To the end of her life my mother never revealed her feelings about what was then considered a shameful birth. I often wonder if even my father knew her secret.

After the wedding, Albin found a carpentry job in the city of Mainz, just across the Rhine from Wiesbaden, and the young couple began to save for their future. They rented a tiny, two-room apartment in a labyrinthine apartment complex in the Rheingauerstrasse where families dwelled close together and shared a toilet down the hall. Small stores and workshops of locksmiths, antique restorers, clockmakers, and a glass-and-framing shop faced one another across the cobblestone courtyard, and the sound of clanking and hammering mingled with the shouts of trade, craft, and commerce filled the air. The smell of fried onions, sausages, and sauerkraut wafted from the windows above, signaling *Mittagessen,* the noon meal, and at the stroke of twelve the men locked up their shops and went upstairs to a set table and whatever the women could afford to cook that day. Most people were poor, yet, as my mother always emphasized, this was *eine gute Gegend,* a nice neighborhood. Small shops lined the Rheingauerstrasse, and even latchkey children were fairly safe, much to the comfort of their working mothers.

Four years into my grandparents' marriage, in August 1914,

World War I began, and soon my grandfather had to leave to fight for the kaiser. My mother was six years old, and her baby brother, Hans, nicknamed Hänschen (little Hans), was just two when their parents' hopes of moving on to a larger apartment with solid oak furniture made in Albin's own workshop were dashed by the so-called Great War.

It was customary for spouses to address each other as Father and Mother once they were parents. Thus in a letter mailed to a coded address on the western front my grandmother wrote on September 26, 1916:

> *Dearest Father, congratulations on your birthday. Our only wish is that you were at home again and that this terrible war had an end. It is your second birthday in enemy country and times are getting harder for you and us. I baked a cake for you but it did not rise. The children ate it anyway and I am sending you a small packet of tobacco for your pipe instead.*

Also in 1916 she wrote:

> *We will get five sacks of potatoes for the winter. They have to last till May for the three of us and we have to pay ahead of time. Many people don't want to buy them for fear that they will rot but what if there are no more stamps to be had later on? I received your money only yesterday and used it as a down payment for the potatoes. Thank you. I also put up 20 pounds of plums that I got from Herr Russ. The good man brought them by instead of taking them to the green market for sale. I bottled them without sugar since we only get $\frac{1}{2}$ pound per month and I am out of it.*

Such honesty and pessimism would be unthinkable for a German soldier's wife in the next world war, when *Schwarzseher* (literally, black seers) were severely punished, often with death.

With a rather morbid sense of humor she wrote in one letter

that Hänschen had told her that he wanted his father to come home and shoot some rabbits for dinner, since surely he had learned how to shoot well out there at the front.

My grandfather's hurriedly written postcards pictured the French countryside and shot-up villages. They always started with "I am still well"—as if he expected disaster to strike at any moment. Once he told my grandmother that he had just come back from the funeral of a comrade who had succumbed to his wounds, and though he does not come out and say it, the matter-of-fact words fail to hide a sense of tremendous sadness. On birthdays he wrote to his children that he would rather be with them and reminded them to be good and obey their mother. Two years after the war started, and with two more to go, he did not mention a hoped-for victory, nationalistic sentiments, heroism, or a soldier's honor, just a longing to have it all done with so they could get on with their lives.

During those years little Albine Pöhlmann and little Emilie Graupner—later my Tante (aunt) Emilie—were fast friends living in the same building across a narrow alley and some darkish hallways from each other. The Graupners, a family with four children, were slightly better off than the Pöhlmanns. Emilie's father, too old to be drafted, owned a workshop for restoring antiques in the courtyard below. From her windows Emilie could see into my grandparents' barren kitchen with its small, chipped, cold-water sink, a two-burner gas stove, and a shelf with a curtain drawn in front of a few pots and pans. Some uneven chairs stood around the brown, wooden table that was used for eating, cooking, homework, writing letters, and anything else requiring a flat surface. The other half of the room held a couple of worn armchairs with a scratched-up, black oak lamp table between them and a stiff, flat sofa, my mother's bed. Hänschen slept in my grandmother's small bedroom with its two wooden bedsteads, a commode, a wardrobe, and a chair that substituted as a night table. My grandfather's exhausting six-day workweek had not allowed him time to make furniture for his family before he left for the war. The odd collection of hand-me-downs would have to do until he could make his own.

Once again Luise had to work full-time ironing in wealthy households to augment my grandfather's military pay. Coming home at night exhausted and irritable, she had little patience with her two lively children, and Mutti often bore the brunt of her ill temper. Albine was small for her age but charged with energy, vivacious, curious, smart, and independent, a frequent ringleader of the street urchins hanging out in the Rheingauerstrasse neighborhood. She was not at all cut out to baby-sit a fat little brother—her mother's favorite—who, according to Tante Emilie, was himself a *sehr böser Bub* (very bad boy).

My grandmother Luise Pöhlmann with her children, Hans and Albine, in Wiesbaden, about 1916.

Tante Emilie witnessed my mother take frequent, harsh beatings when Luise came home to find chores left undone and Hänschen complaining about his sister. Physical punishment was not unusual for the times, and in my mother's home toys, books, and any other form of intellectual stimulation were nonexistent. The ground rules in a German family were the same as in the German state: Punish independence, rebellion against orders, and speaking up (such as little Albine protesting against a perceived injustice); instead, foster unquestioning obedience, submission, orderliness, and hard work.

Anti-Semitism was not sanctioned in Germany at the time, but the undercurrent of it could be felt even in the behavior of children. Whenever the Orthodox Jewish couple who lived with their little boy in my grandmother's apartment complex went for a walk or shopping, the entire gang of children, including Mutti, Hänschen, Emilie, and her brothers, followed them shouting obscenities and rude rhymes. They retreated only when the Jewish father with his enormous, rimmed black hat turned around and shook his cane at them. Years after World War II Emilie Graupner—very old by then—remembered the little Jewish boy, his dark curls and his dark, almond-shaped, serious eyes, and with a heavy, guilty heart wondered what had become of him during the Nazi years. One day her father observed the children's harassment of the Jewish family and forbade Emilie and her brothers to participate in it. Later, in 1932, he and Emilie would help a Jewish shopkeeper on the Rheingauerstrasse pick up the shards of the window smashed by Hitler's henchmen on one of their rampages. Herr Graupner was a moral man, and he and his family voted against Hitler in defiance of a storm trooper who was watching and intimidating voters at the polls. Yet he too bore the German middle-class curse of political passivity, fear of chaos, a wrongly placed trust in law and order, and a total lack of experience with democracy. Trying to shield his children from the evil world of politics and news of volatile alliances and enmities in Europe that had led to the war, he did not allow even his older boys to read the newspapers for fear of their minds being poisoned. He could not see the irony at the time, but a few years later Nazi propaganda would ensure the very thing he struggled to prevent.

□   □

MY MOTHER'S CHILDHOOD IN WIESBADEN with its early hardships, strong friendships, and no doubt educational and exhilarating street experiences came to a sudden end in the summer of 1917. My grandfather's father had died unexpectedly, and Albin wrote to my grandmother from the battlefield that she should pack up and move to his family's house in Selb, which he had inherited through default, as none of his siblings wanted the old place. Sad but dutiful, and without protest, my grandmother said good-bye to her sunny spa city on the Rhine and moved to cold, windy Selb with her children and her few possessions. Albine did not even have time to say good-bye to her dear friend Emilie, who arrived home from charity summer camp to find the Pöhlmann family gone. They missed Emilie's fond send-off only to face the deep resentment of the Pöhlmann relatives, especially Albin's mother, who made life miserable for the three newcomers, forcing them to sleep in a stairwell and giving them limited access to the kitchen without sharing their food.

When the armistice came in 1918, my grandfather walked away from the battlefield, released now from the defeated German army, and made his way to Selb, where he witnessed the fall of the *Kaiserreich* (empire) amidst a revolution, and then the signing of the Treaty of Versailles. This document laid out reparations owed by Germany to the other combatant nations, restrictions on the size and power of the German military, and territorial readjustments intended to punish Germany's aggression. Albine, her brother, her future husband, and all of their friends grew up absorbing the incessant, all-pervasive message that the Treaty of Versailles had been designed to destroy Germany, that it was the main cause of the decadence and disorder of the Weimar Republic and the misery and hopelessness of their youth.

The first thing my grandfather did when he got home was build an addition to his father's cramped house to separate his wife and children from his mother and to hold his new carpentry shop. Shortly after receiving his *Meisterbrief* (master's certificate), he set about opening his business as cabinetmaker and supplier of window frames and doors for builders. On one side of the house a large, white sign with black lettering proudly announced: BAU UND MÖBELSCHREINEREI—ALBIN PÖHLMANN.

The timing of Albin's venture could not have been worse. Having no savings, he struggled with local banks and lenders to obtain

The Pöhlmann house in Selb after my grandfather built the addition, about 1920.

financing for the addition to the house and for the large, complicated carpentry machines he needed, as well as a yardful of lumber. Every pfennig and every minute of his day went into his
fledgling business and repaying his debt, but he was swimming
against the tide of the economic disaster gripping postwar Germany. The business he had counted on was not forthcoming. Few
buildings went up, and even fewer newlywed couples were able to
follow the hallowed tradition of ordering their handmade bedroom and kitchen sets for their first homes. The optimists among
them came to look through my grandfather's furniture magazines
and order what they liked, but most often they could not pay when
the set was ready to be picked up. One particularly detestable bedroom set, with a stylized star motif of painted wood on the glass
doors and headboards, had been painstakingly and flawlessly
painted with a shiny, bright orange-brown fake-wood pattern by
my grandfather. It would molder in storage until his future son-in-
law, Max, recovered it for his and my mother's bedroom. I hated
that furniture until decades later when the fake-wood pattern, so
desirable in the 1920s, was removed and the pale beauty of the natural wood came to the fore.

My grandfather was sickened by the silence of his new carpentry machines. The wood merchants were hounding him for the payments due on the lumber that was freshly stacked in the yard, almost forcing him to declare bankruptcy and bring shame to his family. But Albin, stubborn and innovative as he was, came up with the idea of specializing in coffins, which he would make in all sizes and price ranges. "People always die," he said, unconscious of the sad irony behind the fact that the only way to make a living in a moribund Germany was by banking on death. Indeed the coffins brought enough income that, with the help of his wife and teenage daughter, he could hold on through the fickle ups and long, deep downs of the next thirteen years.

Consumed by the need to survive, the family had little time or opportunity to follow the bizarre happenings in the Reichstag, the parliamentary body of elected representatives that convened in Berlin during the Weimar Republic from 1919 to 1933. Nor did my grandfather know in detail the weakness and ineptness of his chosen party, the Social Democrats, during those last days of the republic. But Mutti said that they were deeply alarmed by the local newspaper headlines of daily violence in the streets of big cities and the chaos that might lead to another Bolshevik Revolution or, worse, all-out civil war.

The move to Selb and the struggle to keep the business alive came at a high cost to my grandmother. She could not get used to the dreary factory town with its harsh climate, severe people, and, to her ear, grating Franconian form of Bavarian speech. For when she would say the loaded words "nach de Griesch," the people of Selb would say "no' m Kraich," both meaning "nach dem Krieg" (after the war). All her hopes for a better life for herself and her fast-growing children had been pinned on the prospect of her husband's business success. Instead of living the bourgeois life she had dreamed about, she found herself once again ironing for wealthy families, even competing with other women for this menial work. Luise Philipine Damm Pöhlmann and her family were hungrier and poorer than they had ever been.

Arbeitslosigkeit and *Inflation* (unemployment and inflation): These twin demons became the daily reality for my grandmother and most of the German middle class during the Weimar years, festering national sores created, as nearly all believed, by the notorious Treaty of Versailles.

2 IN SEARCH OF A FUTURE

MUTTI WAS THIRTEEN WHEN *DIE INFLATION* HIT in 1921. She had finished her obligatory seven years in grade school and had been encouraged by her teachers to go on to a *Gymnasium* (high school). She was very smart and had the desire to continue her education; however, there was no choice but to help the family by finding a job. Resentment and embarrassment over her lack of education would dog her the rest of her life. As it was, she tried to educate herself the cheap way by enrolling for several years in weekly English evening classes, for which she paid eighty pfennig a session. She also studied Esperanto, an artificial language created to become the common world tongue. Its promoters hoped that it would foster greater understanding among all people and reduce the eminence and perceived arrogance of English-speaking countries.

As soon as she graduated from grade school, Mutti began to work six days a week in a small factory that made bed and table linens. She was barely tall enough to reach the sewing machines. Inflation grew worse by the hour. When she received her week's pay in the morning, she had to wait until her lunch break to run with her wad of paper money to the nearest bakery. But by that time the reichsmark, the German currency of the time, had fallen so far that she could not buy a single loaf of bread with her six days' wages. The large, rectangular bills were stamped with a staggering number of zeros; Mutti could not even puzzle out the denominations: millions, billions, more? By November 15, 1923, the high point of the inflation, one U.S. dollar equaled 4,200,000,000,000 reichsmarks.

On days when Mutti was not able to buy bread she searched through the garbage cans outside wealthy people's homes for potato peels and other scraps. During the worst of times my grandmother tied a small blue-and-white-freckled enamel pot with strings around her waist and hid it beneath her long, dark skirt so she could fill it with kitchen scraps and leftovers from the dining rooms of the houses where she ironed laundry. Her family would eagerly wait for her to come home and put the meager offering on the table. Neither woman would ever forget the humiliation of those days, and while my grandmother never talked about these hardships, much of her bitterness must have stemmed from that time.

Not everyone suffered in silence. There were street rallies every day during which speakers promised solutions that never materialized. Increasingly news of turmoil and death in the large cities— always attributed to one faction or another—reached Selb, and even in that small town men got into fistfights and gun duels over politics.

One warm day Mutti decided to attend a labor-union rally during her lunch break. She listened to the speaker, thinking to herself that he was right: workers should rebel against their exploitation and unite in a general strike. She returned to the factory floor, studied the troubled-looking women bent over their sewing machines, and thought, Why not organize a strike right here? Mutti climbed onto a chair and pulled the chain of the main switch, stopping all the machines. It was suddenly quiet in the room. She collected herself and then shouted to her coworkers as loudly as she could that they must strike to protest their worthless wages. Nobody made a sound. Everyone waited tensely for the boss to come and fire Mutti on the spot. Instead, the owner and his wife, already at the brink of bankruptcy, made a brief appearance to announce that they were closing down then and there and sending everyone home. Mutti was sixteen, had been working for three years, and was now jobless.

□ □

THE NEXT THREE YEARS PASSED in a blur of on-and-off work in offices and households. When she wasn't working, Mutti and her friends played sports, hiked, and sang in clubs that allowed them temporary release from their humdrum lives and gave them a sense of German identity. "We need a strong leader!" was an oft-heard refrain.

At the end of 1927, Mutti, desperate for steady work, answered a want ad for a lady's companion on an estate in faraway West Prussia, also known as Pomerania. Incredible as it seemed, she received a positive answer. My grandmother loaned her the money for a one-way ticket, and she set out for Mehrenthin, a tiny railroad station in Pomerania miles from the *Rittergut* (estate) where her job waited. A horse and carriage with a coachman fetched her. They followed a long, sandy country road to an impressive, elegant manor house, where she met her new employers, the Freiherr von Waldow and his wife, the Freifrau. Mutti, like all Germans, was impressed by the small word *von,* but she knew nothing of the rigorous hierarchy of age and eminence among nobility or how a Freifrau ranked.

The eastern landed aristocracy felt deeply threatened by communism on one side and democracy on the other. The democratic impulses of centrist parties also caused them to look to the right for protection of their interests. But the most immediate danger facing the Waldows was the Freifrau's pregnancy. Only a few months after Mutti's arrival, this kind woman died in childbirth, leaving behind the newborn and two-year-old twins. The Freiherr, who had noted my mother's cheerful energy, asked her to stay on to look after the twins. Without hesitation, not least because for the first time in her life she had enough to eat, she donned a nanny's uniform to become a substitute mother for the two Waldow boys.

My mother about 1928.

Pomerania was a place where time had stood still, where the Freiherr in his breeches and shiny boots rode upright and proudly, whip in hand, over endless fields, rigorously supervising the farmhands and servants—only recently freed from serfdom—on his ancestral estate. His authority and at times bizarre privileges were undisputed until Albine, driven by curiosity and a huge appetite, broke one of the old dictates. She showed the other servants that they could reason instead of simply obeying in fear, and she got away with it.

The biggest fall event on the estate was *Schlachttag,* the day on which the fattened pigs were slaughtered and butchered. All hands on the estate were expected to help, from the swineherd to the butcher to the kitchen staff in their white caps and striped aprons that got bloodier and messier as the day wore on. The squeals of dying pigs and the smell of blood filled the autumn air. Some people cleaned the intestines for sausage casings and stuffed them with sausage dough fragrant with garlic and marjoram, while others cut the hams for the smokehouse.

That evening the kitchen staff prepared the best cuts and odd parts of pig along with sausages for the *Schlachttafel* (platter of freshly butchered meat) traditionally served to the Waldow family for dinner. Passing through the huge manor house kitchen, Albine spotted a pair of crispy brown, freshly roasted pig's ears topping the overflowing, delicious-smelling *Schlachttafel.* Not thinking too much about it—there must have been at least a dozen of these ears lying around—she put one on a plate and sat down at the servants' table to enjoy the delicacy. Suddenly the kitchen staff was in an uproar. They had discovered that one pig's ear was missing from the *Schlachttafel!* Mutti, pointing to her plate, admitted her theft to the despairing cook, who replied that it was the Freiherr's absolute privilege to eat the roasted ears of the very first pig slaughtered that day. Eventually Mutti convinced the cook that maybe the Freiherr would not be able to tell which ears came from which pig. The cook, sufficiently recovered, quickly roasted another ear. He grinned and winked at Mutti slyly when the servant who waited at the table carried the refurbished platter to the unsuspecting Freiherr. The great smoked hams, however, were counted and kept under lock and key; otherwise, as Mutti freely admitted, she might have taken one and sent it to her hungry father in Selb.

Her fellow workers on the Waldow estate called Albine *"Der*

Bayer" (the masculine form of "the Bavarian"), as if she was a strange creature from a distant land. This was not without reason. Had she not challenged them to jump into a frozen pond on Good Friday as was customary at her swim club in Selb? And had she not watched with an open mouth in total disbelief as the geese were force-fed an evil-smelling concoction for weeks to fatten them up for the autumn day on which they were plugged and killed? Had she not eaten the Freiherr's pig's ear?

After two years as a nanny Mutti tired of the Prussian lord-servant relationship, the yea-saying and curtsying before the Freiherr. After giving notice, she decided that she would hike through a part of Finland before returning home. All by herself she set off with only a backpack. She must have taken a ferry across a stretch of the Baltic Sea and buses and trains to the lake region she wanted to explore, but for me the story began when she had crossed a border into Finland and started on her walk. She stayed overnight in Finnish villages or simply slept out in the woods, making little contact with the Finnish people she passed on her journey. As often as I would ask for the Finnish story, she told me that she felt herself to be a *Wanderer* (wayfarer) who goes on a pilgrimage looking for *"die blaue Blume,"* a mythical blue flower that transformed the seeker and provided insight into the oneness of humans with nature. Mutti never worried about being a woman wandering alone in the untamed, foreign countryside, crossing without fear the expanses of brown and yellow wetlands that swayed under her steps. She passed countless ink-black lakes and walked through vast, silvery birch forests that rustled softly in the slightest wind. At times she moved through this magic world by moonlight. An elk or a rabbit would startle her and be equally startled by her presence.

Mutti knew no other woman who had challenged herself in this courageous way. One day I realized that, as she walked in search of *die blaue Blume,* she dreamed not of philosophical or intellectual enlightenment espoused by German Romanticism but of her future as a mother and wife with a strong, handsome husband who had a steady job in a country where there was peace and order. She wished for many children, preferably six boys. She had loved the two Waldow boys very much and always envied her brother who, though younger than she, held the superior position as the male child. But most important of all, she would raise her children as a full-time mother, unlike her own mother, who had left her and Hans alone day after day to toil at a thankless job.

Finally, in February 1930, Albine returned to Selb. The Pöhlmanns, after a brief reprieve, were once again caught in the throes of a world financial crisis ushered in by the crash on Wall Street. This renewed downturn gave the Nazis a new lease on life, bringing Adolf Hitler, who had been jailed and gone underground (on Obersalzberg), back into the public eye. Mutti watched and listened, and much of what he spouted seemed to speak to her own bitter experience—and to her hope.

Still, Albine was only twenty-three, and in the midst of continued economic disaster and political turmoil, she fell in love. On an

My mother's childhood friend Emilie visits in Selb in 1930.

outing with her hiking club, the *Wandervögel* (wandering birds), Albine met Max Paul. He was tall and slender, with blue eyes, blond hair brushed back above a high forehead, and a prominent nose that my sister Ingrid would inherit, along with his very fair, sunburn-prone skin. He possessed the intelligent face of a book reader, had favorite poets, loved mountains, folk songs, and, of course, Mozart. He and Mutti became pen pals and secretly courted by mail, for he soon moved to Berchtesgaden in South Bavaria for that elusive commodity, a steady job.

Max's life too had been hard and poor. His mother had died of consumption when he was but one year old, making it necessary for his Czech grandmother, Kohout, who lived across the border in Czechoslovakia, to raise him until his father remarried. Marie Paul, his new stepmother, fetched him back and gave him and a baby half-sister, Frieda, born a few years later, a loving home.

Most people in Selb worked in one of the china factories that had been founded there after kaolin, the clay from which china is made, was discovered in the region. Among the factories that provided the bulk of the employment in town were Rosenthal, Heinrich, Krautheim, and Hutschenreuther, the oldest, founded in 1814.

Except for my father, who thanks to his talent was trained in the Rosenthal art department to hand-paint the flowers, birds, and latest designs on the most expensive china, the Pauls traditionally worked at Heinrich. Their table was set only with Heinrich china; their gifts were always Heinrich-manufactured figurines, vases, and bowls. Their lives were regulated by the Heinrich factory whistle, and their lungs were destroyed by the fine, sharp dust they breathed day in and day out. During frequent periods of unemployment they stood in line to collect the unemployment insurance that would buy nothing if they did not reach the grocery before it had become worthless. At least they could count on this regular support; my Pöhlmann grandfather, with his unprofitable business and his debts, was worse off. Nonetheless, the owners of houses and small businesses looked down on the factory workers, assuring that Mutti's liaison with Max would cause an uproar once her family found out about it.

In 1930 Max accepted a job offer in Berchtesgaden, a developing tourist town in the Bavarian Alps, where he joined a team of porcelain painters in the newly opened Porzellanmalerei Adler (workshop for hand-painted porcelain). Herr Waldemar Adler, also a painter trained in Selb, had been able to raise the capital— some said by marrying a rich woman—for this venture, which would offer fine white china with hand-painted alpine flowers to an increasing number of tourists. The desperate poverty of the local population had begun to improve by the mid-1800s, when mountaineering and summer villas in the Alps had become fashionable among the wealthy. Everyone seemed to have heard that the world traveler Alexander von Humboldt called the valley the most beautiful spot on earth, but no one knew that a Dr. Sigmund Freud came many a summer weekend from Salzburg to enjoy the hiking and walking. A few summer villas, elegant hotels, picturesque bed-and-breakfasts, cafés, eateries, and all the trimmings of a *Luftkurort*—a fresh-air resort complete with sanatoriums—had developed long before Hitler discovered the valley and made Obersalzberg his *Wahlheimat* (chosen home).

Max, Albine, her brother, who was no longer Hänschen but Hans, and many of their impatient young friends were easy prey for Hitler. After years of being made to feel like beggars and scum, they lent an eager ear to the man who told them that Germany was not only a worthy nation but a superior one. Anyone who promised economic stability would capture the nation's mind and soul as well. Of all the Weimar politicians, only Hitler understood fully that playing up patriotism and making false promises to every interest group would garner a following. And most important, perhaps, he realized that instilling fear of a vaguely defined enemy—the "conspirators of world Jewry"—would bring a suspicious and traumatized people, including my own mother and father, to his side.

Mutti documented her tiny contributions to the NSDAP (Nationalsozialistische Deutsche Arbeiterpartei, or German National

My mother's monthly account for October 1932 showing one contribution to the Nazi Party (NSDAP) on October 7 and one to Hitler on October 15. One reichsmark equaled approximately 23 cents.

Socialist Workers' Party, Nazi for short) in the small brown cardboard accounting booklet in which she traced every expenditure of her incredibly frugal life. In December 1930 she entered the purchase of a fifty-pfennig ticket to the Nazi Party's Christmas event and a contribution of a little china pitcher, perhaps for an auction, which cost her another fifty pfennig. Over the next two years irregular contributions to the NSDAP added up to a total of 9.15 reichsmarks, with one final gift of 1 reichsmark earmarked for Hitler personally and made perhaps at a rally. She and her cohorts were part of the jubilant crowds when showman Hitler staged his displays of marching storm troopers surrounded by seas of swastika flags, but they were certainly not the source of the large sums needed to secure his dictatorship. That money and support came from wealthy interests that, equally scared of communism and democracy, hoped to control this strange little man.

By the summer of 1932 Mutti must have told at least her mother about Max, since she entered a loan from her in the scruffy little accounting book and in the expense column noted the price of a train ticket to Berchtesgaden. During her two-week visit with Max she explored the mountains and fell in love with them too. For three reichsmarks she took a solo bus trip to ancient Salzburg across the border in Austria while Max was at work, but before she left, during a stroll at the end of a ripe summer day, he proposed to her. On the way back to Selb she paid extra for the express train from Bayreuth to Selb, as if she couldn't wait to begin preparations for her wedding.

"Nun aber bleibet Glaube, Hoffnung, Liebe, diese drei; aber die Liebe ist die Größte unter ihnen" (Now there remains faith, hope, and love, these three; but the greatest of them is love). On January 7, 1933, the minister of the Lutheran church in Selb spoke these words from 1 Corinthians 13, chosen by my parents for their wedding ceremony, and presented them with a New Testament at the end of the service. At the civil ceremony in the old town hall they were handed the *Deutsches Einheits-Familien-Stammbuch mit Familienregister* (general German family genealogical register)—a small, linen-bound, reddish brown book containing formatted pages framed in black in which to document their family history, marriages, births, dates of baptisms, and deaths. The *Stammbuch*'s introduction encouraged the young couple to research their family history, note the special talents, educational achievements, and characteristics of family members, and provide as much information as possible "for the enjoyment and benefit of future generations." It also contained a brief description of the church

My mother and my father, Max Paul, on their wedding day, January 7, 1933.

laws—both Catholic and Lutheran—regarding marriage, as well as a summary of state laws pertaining to the rights and duties of man and woman in a marriage: "The man is the head of the family. The woman takes his name. The state assigns to him the right to decide where they live, their home, and all decisions regarding married life." There was no mention of race or ethnicity, and among the list of suggested names for girls were Jewish ones like Ruth. This would soon change.

Not surprisingly, my maternal grandparents had been dead set against their daughter marrying my father, the son of mere factory workers. The additional fact that he was a fledgling artist did nothing to endear him to them. They had a teacher or civil servant with a secure job and a future pension in mind for their daughter, but my strong-willed mother prevailed. She followed my father to Berchtesgaden, where they found—not by design—an apartment on the very mountain that Hitler had chosen as his retreat and future headquarters and from which he unleashed his madness on the world.

A year later, I was born into the Third Reich.

part two: 1934–1939

HITLER'S WILLING FOLLOWERS

□ □
□ □

A FEW GOOD YEARS
1934 TO 1939

Although my father had left the Nazi Party in 1932
in a personal disengagement from politics, he
continued to believe in Hitler wholeheartedly. He
and my mother had painted the walls of their new
home in Haus Linden a luminous light yellow and
the ceilings snow white, colors that brought cheer
on rainy days and conveyed my parents' optimism
about Vati's steady income and Mutti's ability to be
a full-time mother. Hitler's portrait hung above the
dark sofa in the family room and his presence
influenced our domestic lives, our thoughts, and the
stories and memories I gathered. However, some of
the momentous political events of those early years
were not talked about at least within my earshot.
Soon after my birth, the Führer ordered
the massacre of a large number of his old fighting
comrades, including the former leader of the S.A.,
his friend, Ernst Röhm, and other foes. They were
accused of conspiracy and of being vile, incorrigible
homosexuals who did not deserve to be treated as
human beings. I heard no tales of the *Kristallnacht*
that so infamously and unashamedly revealed the
intent to dehumanize Jews. These ominous portents
on the seemingly bright horizon were smoothed over
by the Nazi leaderships' frenzied moral outrage and

denunciation of whole segments of the population. Silently my father and mother held on to their delusion that indeed a happy future lay ahead in our cheery home with Hitler's red wax portrait watching over us.

□   □
□   □

THE RITUALS OF LIFE

I was born on May 28, 1934. The evening before, an owl family had settled on the fence posts near our house and hooted eerily into the night. Mutti desperately wanted the hooting to be a good omen, a sign that Hitler would bring her and her family prosperity and peace. It was more than a year after my parents' wedding and Hitler's power grab. My mother and father settled into their cozy, small, two-bedroom apartment on the ground floor of a picturesque cottage on Salzberg (Salt Mountain) in Berchtesgaden, enjoying a sense of modest well-being that neither of them had experienced before. Mutti was twenty-six and Vati (Daddy) twenty-nine, both happily expecting a child they hoped would grow up proud to be a German.

The next day the owls were gone, replaced by flitting swallows and a cloudless sky. The sun was smiling a shiny welcome into the windows of Haus Linden, our home with green shutters and heart-shaped cutouts in the second-floor balcony. I slipped from my mother's womb without much difficulty onto the snowy white, carefully ironed linen sheets, protected, no doubt, from any mess with equally white flannel cloths. Mutti's friend Emilie (my soon-to-be honorary *Tante*) had come from Wiesbaden to assist the local midwife in Mutti's *schwere Stunde*—her difficult hour, as a woman's labor in childbirth was called. "It's a girl!" Tante Emilie announced proudly, as if it was her doing, and my mother, even though she had very much wanted a boy, was glad that I screamed loudly and was obviously strong and healthy.

Max, who like most fathers through the ages had been banned

View of Berchtesgaden with Watzmann, the second-highest mountain in Germany.

from the birthing room, finally stopped his restless pacing and came in to see his young wife and slightly pummeled new daughter. He was happy and relieved that all had gone well, and while I had deprived him of a firstborn son, I was a sound specimen and would soon make a room for myself in his heart. Tante Susi, as I would be allowed to call Frau Reitlechner, our upstairs neighbor, and Trudi, her teenage daughter, were told of my safe arrival and came down right away to get a glimpse of me, now calm, clean, and wrapped tightly in a thick, soft, white flannel square with a light blue crocheted rim. Trudi was already eager to wheel the baby out in the fashionable baby carriage that the family of Professor Linde, who lived in the villa Schiedkoepfl up the road, had handed on to my mother.

A while later, feeling superfluous, even unwelcome, among the busy womenfolk, my father walked down the mountain and up the other side to the town hall of Berchtesgaden, where he entered my name into the register of births. Climbing higher still, he reached the small Lutheran church and parsonage and set a date for my christening with the pastor. When he returned home from the long walk, he announced out of the blue that at the last moment he had changed his mind about my name and had entered Irmgard Albine into the registry instead of the Helga Albine that he and my mother had agreed upon. There were no telephones, of course, and his unilateral decision had saved him a walk of at least forty-five minutes each way. Perhaps my mother was too tired to question my father's impulsive action, or maybe she too liked Irmgard better. He had, after all, kept her name as my middle name. Friends teased Vati about it, but he and Mutti smiled conspiratorially when the story was told, saying that they loved the name Irmgard; I too have always liked my name, even when it was abbreviated to Irmi.

Years later I discovered a curious entry in my mother's scruffy old accounting booklet for "funeral expenses" of 12.35 reichsmarks a whole year before I was born. The town register revealed that my mother had then lost a one-day-old baby girl named Irmgard. I wondered why I had never been told—was this child simply premature, or was she born too soon after my parents' wedding to be "honorable"? Perhaps Vati had wanted to keep the memory of his very first child alive by giving me her name. After my initial anger at being a secondhand Irmgard and my bafflement at the secretive nature of adults, I chose the story as something to remember my father by. Mutti never talked about the dead baby, and I never asked.

By the time of my birth the most important thing was that both Helga and Irmgard were names of Germanic origin. In 1934 when I was born into our mountain paradise the Nazis were in full control of all branches of government, the military, and the media. And they had begun to infiltrate all aspects of life and to dictate the everyday details of family decisions: our education, the books and the news we read, how we greeted one another—even the names parents gave their children. The Nazi propaganda machine stressed the superiority and importance of things Germanic, Nordic, and Celtic, and names were among the most important badges of this identity. From now on girls would be called Gudrun, Gertraud, Hildegard, Brunhilde, Sigrid, Ingrid, Edeltraud, or the more exotic Gotelinde, Gerlinde, Ortrun, or Heidrun. Old-time Berchtesgaden families steeped in the Catholic traditions still baptized their daughters after saints—Maria, Katharina, Anna, or Elisabeth—and celebrated *Namenstag*, the day of their namesake saint, rather than their birthday. But the custom was quickly eroding even among them, as a whole nation cleansed its list of all possible non-Germanic names—especially, of course, Jewish names—to conform to the wishes of the Nazi state.

Two weeks after I was born, on the day of my baptism, my mother, Tante Emilie, and my father's half-sister, Frieda, who was my godmother, dressed me in a white outfit and carried me on a lacy white pillow to the Lutheran church in Berchtesgaden. It was a long walk, down into the valley and up the other side, but no one thought anything of it. Cars were only for the very wealthy, and the stony, sandy roads were far too steep and bumpy for a baby carriage. Herr Pfarrer Krafft, the Lutheran minister, performed what was by all accounts a rather perfunctory ceremony, and after the christening, I, now Irmgard Albine Luise—before God—was carried home safely in my father's arms while my mother, still a little wobbly on her feet, tried to keep up. The Reitlechner family awaited the christening party with freshly brewed coffee, moist, yellow *Königskuchen* (pound cake), and shiny *Apfeltorte* (apple tart) that the women had baked for the occasion. I was put back into my pretty, white-lined willow basket fastened to a wooden undercarriage with small wooden wheels. The grown-ups, meanwhile, sat down to their celebratory *Kaffeeklatsch* at the table set with my mother's best china on top of the starched, white tablecloth that she herself had embroidered with a light blue and dark blue cross-stitch pattern. Thus ended my only visit to church until about a dozen years later.

□ □

FROM THE BEGINNING MY BIRTHDAYS and those of other family members were the most significant and joyous markers of the year outside of Christmas. However, growing up in Bavaria meant living by a calendar studded with feast days: days for Sankt Peter and Sankt Paul, Michaelitag (Saint Michael's Day), Maria's Verkuendigung (Mary's Annunciation), Maria's Himmelfahrt (Mary's Ascension), Christi Himmelfahrt (Christ's Ascension), Aller Heiligen (All Souls' Day), the feast of Fronleichnam (Corpus Christi Day), and then some. Between them and the new Nazi holidays, you could watch a march or walk in a procession every couple of weeks. It seemed as if marching or walking in long, orderly rows for one mysterious reason or another was one of my country's favorite pastimes.

Many of the traditions in the Berchtesgaden valley stemmed from ancient customs and myths that had been changed, overlaid, and added to over hundreds of years of Christian interpretations and beliefs. As the Nazis began to impose their radical interpretation of our Germanic heritage and Aryan destiny by altering the meanings of familiar holiday symbols and practices, we began to integrate those meanings and practices into our lives, just as generations of people in the valley had done before. To me, growing up with these changes, they seemed quite normal. Usually we just doubled up on the old and the new, feeling it was all part and parcel of a better Germany. If what was demanded was too inconvenient or absurd, we ignored it, but only in private.

Weihnachtszeit (Christmas season) or *Advent* in Berchtesgaden was a magical time of year. The Nazis, knowing full well the deep impressions the traditions and pageantry of this holiday made on children and adults alike, tried to put their imprint on every aspect of it. By mid-December, the mountains were blanketed with snow that would cover the entire valley for months. From the day we made our Advent wreath and put four red candles on it—one to be lit on each of the Sundays leading up to *Heiligabend* (Holy Night, or Christmas Eve)—preparing for Christmas was part of our everyday life. Mutti made spiced cookie dough from a recipe out of her handwritten cook-

book. She let me mold my own small lump of shiny brown dough that along with hers was stored in a covered stoneware bowl on top of the orange-flamed wardrobe in the unheated bedroom to let them rest.

Over the next few weeks, whenever the oven in the wood-fired kitchen stove was at the right temperature, Mutti sliced a thick slab from the fragrant loaf, rolled it out, and cut it into cookie shapes. As soon as I could look over the table's edge, standing on a stool, I

My father holding me, age ten months.

used my own child-size wooden rolling pin with red handles to make cookies in the shapes of stars, bells, hearts, Santa Claus, and trees and decorate them with peeled white almonds. *"Es riecht nach Weihnachten"* (It smells of Christmas), Vati said when he came home on a baking day. If Mutti felt generous, she'd let him try a few of the hard, crisp *Pfefferkuchen* before she consigned the rest of them to a large silvery tin, where they would soften and their flavors meld and mellow. By the time *Heiligabend* came around, at least a dozen different kinds of cookies had been baked in heavy competition with other *Hausfrauen,* each with her secret and well-guarded family recipes. Now, however, the Nazis urged the women to form their dough into Nordic trees of life or Celtic runes. My mother made a few attempts at this—she even had a pattern for the suggested shapes—but the misshapen sausages that came out of the oven earned her only ridicule from my father and the Reitlechners, and she went back to our traditional forms of stars, half-moons, rings, and hearts.

The *Weihnachtsstollen* (Christmas bread) came last. Mutti was partial to a *Dresdner Stollen,* a rich and heavy loaf that was served a few thin slices at a time. She and the townswomen marveled at the fact that with employment up and steady incomes they were able to buy all the butter, sugar, eggs, vanilla sugar, essence of rum, lemons, and almonds needed to make a masterpiece. This feeling of plenty was still novel to them, and they thanked the Führer for it.

The word *Weihnacht* (holy night) may have come from pagan times but had for ages stood for the blessing brought by the birth of Jesus. The Nazis, however, began to promote a different name for the holiday, calling it Julfest (Yuletide) or Rauhnacht (rough night) to emphasize a neopagan, Nordic/Germanic concept that focused on the winter solstice, the harsh, dark times that required forbearance and strength, followed by the long-awaited return of the sun. The notion of celebrating the sun appealed to my no-longer-churchgoing parents, especially to Mutti. But even she never used any word for the holiday other than *Weihnachten.*

The Nazi zealots also undertook to change Saint Nikolaus

(Santa Claus), the old saint who showed himself to the children of Berchtesgaden on the evening of December 6. The Nikolaus I knew first was dressed in the white-and-gold vestures of a bishop, his white-gloved hands holding a crooked staff, an impressive, tall miter sitting atop his head. According to ancient mountain customs he was accompanied by a bunch of wild devils wrapped in straw, wearing carved wooden masks with horns meant to drive out bad spirits. Every year I was scared out of my wits just from the noise of cowbells and chains that grew louder as the group approached Haus Linden. Vati, however, opened the door only to Saint Nikolaus, who expected to hear a pious little Christmas song and a promise that I had been good all year. After a blessing and the gift of a small burlap sack with apples, nuts, cookies, and golden chocolate coins, he assured us that he would tell the Christ child that I deserved Christmas presents and then left some willow switches with my parents just in case.

The Nazis sought to replace the saintly bishop, messenger from the Christ child, with the *Weihnachtsmann* (Father Christmas), a bearded man clad in red who came from the frozen Nordic sea. For him we sang "Der Weihnachtsmann wo kommt er her, über Berge und Felder, durch Wiesen und Waelder, vom kalten Meer" (The Christmas man, where does he come from? Over mountains and fields, meadow and woods, from the cold sea). Finally we let in Klaus Ruprecht, a grizzled old man riding in from the woods on a donkey (he left the donkey outside hidden in the dark, of course). Him we greeted with a silly little staccato tune with the words "Knecht Ruprecht aus dem Walde, kommt zu uns nun balde. Bringt uns gute Sachen mit nach gutem Brauch und alter Sitt, ria ria ria rullala" (Knecht Ruprecht from the forest will be coming soon. He will bring us good things according to old traditions and good customs). I became quite confused by these different harbingers of Christmas who showed up over the years, but I never lost faith that one of them would come on December 6, make me tremble with excitement, and raise my anticipation of the real thing: Christmas Eve.

A few days before December 24, my father put a handsaw into his grayish green rucksack and at dusk went out to cut a young spruce tree he and Mutti had secretly earmarked during the summer in a public or farmer's wood. He dragged it home through the snow to a hiding spot behind the house. I have to admit that stealing the Christmas tree rather than spending scarce money for it was the pervasive tradition, and no Nazi official tried to do much about it. As a matter of fact, the relatively new custom of the evergreen *Tannenbaum* (spruce) and the evergreen branches, garlands, and wreaths fit well with Nordic symbolism and pagan ideas.

Christmas Eve was always a cold, often snowy day. Vati fired up the cast iron stove in the big bedroom until the pipe glowed. At three o'clock in the afternoon the whole family dressed warmly enough to step outside to hear the church bells in the valley "ringing in" the Christ child and the *Weihnachtsschuetzen* (Christmas shooters) making a great racket with large, old-fashioned, wooden pistols that were passed on from father to son. Most German clubs had been subsumed into Nazi organizations, but the *Weihnachtsschuetzenverein* (Christmas shooters club) tenaciously held on to its existence and its mission to preserve local traditions. The clubs—each village in the valley had its own chapter—were a thorn in the eyes of Martin Bormann and local Nazis who felt they should be part of the Hitler Youth or at least under the leadership of those who would teach Nazi doctrine. Since the clubs were close to the ever-suspect Catholic church, provided a means of gathering and unobserved conversation, and had access to gunpowder, they seemed to present a real danger. However, since Hitler himself was an honorary member, no one dared disperse the association.

We children went back into the warm bedroom until the tinkling of a small bell called us to the open door of the living room lit only by the candles on the tree. Unlike the gaudy Berchtesgaden tree, with brightly painted miniature toys, stars made of straw and wood shavings, little red apples, and bright red candles, Vati's signature tree had snow-white candles, silver tinsel, and frosted silver balls. I loved the calm glimmer of ours; we always had it that way.

The women of Haus Linden—Mutti, Tante Susi, Trudi, and later my sister and I—sang together throughout the year, but on *Heiligabend* the singing before the tree was obligatory and for my taste far too long. With increased infiltration of our traditions by the Nazis we now sang all of the new songs that we learned from Trudi, who was in the Hitler Youth, after the old carols we had always known. The new songs glorified not Mary and the birth of Christ but German motherhood and winter solstice with the promise of the return of the sun. *"Hohe Nacht der Klaren Sterne"* ("High Night of Clear Stars") was my favorite new song, especially the verse: "Mütter euch sind alle Feuer, alle Sterne aufgestellt; Mütter tief in euren Herzen schlägt das Herz der jungen Welt" (Mothers, all stars and fires are lit for you; mothers, deep within your hearts beats the heart of a new world). For a girl someday headed for womanhood and motherhood, it was a seductive text aimed straight for my heart. At last, in front of the now half-burned candles, Mutti began the final song, which was and always would be "Stille Nacht, Heilige Nacht" ("Silent Night, Holy Night"), focusing our attention back to God's Son and the religion that had been the backbone of German culture for a thousand years. This more than any other song made my Christmas. It had been composed in a nearby Austrian village, and we sang it only on Christmas Eve.

Our presents were not wrapped—who would think of such waste even in these better times?—and were, as Mutti's expense account confirmed, extremely modest and outrageously practical. There was the obligatory heavy underwear from the grandmothers, and the knitted gloves and hats. The *Puppenstube*, a dollhouse consisting of two open rooms next to each other with furniture made by my grandfather, reappeared after eleven months in storage. Each year the furniture would be rearranged and something added, such as fresh curtains a new, tiny china tea set. My dolls too reappeared after a mysterious absence, with new dresses, coats, and hats, all, of course, secretly hand-stitched by my mother. We stayed up as long as we wanted on Christmas Eve. Before midnight we heard the jingling of bells on the sleds of the farmers who passed the house on their way to celebrate mass in the *Stiftskirche* (cloister church). I was told that a thousand candles lit the nave that, despite Hitler's proximity on the mountain, echoed only with Christian songs.

Months later, shortly before Palm Sunday, Mutti asked one of the neighborhood boys to bring her a *Palmbaum* (palm tree). Living nowhere near where palms grew, young farm boys tied together pussy willow branches, decorated them with brightly dyed ribbons of wood shavings, and carried them to Palm Sunday mass for blessings. The bundles were supposed to commemorate Jesus' entry into Jerusalem, but Mutti found the Nazi interpretation that this was a fertility rite more appealing. For a little pocket money Anderl Schwab, the landlord's grandson, brought a bush that we stuck in Vati's rock garden while the farmers put their bush out into their fields or behind the crucifix that hung in a corner of their living rooms. Outside, the ribbons of the willow bushes fluttered in the wind on the greening meadows and eventually faded in the sun.

Inevitably Palm Sunday was followed by Good Friday, the highest of Protestant holidays, filled with somber services and Bach chorales. Both the Nazis and my parents mostly ignored it, except that Mutti still honored her parents' rule of no meat on Fridays, especially Good Friday.

Easter, to the contrary, sprouted many a new Nazi song in praise of the fresh green and the reawakening of nature. The traditions of Easter, the eggs and the *Osterhase* (Easter bunny), were heathen enough, making change less necessary. Observant Catholics and Protestants—which few of our friends were—went to church, of course, but for my family Easter was simply a jubilant marking of the end of winter. The cold and the snow that still lay in store suddenly seemed bearable. Someday soon the sleds and the skis would be put away and the indoors would once again take sec-

My father and mother skiing near Haus Linden. The wooden skis were made for them by the local ski maker.

ond place. There must have been snowy and slushy Easter Sundays, but those I remember were glorious spring days when you could watch the snow melt and the tiny deep blue spring gentian, primroses, and soldanella appear.

Under Trudi's instructions I—later my sister too—built soft, round Easter nests from the moss that we pulled in large pieces from old wood or rocks and shaped with great care at the base of a tree trunk. On Easter morning we ran out into the woods, wool sweaters slipped hastily over our pajamas, to check if the Easter bunny had indeed left a few chocolate eggs or perhaps a real, colored egg in the moss nests or other hiding places.

The Nazis declared several holidays of their own and held on to May Day, the first of May, as a nod to the productivity and industry of German workers—but decidedly not to celebrate labor unions, which they had brutally eliminated after the May Day celebration in 1933. The day was now called *Nationaler Feiertag des Deutschen Volkes* (national holiday of the German people), but *Tag der Arbeit* (day of labor) remained the common name. Regardless of official ceremonies and marches, in Berchtesgaden the first of May was a prime day for skiing in the high mountains or for all-day family outings.

November 9, in contrast, was a somber and politically laden holiday that we could not escape. I knew even before I went to school that the day commemorated the 1923 march by the S.A., Hitler's Sturmabteilung (storm troopers), on the War Ministry in Munich after Hitler's attempted beer-hall Putsch. Sixteen of the storm troopers were shot while Hitler fled the mêlée. He was soon caught and after a trial went to jail. Nazi propaganda exploited the episode by turning the killed S.A. men into martyrs and Hitler into a wronged hero who had suffered for his people. The "Horst Wessel Song" composed for the occasion proclaimed: "Kameraden die rot Front und Reaktion erschossen, marschiern im Geist in unsern Reihen mit" (Comrades who were shot by the Red front and the Reactionaries are marching with us in spirit). For years I had no idea what the words meant, but since I thought I should know, I never dared ask. The song, like many Nazi songs, had a driving, militaristic beat that made me want to march along with whoever was marching, men or ghosts. Most of the new songs composed

The swastika flag shadows Berchtesgaden's streets.

for the various occasions in need of a Nazi imprint were rotten compositions with bad lyrics, but they were eminently singable and persuasive in a basic, primitive way. I was easy prey for manipulation by music, since like all Germans, I loved music as a medium that could tell a compelling story, express deep feelings, and arouse great passion.

Even the smallest child knew that Adolf Hitler's birthday was April 20. On this day, more abundantly than on any other, the red flags with the black swastika against a white circle were hoisted all over town. They flew from the windows and balconies along the main street, the town hall, the post office, and the schools, and in the gardens of restaurants and inns. My family, however, did not ever own or fly a swastika flag. I took this to mean that my parents' Nazism was a mixed bag of enthusiasm and avoidance when possible of the most inconvenient and absurd decrees and customs; besides, my father disliked crowds, marching, and uniforms. After one of those birthday parades Trudi brought home a tiny swastika flag on a wooden stick. It was still around when we built a snow castle the following winter, and with Vati's approval we stuck it over the entryway. Usually Hitler spent his birthday on Obersalzberg, prompting the town paper to run pictures of local dignitaries making speeches and Hitler smiling paternally at local children congratulating him with bunches of alpine flowers. During one of the war years Mutti's only entry in her diary on April 20 was "Heute ist Hitler's Geburtstag" (Today is Hitler's birthday).

4 "HEIL HITLER"

IN BETWEEN HOLIDAYS MY FATHER WENT TO WORK in the Adler workshop every day except Sunday, while Mutti, as she had dreamt when she walked over the moors of Finland, was a full-time homemaker and mother, thrifty as ever, and very content. Every morning I waved to Vati till he disappeared on the trail through the woods, and later met him a little ways down the trail when he came home for lunch, the main meal of the day. Herr Adler, Vati's boss, was what my mother contemptuously called a "Nazi fanatic." Strangely enough, what made her differentiate between him and all the other people who were middle-of-the-road or forced Nazis was quite clear to me. I learned to discern the subtle differences in conversations, in gestures and phrases of greeting, the deferential mention of "our Führer" as opposed to the overly familiar and therefore disrespectful "Adolf" that Tante Susi and Onkel Peppi used. Quite likely Herr Adler's fanatical and early devotion to Hitler won him the order to decorate Hitler's own dinner set for the Berghof, his newly reconstructed mountain home, with alpine flowers. The contract brought Hitler right into my father's workweek, making me tremendously proud of him. I told anyone who asked me what he did that he painted flowers for the Führer. The fact that the Führer preferred simple flowers on white china to the fancy gold and cobalt blue decorations that most heads of state demanded endeared him to the people and to me, for I loved flowers too. Soon everyone wanted to own souvenirs and china adorned with hand-painted edelweiss, gentian, alpine primroses, and anemones. The Adler workshop was thriving.

Decorative bowls with alpine flowers painted by my father.

Unfortunately, Vati's long work hours did not translate into an ample income. Mutti's weekly household money was just enough to meet our modest, basic needs, making her thrift a necessary virtue. My toys and few books, the annual trip to visit my grandparents, and small savings toward the house we would buy one day were all beyond her tight budget. We could afford them because over my father's objections—he hated strangers in the house— Mutti rented out my bedroom to summer guests who flocked in increasing numbers to Berchtesgaden to breathe the same air as Hitler and perhaps even get a glimpse of him.

During the summer months the *Fremden* (foreigners, as they were called here in this Bavarian valley even though they came mostly from within Germany) took breakfast in our kitchen or in front of its window, which had a partial view of Watzmann, Germany's second-highest mountain. They would ask me how to get to Obersalzberg, where Hitler lived, from Untersalzberg, where we lived. Once I had overcome my shyness I gave precocious answers our guests found amusing. I was often invited along on hikes and the tour into the salt mines deep inside our mountain. I learned to my amazement that the Salzberg was not, as I had imagined, filled with white salt but was made of hard rocks that required a great deal of work by miners and machines before they were transformed into Mutti's cooking salt. "White gold," the guide called the precious mineral, and I thought that was more fitting than salt for Hitler's mountain.

The best part of having my room rented out was that even though at three I considered myself a big girl, I was for a short time moved back into my parents' bedroom to sleep in the large, white crib that my Pöhlmann grandfather had made for me and shipped from Selb when I was born. After the last guests had left along with the swallows, the meadows turned brown and the geraniums were taken in from the balconies or died in an early frost. The fall holiday season began anew with November 9, and the marching and the drumbeat continued.

□   □

AMONG THE LITTLE BOYS AND GIRLS who came to play with me was Ruth Ungerer. She had been born a week before me in a house up the road, even though I had been expected first. The two young mothers competed fiercely over their babies' development, comparing the first smile, first word, first steps, and progress of potty training. Ruthchen (little Ruth) had a headful of hair from the day she was born, whereas I, much to Mutti's concern, had none until I was a year old. Ruthchen was a constant presence in my very early life, so I was amazed when Mutti told me one day that Ruthchen was no longer Ruth but Ingrid—one of the most favored Germanic names. "Ruth is a Jewish name," Mutti explained without obvious malice in her voice, "and with her father joining the border police [he had been a barber] it is better for her not to have a Jewish name." I had no idea what Jewish was, but it could not be good if you had to give up your name because of it. The Ungerer family was moved to Austria quickly, making it impossible for me to remember my playmate by any name other than Ruthchen until we met again.

In the winter of 1936–37 my Onkel Hans, Mutti's brother, had written from Selb: "I have finally found a job in Lettin near Halle on the Saale and Emma and I plan to get married as soon as we can arrange it." Mutti and Vati rejoiced. Onkel Hans and Emma Fischer had been dating since their late teens and had been eagerly waiting for Hans to find a steady job so they could be married and begin a family. Along with many impatient young men, he had become an ardent Hitler supporter. To my grandfather's disappointment, he had also decided to become an accountant instead of a carpenter who would take over the family business. Hans had seen what kind of life a small business afforded and preferred to be employed in a white-collar job that came with a pension. Retirement with a pension had become an obsession with middle-class Germans, even the young, having witnessed again and again the loss of all their private savings.

Mutti and Vati did not travel to Selb for the wedding. By and by we received a wedding picture, and I thought that my new Tante Emma and Onkel Hans made a very handsome young couple. There were no polka dots for Emma, such as Mutti had had on her wedding dress, but—as was suitable for an accountant's and future corporate vice president's wife—she wore a long white dress. An embroidered veil lay fashionably loose halfway across her forehead and over her carefully coiffed hair. She seemed extravagantly beautiful to my almost three-year-old self, and I told Mutti that I planned to look just like that when I married Vati.

After their wedding ceremony at the town hall Hans and Emma were handed the new, official *Familien Stammbuch*. It had been completely revised by the Nazis since my parents had received theirs and no longer contained the sentence "Schwer lastet auf dem Deutschen Volk die Not der Zeit" (The misery of our times weighs heavily on the German people), the official recognition by the Weimar government of those impossibly difficult times. The record-keeping function of the *Familien Stammbuch* had not changed, but now it had become an instrument of control and surveillance over each and every German family, mandating that

young couples prove their racial purity back over several generations. Two introductory essays addressed racial hygiene and the
need for racial purity. A certain Dr. Achim Gercke, expert for racial
research of the Reichsministerium des Innern (Department of the
Interior), wrote, "Clearly it is necessary that everyone must con-
serve his kin, connect with German blood of equal quality and
build a healthy and numerous generation. This generation will
represent an invincible Germany that in the purity of its blood and
the strength of its race will fulfill its great tasks in the world."
Meanwhile, taking some of the burden of racial cleansing off the
individual, university professor Dr. F. Lenz told the newlyweds
that "the measures necessary to maintain the purity of our [the
German] race are to a large degree the task of the State which can-
not be addressed here."

The new *Stammbuch* also stated that anyone marrying a non-
Aryan endangered his or her legal standing as a German citizen.
Average middle-class Germans were not used to questioning the
pronouncements of people of rank, especially people in authority
or with academic titles, and it is not surprising that no one questioned these declarations but instead—if they read them at all—
decided they could live with them. Onkel Hans conscientiously
filled out the required data as far back as his great-grandparents,
distressed perhaps that while they were pure Germans, they were
all so very, very poor.

□   □

SHORTLY AFTER MY THIRD BIRTHDAY, in the early summer of
1937, my father taught me to stand up straight and raise my right
arm in the "Heil Hitler" greeting. We stood in front of the Führer's
portrait, a small, red wax relief in an antiqued gold frame cast by
my father's friend Schego as a wedding present. I laughed at first
and thought we were playing some kind of game but quickly realized that Vati was dead serious. He insisted that I thrust my small
arm forward in just the right way. This would be the greeting I
would use in town and with strangers and especially if a swastika

flag was carried past. With the Reitlechners and other close friends and neighbors I could still shake hands, curtsy, and say "Gruess Gott" (God greet you), the comfortable, old Bavarian way of wishing one another Godspeed. I listened but by then was much more interested in running outside to my new sandbox. Vati had filled a wooden soap crate with white sand from the edges of the Larusbach, a swift mountain stream tumbling down a rocky bed from Hitler's Obersalzberg. Having such a fine new plaything took my mind off the vexing problem of how exactly I would discern when to greet people in God's name and when in Hitler's.

Young children greeting Hitler with the Nazi salute on Obersalzberg.

5 OMINOUS UNDERCURRENTS

A FEW WEEKS AFTER THE 1937 SUMMER SOLSTICE—
Johannistag (Saint John's Day) for Catholics—Mutti told me that
any day now a stork with a strong, orange beak would bring me a
little baby brother or sister. In those days pregnant women carried
their babies with extreme discretion and modesty, usually just
moving a few buttons on their dirndl dresses and letting the
pinafores slip above their bellies. No one would dream of pointing
out the state of affairs to a three-year-old. My energetic, dark-
haired, rather short Tante Emilie had arrived a few days before the
new baby's due date to help my mother once again and to look
after me for a few weeks. I greeted her joyfully and proudly with
my brand-new "Heil Hitler!" She stopped just inside the door,
looked at me, and without losing a beat said that I knew my greeting very well but that she liked the old "Gruess Gott" or "Guten
Tag" (good day) better. I was taken aback and disappointed, as I
had expected nothing but a "Heil Hitler" in return, but quickly decided that it was time to run to her and give her a hug.

Tante Emilie had not married—she blamed it on a dearth of
young men after World War I—but had a degree in home econom-
ics and was usually either teaching at or managing the household
of a hospital, training institution, or youth center. She was a bit of
a busybody and with her rigorous concepts of hygiene found fault
even with Mutti's immaculate home, rearranging and cleaning the
minute she arrived. She was an optimist—rare in our land—who
would usually find something good in any situation, a moment to
laugh about or to be amused by. The two women giggled over

things I did not understand while they kept busy with refurbishing my baby things in preparation for the new arrival. Both were good seamstresses who had made their own up-to-date flapper dresses in the 1920s and knew how to line a bassinet as well as copy the newest fashions sported by the spouses of the Nazi bosses or, until she left Germany, by Marlene Dietrich.

On July 12, 1937, an invisible stork brought my little sister. She was named Ingrid Emma—obviously there was no getting away from Ingrid—and I realized that it would be a long time before she would become a playmate. Instead, she spent her time sleeping and being nursed by Mutti. Knowing how much my mother had wanted a boy, I hoped that, contrary to all evidence, her wish would still come true if only I believed it. For a few days I insisted that I had a little brother, and only when a neighbor pointed out that Ingrid was a peculiar name for a boy did I accept that indeed she was only a girl, just like me.

As he had done when I was born, Vati went off to the town registry and the parsonage at the Lutheran church way up the other side of the valley. Once again he came home with important news: There would be no christening for Ingrid because he had officially withdrawn from the Evangelical Lutheran Church and joined the 5 percent of Germans who had become *Gottgläubig*, a new, optional "religion" thought up and synthesized by the Nazis and Hitler. I pouted and bravely told my father that he should have asked me before he took such a step. I had looked forward to taking the baby to church on the white lace pillow and having a *Kaffee und Kuchen* party for her christening. Yet, along with a tiny baby who could not play with me, I lost out on that too. As consolation I was promised a party without the baptism to welcome Ingrid Emma. Although now we were *Gottgläubig*, throughout the existence of the Third Reich I never learned the slightest thing about our new beliefs or values—not even if we believed in God or not—most likely because none were ever thought up. Perhaps Vati, who had never been a fan of the church and in his younger days had actively rebelled against it, felt more comfortable with the nebulous *Gottgläubigkeit*.

The decision not to christen the new child upset my Pöhlmann grandmother, a devout Lutheran. She scolded my mother for giving in to my father's newfangled ideas, but Mutti said that she herself was sick of churches holding us captive and fully agreed with Vati's decision. I knew of this family debate only by hearsay but in any case had no voice in the matter. Ingrid, with a fluff of white-blond hair and, as everyone noted, a likeness to my father, was a fat, happy baby and clearly seemed none the worse for her lack of christening.

Trudi, my idol, tried to distribute her love evenly between us, but I was not happy that Ingrid Emma was now being wheeled up and down the road in my baby carriage. Besides, Vati would come home these days and check out the baby before he told me about his day and what flowers he had painted. I resented the huge amount of time Mutti seemed to be spending with the baby. All day long she was either nursing it, cooking the mushy food it could eventually eat, and endlessly washing and hanging diapers, baby clothes, and bibs.

With this second baby my mother rarely referred to her battered baby book. She grated fewer carrots for the fresh, vitamin-rich juice that had given my skin an orange hue. I, however, found looking at that slim, light-green paperback deeply fascinating and was awed by its all-too-realistic, gruesome pictures of malnourished and sick babies with their rickets and smallpox. I suggested that Mutti and I should check Ingrid's small body for signs of these terrifying diseases, but she assured me that according to the chart and the rented baby scale, my little sister was doing just fine. The green paperback, written in the late 1920s, had been meant for a miserably poor middle-class readership. It was filled with hints for how to deal with tiny, windowless city apartments with no heat or fresh air, or with the inability to take the baby outdoors or to hang its wet, hand-washed diapers outside to dry. Mutti would look sad when she saw the pictures and say, "It's good that our children were born here in the mountains with all this fresh air and sunshine." She was amused that the authors of the green book found it necessary to warn against toughening the baby in ice-cold water. "Must have been a Prussian custom, for who else would think of such a thing," she said, shaking her head. Our lack of early hardening was no deterrent when she taught me how to swim in our glacial mountain lakes.

ONE WARM, SUNNY DAY while my mother and Ingrid were sleeping, Tante Emilie and I swent for a walk. It was the time of high grasses, bluebells, yellow-eyed daisies, and tall, pink clover, and we picked a large bouquet for my mother. Suddenly the peaceful, fragrant summer day was interrupted by the sound of shouts on the road to Obersalzberg. I stated matter-of-factly: "That's probably the Führer driving up to the Berghof, or perhaps Hermann Göring or Dr. Goebbels." I was repeating the words that I had heard from the grown-ups when we saw the black cars driving up the mountain, and I felt myself to be a very smart guide for my aunt. In spite of herself, Tante Emilie became very curious, and we ran toward the main road. Hitler's trip up the mountain that day must have been widely announced because we joined an enthusiastic horde of onlookers lining the road, waving and cheering. As always when a large crowd was at attention, Hitler stood up in his open, black Mercedes with the red leather upholstery. His arm was stretched out straight, and I asked Tante Emilie in a whisper whether he hailed himself, and she said he did it to recognize our adulation. His entourage followed in the black signature cars.

Apparently Tante Emilie had made up her mind that she would not raise her arm to greet either the Führer or the swastika flag fluttering next to the Mercedes emblem, an encircled star, on his car. I, of course, happily raised my arm and called out "Heil Hitler" with the rest of the crowd. As the big, black limousine passed by, even I could see the Führer's face. Tante Emilie kept her arm close by her side at first, but then, probably realizing that she risked imprisonment or worse, she raised it slowly, without shouting. The dispersing crowd was happy to have seen the Leader, but on our way home, I heard Tante Emilie grumbling to herself. "How could I have been so weak as to let myself do that?" Years later she told me that as the car moved by at its unhurried pace, Hitler's black eyes fastened on her and kept staring at her until, as if hypnotized, she raised her arm in the salute she hated. Tante Emilie could never forget this victory of Hitler's will over hers.

Back at Haus Linden my little sister was sleeping sweetly in her *Stubenwagen*, the same wooden-wheeled indoor baby carriage, hung with clouds of pretty, white organza, that had once held me. She winced in her sleep, and my mother and Tante Emilie laughed at her funny, wrinkled nose. When my father came home that evening, we told him of our encounter with Hitler, but Tante Emilie omitted the fact that she had not wanted to greet him. Throughout her stay Vati let it be known that he was critical of Tante Emilie's lack of enthusiasm, and I was utterly bewildered that two people I loved could disagree so strongly. I kept looking for clues about which one to listen to, to believe, and to follow.

Tante Emilie and my parents had moved in opposite directions. Emilie had never been and never would be a Nazi, and tried to maintain her distance and show her disdain for the regime, actions that became increasingly risky. She refused to participate in Party-sponsored women's groups until the middle of World War II, when she was told she would lose her job unless she attended the weekly women's group meetings and subscribed to a Nazi newspaper. Mutti said to her, "You are in the wrong camp." The result of this rift was an avoidance of political debate, especially, it seemed, when my father was home. The views of my parents and Tante Emilie were too far apart to risk a conversation that could have no good outcome. The risk was not betrayal as much as the loss of their friendship when all the two young women wanted was to make up for their lost youth and enjoy what they had gained.

"Good Man Hitler" endeared himself to innumerable middle-class women by proclaiming that German mothers with many children were the very basis of a strong, healthy nation. Unlike the extermination programs, the breeding programs were yet unrealized on a massive scale but were forming in Hitler's mind for a future time. Within my own mother's heart—she still hoped for a bunch of boys—the Nazi support of motherhood and full-time homemakers struck a deep chord. She was grateful that unlike her mother she was able to enjoy the luxury of staying home with her children, and she relished the fact that we were well fed and had a small but adequate supply of diapers, cotton wraps, caps, and booties. Did she want to raise her dream boys for the Führer, for his army, to create the super race? I will never know because we never talked about it.

The Party organized ceremonies to honor mothers with six or more children. Mutti took me along to one of these events one gray winter evening. I heard the drone of long speeches and the singing of new songs and saw the presentation of the Mutterkreuz (Mother's Cross) to the honoree, a stout woman in a dark blue, long-sleeved dirndl dress on which the silvery medal shone. Magda Goebbels, wife of the propaganda minister and more or less our neighbor on Obersalzberg, was, with her seven children, the most famous of the Mutterkreuz recipients. Most of the mothers thus honored in Berchtesgaden, however, were Catholic farm women who had always borne many, many children, unlike the majority of educated, emancipated German women of the 1920s and most of the wives of the higher-up Nazis. Hitler himself claimed he was too busy ruling Germany to marry and father children. The motherly housewives who were honored did not know that top-notch professionals like the filmmaker Leni Riefenstahl or Hanna Reitsch, a famous test pilot who would share Hitler's last days in the Berlin bunker, were the women he most respected.

□   □

ONE ADVANTAGE OF MUTTI'S PREOCCUPATION with Ingrid was that I gained far greater freedom to explore the world on my own; soon the entire neighborhood became my playground. Haus Linden stood at the edge of the woods and meadows of the Stadlerlehen, the estate and wonderful parkland of Frau Villnow, a well-to-do divorcée from Pomerania who had bought the old farm years earlier. The farmhouse had become a villa, but the stable and the gray, weathered barn were left intact. Benches for sunset watching stood under old linden trees, and gravel paths wound through mixed forest and upwards-rolling meadows. A few fine, strong horses and a few cows were kept by Herr Dehmel, the caretaker from Pomerania who with his family had accompanied Frau Villnow to Berchtesgaden and lived in a cottage on the estate.

I loved to roam the estate with my neighborhood friends. Surprisingly, the stout and arrogant Frau Villnow tolerated our explorations of the park and our using the gymnastics equipment that she had installed for her now grown son. Three of the four Dehmel girls were always part of the group of neighborhood children that played together in the park. The fourth girl had an illness of some kind and never came outside to play. Albert, their older brother, was beyond our childish games and had already signed on for the Hitlerjugend (Hitler Youth), and we looked at him with awe. White-blond Hildegard, the youngest of the three sisters who played with us, was a somewhat peculiar-looking, slow child with very small eyes and seemingly little response to the world around her. Her two older sisters, Else and Gisela, were incredibly patient with Hildegard and carefully helped her get through a fence or sat her down on a lump of grass or moss so that she could see us while she gently rocked her body back and forth, back and forth.

□   □

ONE AFTERNOON (IT MUST HAVE BEEN MONDAY, wash day, because they were hanging their linens on the wires strung across the small, sloping meadow in front of our house), Tante Susi and my mother talked quietly with serious, worried faces. I loved to listen to grown-up gossip and moved closer to hear what the two women were saying. "One of the Dehmel children, the mongoloid one that's never outside, was picked up by the Health Service a few weeks ago, and now they've said she's dead from a cold," said my mother. Tante Susi with her pretty bobbed haircut shook her head. "That child was retarded worse than Hildegard," she mused, adding after a moment, "Well, it's probably true, her dying from a cold, I mean." Mutti bent down for another blindingly white sheet from the tin tub and sighed. I began to pick some white, pink-rimmed daisies as I mulled things over. Just that morning I had played with Else, Gisela, and Hildegard and knew they were fine. I began to wonder about the sister who had never played outside. What did it mean, she was taken away? She died from a cold? Would they take me away if I had a cold, and would I die too? I was infected by the feeling of unease I had sensed during the two women's conversation but, as quickly as they had, convinced myself that there was nothing to fear. Certainly Mutti and Vati would never let anyone take me away.

□ □

WHAT I DID NOT KNOW, and what the adults refused to believe or face, was that Hitler's euthanasia program, while still shrouded in secrecy and as much as possible hidden from the general public, was up and running. And if Mutti had heard rumors or suspected foul play concerning the Dehmel baby, she would have convinced herself that Hitler himself would not condone such murder. Herr and Frau Dehmel too did not question the authorities about their little girl's death but must have suspected that at the very least she was not cared for in the institution that took her. With deep silence, cunning, and determination, they succeeded throughout the Nazi years, right there on Hitler's mountain, in hiding and saving Hildegard, who so obviously was an afflicted child as well. They did not send her to school, use public health services, or do anything else that might bring her to the authorities' attention. The fear of having their child killed by the Nazis for her defect far outweighed the risk they took by not having her inoculated or ever visit a doctor. Else, Gisela, and Albert, the healthy siblings, were told to answer any questions regarding Hildegard with "I don't know." It worked, perhaps by sheer luck and because no one in the neighborhood who knew about her condition thought of turning to the authorities.

On the other hand, none of them had the moral courage to voice their suspicions openly and speak up against euthanasia. Fear of Nazi retribution and the wish to be left alone was a large part of this cowardice. Ironically, Herr Dehmel was one of the three men I knew who wore the brown S.A. uniform when the occasion arose; the other two were my father's boss, Herr Adler, and the painter Hans Schuster. Else would point out to us how shiny her father's boots and belt were, and with the enormous respect that was accorded the uniform I could see how different he looked out of his field and stable clothes.

Around the same time that I had been scared by the story of the sick little girl, Tante Susi's brother, Ferdl, came to visit her. We knew that he had just been released from Buchenwald, a new kind of

prison called K.Z. or *Konzentrationslager*—concentration camp. Tante Susi was visibly shaken on seeing how old and diminished he looked. They talked about their other sisters and brothers, the weather, everything except the concentration camp, waiting, perhaps, until I left the room. Onkel Ferdl, as Trudi called him, had been accused of making a small contribution to the Communist

A brooding Hitler walking on Obersalzberg.

Party and received a two-year sentence. On leaving the camp, he was told not to say a word about his experience or what he saw, not even to his family. Tante Susi told my parents that he had told her nothing because he feared he would be sent back. It could mean death for him. What my parents made of this information I don't know. Did they ignore it and stash it away in some secret part of their mind because they had no choice? They did not mention anything unusual about Ferdl's visit, leaving me to wonder why such a gentle, kind man would be in danger of losing his life. So far the only person I had known who had died was Kathi, a very old relative of the landlady who lived in a first-floor room in the big Haus Linden. No one grieved greatly when she died. It was to be expected, Mutti said, and put on her black skirt and jacket for the funeral. But things were very different with Onkel Ferdl. That much I knew even if Mutti and Vati cut short my childish questions about him. I realized that the concentration camp was the worst thing that could happen to a person and decided I would never get into the kind of trouble that would send me there.

I did not know that being Jewish was the main reason for being sent to a K.Z., and of course, my passport and certified Aryan ancestry assured that I would not get into that kind of trouble. The hate campaign against Jews had reached the valley already in 1933 when a black-framed ad in the local paper called for a boycott of Jewish businesses and publications. My parents must have heard about the Kristallnacht (night of broken glass) of November 9, 1938, when storm troopers, with help from the public, had destroyed close to two hundred synagogues, homes, and shops that belonged to Jews throughout Germany and Austria, including a few in our neighboring town of Bad Reichenhall. Yet there were no stories in my family of either friendly or hostile encounters with Jews.

Supposedly there were only two Jewish families in the Berchtesgaden valley in 1933; perhaps they had all left, like the Eichengruen family who sold their summer cottage on Obersalzberg in disgust in 1932 after Hitler and his S.A. roughnecks moved in next door and began to harass them. In 1937, when Hitler and his henchmen took over all of the upper mountain, the Eichengruen house and a neighboring farm were torn down and burned to make room for Martin Bormann's garden. The head of the family, Dr. Arthur Eichengruen was a prominent chemist under whose research direction the Bayer pharmaceutical company had developed aspirin. He built his own company, the Cellon-Werke, held about sixty patents, among them those for early synthetic fibers, noninflammable film, and numerous important medical inventions. His third wife was an Aryan German, which for a few years afforded him some protection. Stubbornly and naïvely, he never stopped believing that National Socialism was like a temporary illness—it would simply pass—and thus there was no need to leave Germany. He was eventually robbed of his entire wealth, his company, and his degrees. In 1943 he was sent to Theresienstadt, where he remained until he was freed in 1945 at the age of seventy-eight.

We had not known the Eichengruens or learned about their fate until I read about them many years later. However, lack of direct encounter with Jewish Germans did not mean that I did not absorb the general atmosphere of anti-Semitism and the contempt in which Jews were held, no matter how German they knew themselves to be. By osmosis rather than formal instruction I picked up the primitive and rudimentary impression that anything created by or connected with Jews was inferior, decadent, and dangerous. In my eleven years under Nazi rule no one tried to refute these claims. To do so might have spelled doom.

On certain days of the week I interrupted my games in the Stadlerpark to go shopping with Mutti in the *Markt* (commercial center), the actual town of Berchtesgaden. Since ancient times the people who settled in surrounding hamlets and villages undertook the often arduous trip up and down valleys and mountains to the *Markt* to purchase household supplies and transport them home in rucksacks, straw baskets, or oxcarts. Many of the villages had grown large enough for a small grocery store, a butcher, or a baker to make a living, but for fabric, candles, hardware, pots and pans, the barber, the printer, the blacksmith, and often the tailor, people still made the laborious journey to the old *Markt*. No one I knew had a refrigerator, even though Professor Linde, who had invented refrigeration, had a large summer villa on Salzberg and a beautiful walk named after him. Instead we bought small amounts of perishable food every few days and stored it in the fragrant, dark potato-and-apple cellar underneath the house or in the pantry outside the kitchen door. Strong as he was, Vati carried home the heavy staples on Saturday evenings after work. Knowing what would keep best where and under what conditions was a skill at which Mutti, Tante Susi, and their friends excelled.

Before we went downtown I had to hold my chafed knees still for cleaning and then put on a fresh playsuit. Mutti slipped into a clean white blouse and a freshly ironed, brightly colored dirndl jumper—you never knew who you would meet—and tied the bands of her white pinafore into a bow at the back. Her yellow-and-black-patterned typical Berchtesgaden straw basket hanging

S.S. troops raise flags at their barracks on Obersalzberg.

over one arm, she carried Ingrid upstairs to Tante Susi's. One behind the other, Mutti and I began to walk down the steep, slippery
shortcut through the woods to the river Ache. In about twenty
minutes we crossed the strong, newly rebuilt bridge, and I made
Mutti stop for a while in the middle so I could look down into the
froth of the deeply green glacial river in its stony bed, rushing toward Austria.

At the end of the bridge stood a small but solid stone guardhouse from which two S.S. guards watched the comings and go-
ings on the bridge, the first barrier to the Obersalzbergstrasse and
Hitler's quarters. The guards on duty knew the local people and instead of asking for our identification casually waved us on; we said
"Heil Hitler" as we passed. I knew that the guards were a police
force of some kind and that the police were always on the lookout
for bad conduct. I stopped hopping and skipping and was on my
best behavior when we passed by them, and for good measure I
held Mutti's hand tightly. What if suddenly I did something that
would change the guards' benevolence to anger? Almost without
my knowing, a little anxiety, a basic fear of authority, had contami-
nated my carefree mood, and an undercurrent of unease dimmed
the joy of the shopping trip at least for a short time. On the way
home we again passed the guards. Without being aware of the cynicism in what she was saying, Mutti pointed out that while these
S.S. men were guarding Hitler we too fell under their protection
and lived on a mountain free of crime, which made me feel sheltered from evil and more comfortable with their presence.

6 MEETING HITLER

I N THE FALL OF 1937 MY PÖHLMANN GRANDPAR-
ents came for a visit to meet Ingrid Emma, their new granddaughter. Both duly admired the healthy, smiley baby, and to my delight
Grossvati (Grandpa) was also amused by my antics and laughed
heartily when I offered him all the potatoes and spinach on my
dinner plate in return for his sausage. However, the degree to
which my parents and my grandparents diverged in their views on
Hitler and his politics had reached a new high. Most of their discussions, encouraged perhaps by Hitler's presence on the mountain, ended in verbal clashes followed by hostile silences. Grossvati
called Hitler a fly-by-night, no-good maniac who had seduced the
German people and addled their collective minds and would ulti-
mately betray them.

Hitler's path to Obersalzberg had been interwoven with the ups
and downs of his political fortunes. At first, when a warrant was
out for his arrest by the Bavarian state police, he was able to hide in
a small wooden hut on the mountain. Then, while also building
his power base, he finished writing *Mein Kampf* (published in 1925
to disappointing sales) in the summer cottage that he rented inex-
pensively from wealthy friends, and finally he ruled Germany and
planned to conquer the world from the completely reconstructed,
rather unwieldy residence he called the Berghof.

On the last day of my grandparents' visit Mutti persuaded her
reluctant elders to join us in a stroll up to the Obersalzberg to try
and see the new Berghof, now the center of a large, ever more
tightly sealed *Führergebiet* (leader's territory). The walk became a

historic event for my family, but the accounts of the event and the way I remember them—I was very young—have differed depending on who told the story. Strange, seemingly unimportant trivialities, such as the pale autumn crocuses that grew along the road, have remained with me vividly. But details of the exact trails we took, where we entered through the tall, barbed-wire fence that would soon close off the mountain to the unauthorized (I remember my grandfather commenting on it with contempt), the state of construction of each of the buildings we passed—in fact, the exact date—have from the beginning taken a backseat to the main event of meeting Hitler.

I remember it as a wonderfully warm autumn day on which fallen leaves rustled at my every step. As we made our way uphill the conversations between the grown-ups led to the same clashes they had at home. Mutti and Vati praised Hitler for saving Germany, and Grossvati maligned everything the Führer had done. I didn't understand the debates, and their vehemence made me feel anxious and helpless. I wondered who was right and who was wrong, since both sides carried the weight of authority. Hiking had made me thirsty, and in an attempt to divert the grown-ups from talking about Hitler I asked that we stop for a hot chocolate and *Apfelstrudel.* Unfortunately my request only intensified their argument, completely ruining this sun-dappled, intensely colorful autumn afternoon. "No, we can't," said Grossvati, "because there are no longer any inns and restaurants left for us here on Obersalzberg. Hitler and his friend Martin Bormann saw to that." Tante Susi with her keen ear for gossip had told him about Bormann's crude and merciless methods of evicting the inhabitants of Obersalzberg. Her words had scared me into thinking that Bormann might take our house as well, leaving us without a home. Seeing that I was upset about this possibility, she reassured me that Hitler had enough land now for his headquarters and would not want to come this far down the mountain.

Once the decision had been made to eliminate the old settlements and forge a completely insular and secured *Führergebiet* for

Bormann removed roofs from occupied homes to force their owners out.

Hitler, Bormann had evicted the inhabitants with great speed. The homes were destroyed and burned to make room for the Nazi leadership. Eighteen ancient farms, three inns, six bed-and-breakfasts, a large children's sanatorium, several hotels, and at least thirty-five private homes, villas, shops, and small artisan businesses were forcefully acquired most often for laughably small amounts of money. Families who had farmed and lived on the old Obersalzberg for generations had, even in the middle of winter, their roofs removed or their roads closed off if they balked at leaving or dared ask for greater compensation than the pittance Bormann offered. Years later I learned that the uncle of my grade-school classmate Trauderl Koller was sent to the Dachau concentration camp for two years merely for handing Hitler a letter requesting that he might continue his photo business on the mountain. Neither Trauderl nor Dorothea Lochner, another classmate whose family lost their ancestral home up on Obersalzberg, ever talked about it, not even after the Third Reich had collapsed. At the time a decree by Nazi authorities in the local newspaper announced that anyone who spread gossip about an Obersalzberg affair would be declared an enemy of the state and sent to a concentration camp. Grossvati was livid about his son-in-law's casual, accepting attitude of what he thought was a vile threat.

The population of Berchtesgaden—46.8 percent of whom had voted for Hitler—was torn between pride that Hitler had chosen to settle on the high plateau of Obersalzberg, his old hangout, and anger at the violence done to the old settlement and its inhabitants. My parents agreed that our leader deserved to have an impressive setting from which to represent Germany before other heads of state, and found his love of the mountains endearing.

Grossvati saw the radical takeover and changes as symbols of the Nazis' seemingly limitless, dangerous power. Vati pointed out that along with the new Berchtesgaden railroad station, a new branch of the Reichskanzlei (state chancellery), and the road construction from Munich to the mountains, this was the largest building project in all of Germany. It created more than three thousand jobs (up to six thousand later on) for local men and an increasing number of foreign workers. The foreign laborers, even though they were not slave labor, were ill fed and housed in stark, ugly barracks that we passed below the large new movie theater that was still under construction. Mutti stoked the fire, asking her father pointedly why he was not grateful that Hitler had ended the downward spiral of the twenties and that finally he made a living with his carpentry.

I left them to their argument, jumping over the huge puddles that had formed among vast piles of debris, and halted at the sight of the gigantic construction machine with wheels as tall as my father coming toward me. The monster stopped and I thought the Führer was indeed a very rich and powerful man to own such machines. A complex of S.S. barracks with a yard for marching, administrative buildings, a post office, the refurbished Hotel Platterhof, the movie theater—in short, a whole, rather sterile, ugly city interspersed with parking lots—was being created.

Not getting anywhere with his opinion, Grossvati looked upset and sad. I tried to find a few autumn flowers in the muddy grass

alongside the road to make him smile. But the boots of the workers, their machines, and the shoes of the crowds had trampled and killed any that might have grown here.

We approached the Berghof from above, and from a knoll we got the first glimpse of the new, domineering white structure that bore no similarity to the modest, rustic cottage my parents had known as Haus Wachenfeld. Mutti may have pointed out the other villas and homes of the Nazi elite that had replaced the old farms and flocked in a maelstrom around Adolf Hitler. The sheer south face of Untersberg, a stocky, stretched-out mountain—half in Germany and half in Austria—rose up across the valley. According to myth, deep inside Untersberg, Kaiser Friedrich I, known as Barbarossa (Redbeard), slept with his knights around a marble table. At a time when the black ravens would cease to circle the mountain, Barbarossa would awaken, blow his fanfare, and come out to wage his final, victorious battle. I had no idea why and against whom he would fight, but I loved the idea of the great kaiser of ancient times with his beautiful crown and his long red beard riding from the depths of the mountain followed by his handsome knights on their steeds. It was said that Hitler loved the Untersberg perhaps because he felt that the time of his own great, victorious battle for an empire had arrived.

Throughout the walk my grandmother had said little. In her long black skirt and black blouse, and with her very black hair, she was the opposite of my suntanned, blond mother in the pretty dirndl dress that Vati had admired before we left for our walk. Grossmutti, being twelve years older than my grandfather, was breathing hard to keep up with us, especially on the trek up the mountain.

On approaching the Berghof we joined a restless crowd of people milling around and waiting outside a fence. Even this late in the fall tourists were plentiful in Berchtesgaden, and most of them made the pilgrimage up the mountain in hopes of seeing Hitler

The Berghof, Hitler's mountain home, with Hoher Göll in the background.

himself. They jostled for better positions to take pictures of the house with its famous, large picture window and the rolling land

Hitler greeting admirers on Obersalzberg.

that in every direction led the eye on toward the high, jagged, or stocky mountains that enclosed the valley. An expectant murmur was in the air, a sense of anticipation, and everyone was ready to raise his arm and scream "Heil mein Führer!" at a moment's notice.

Then it happened. Hitler came out and I ended up sitting on his lap and family history was made. I remember being ill at ease perched on his knee and suspiciously studying his mustache, his slicked-back, oily hair, and the amazingly straight side part, while at the same time acutely sensing the importance of the moment and of the man. The applauding crowd disconcerted me as well, but I smiled bravely, checking every few seconds to make sure my family was close by. An official photographer snapped a photo. At one moment I saw my grandfather turning away brusquely, striking the air angrily with his cane, trying to find an escape through the people. He had obviously

Hitler with two children on his knee.

had enough of the spectacle, feeling most likely that his granddaughter was being misused by the man for whom he had nothing
but contempt.

I was greatly relieved when Hitler let me go, got up from his
crouching position, and stiffly turned back to the Berghof. The audience with the Führer was over, and everyone would go home

bragging about having seen him. Mutti beamed at me, and Vati gave me a "well done" nudge on my shoulder.

After the encounter with the man that I would one day consider a monster, I began to feel cold in my summer dress. A bank of dreary, gray clouds was moving into the valley, a sign that it would soon rain. On the mountains it would snow, bringing to an end the *Altweibersommer* (Indian summer—literally, old women's summer) we had enjoyed.

Back at Haus Linden we picked up baby Ingrid from the Reitlechners'. With glee I noticed that no one paid her any attention once Mutti told the whole exciting story of my meeting with Hitler, and Tante Susi joked that I had become an important person. I basked in the admiration that this short, unintended moment on Hitler's lap brought me and felt lucky to live so near the Führer. I was developing, quite according to Nazi plans, into a true little Nazi child in spite of my grandfather's ire.

At bedtime I asked Mutti why Grossvati did not like Hitler and was cross about my sitting on his knee. She thought for a moment before explaining that while her father was wrong about the Führer, he would probably not change his mind and because he was her father we must let him be.

It made no difference that, for all we knew, the picture of Hitler and me was not released to the public; the story alone was an enviable tale that brought awed attention from friends, teachers, visitors, and acquaintances whenever it was told, which was often. Whenever my grandfather heard it being rehashed, he snorted with scorn. In May 1945 it was quietly buried along with so much else, and as the crimes of Hitler's regime became known I felt poisoned and dirtied by my contact with the greatest criminal of all times.

Around the time I met Hitler I began to have a nightmare of a horrible, black monster sitting heavily on my chest, eyes aglow like coals, a forked devil's tongue lashing out toward my face, and its fangs ready to rip into my covers. I knew I must keep the covers smooth at all cost, but I had no strength and could not move under the weight of the beast until finally I awoke crying. This nightmare recurred with increasing frequency as our orderly, ordinary lives unraveled in the Second World War.

My grandparents' visit ended the next morning. Vati had left for work, saying a quick good-bye before Mutti and I took them to the railroad station, the grand, new building at the very end of the rail line from Munich. We left the house in a chilly, annoying drizzle of the kind that left one uncertain whether to open an umbrella or let the dampness wet one's face. My grandparents used for the first time the overcoats they had brought and I my gray loden coat that Mutti had fished out of the chest with winter clothes. It smelled pleasantly, I thought, of mothballs. From the balcony Tante Susi with Ingrid on her arm waved and wished my grandparents a good journey, and Mutti lifted the aged suitcases of imitation leather onto our small, wooden cart. I helped Grossvati slow down the cart until the steep Obersalzbergstrasse flattened out and we crossed the bridge over the Ache. On the level stretch to the station Mutti and her parents talked about the train changes they needed to make to get back to Selb and about plans for our visit with them the following summer. I asked why a hole had been blasted into the rocks on top of which part of the town was built. Mutti said that it was the beginning of Hitler's direct rail line to Salzburg and the south. Predictably my grandfather immediately asserted that this was a crazy waste of money, since the bus and the road along the Ache and the train that required only one change seemed perfectly adequate. It was his parting shot, but Mutti just shrugged.

The conductor called out to the few people milling on the platform to board the train. I said "Auf Wiedersehen" and not "Heil Hitler," shook my grandparents hands, and curtsied. Giving me last-minute admonitions to be a good girl, my tall, slender grandfather hugged me, while Mutti helped her mother into the train and lifted the suitcases up the iron steps. The whistle blew, and the train pulled away and picked up speed. By the time Grossvati's and Grossmutti's waving white handkerchiefs disappeared, I had almost forgotten the discord that had marred their visit. At last our little family was back to normal, to one wavelength, to consensus. Mutti lifted me into the pull cart and began to run all the way to the bridge, finally able to fully enjoy the fact that Adolf Hitler himself had sought out her little girl and that there was no one to dispute the honor it brought. We exchanged a few words with the S.S. guards at the bridge before we headed up the mountain once more in the direction of Hitler's abode. I saw the Führer drive up or down the Obersalzbergstrasse quite a few times over the next few years but never came that close to him again.

7 GATHERING CLOUDS

By 1938 THE DISCUSSIONS AMONG ADULTS SEEMED to grow more excited. That year Vati showed me pictures of German troops being greeted in the city of Salzburg by ecstatic Austrians who were celebrating their homecoming to the German Reich. Salzburg's ancient cathedral square was awash in swastika flags. The border crossing into Austria at Schellenberg near Berchtesgaden was reopened, and Vati promised we would all visit Salzburg soon and without need of a passport. The Pöhlmann and Paul families were relieved when the Sudetenland was ceded to Hitler because Selb was right at the border of Czechoslovakia and any armed conflict might have engulfed them very quickly. The Czech branch of my father's family, the Kohouts, had always maintained contact, and now the back-and-forth was made even easier.

On Saturday evenings when friends came to visit after supper, the noisy evening debates among the men—Onkel Peppi, Hans Schuster, Schego, Vati—grew, in my opinion, extremely tiresome, and I often wished they would stop and instead talk about things that made them laugh and me happy. But again and again the men got into disputes over a rumor, or the news, or the right or wrong of Adolf Hitler's strategy vis-à-vis our enemies in the west and in the east. They talked about the need for *Lebensraum* (room to live), a concept promulgated by Hitler to justify expansion of the Reich, and tried to guess what Russia and each of the European countries had in mind. Mutti was in love with the idea of *Lebensraum* because of the adventure it would offer and said that she would be happy to go and settle on a farm in an eastern territory. For reasons I could never figure out, she fancied Madagascar, rather in an opposite direction, as a place to migrate to. I had no idea what caused this wish to move on, and told her that if she left, Vati and I would stay at Haus Linden.

My sister, Ingrid, and I playing in our sandbox made from a grocer's crate and filled with sand from a mountain stream.

On evenings when neighbors or colleagues who were not part of the close-knit group of friends visited, conversation was quiet and convivial. But among the smaller circle, emotions ran high. Often they argued into the night, and at bedtime I pulled my duvet over my ears to muffle their excited voices. One evening Onkel Peppi, who had a fierce temper, got so angry that he punched a hole through the thin wall between the living room and the adjoining bedroom. While the landlord fixed the jagged hole with plasterboard, the women whispered about this outburst and the dispute that had caused it. Mutti hinted that Onkel Peppi had called Adolf, as the Reitlechners disrespectfully referred to Hitler,

A last prewar picnic at the Liegeret Alm with *(from left to right)* Onkel Peppi, Tante Susi, myself, Ingrid, Mutti, and Vati, the photographer.

a warmonger, emphasizing his statement with his fist. I hoped in vain that this outburst signaled an end to the shouting, for it scared me. But as I already knew, the clash of values extended beyond my parents and their friends; it existed even within our own family, between my parents and my grandparents.

Nature took no notice of human disputes, and she invited the four of us to make Sunday expeditions in almost any season, but Nazi voices managed to intrude even on them. Once, returning from a boating trip on Königssee, our famed fjordlike lake, we ended a perfect day in the garden of an inn. The chestnut trees overhead were studded with the white candles of their blossoms. As we waited for our coffee, cake, and hot chocolate, a voice began to blare from a radio out the window of the inn. Vati got up to listen to Dr. Goebbels's speech—I don't know what it was about—and the peace of the afternoon was shattered.

Among the endless variety of Sunday outings were those that took us past one of the many beautiful or merely quaint village churches or pilgrimage chapels that dotted our landscape. Every hamlet in the side valleys or on the grassy plateaus had its own Catholic church, always next to at least one inn. If we were not too late or too tired, we would enter the coolness of these churches in the villages of Ramsau, Ettenberg, Oberau, and Maria Gern and admire their painted ceilings, carved, gold-covered altars, and statues of Mary, the saints, and the apostles. Only Vati could remember the names of the wood-carvers and the workshops where they had been trained in Austria or Bavaria. Naturally we did not cross ourselves with the sacred water at the entrance, but Vati insisted that we children not run around or talk loudly.

If our walk ended inside the Kunterweg Chapel above Ramsau, we stretched our necks and bent our heads back to see the rococo ceiling painting, done in 1733 by one Innozenz Warathi from Burghausen. It portrayed and commemorated the victory of the Virgin over the Protestant heretics who were driven from Berchtesgaden and nearby Austrian villages after the end of the Thirty Years' War (1618–1648), which followed the Reformation. Vati pointed out that the outright hostilities between Protestants and Catholics were long over and that, in addition, thanks to Hitler, we did not have to belong to either of these religions.

At the end of these often long excursions I would get very cranky, but at a crucial burnout point Mutti would start singing a *Wanderlied* (hiking song), and I could not help but sing along; even Vati, who carried Ingrid on his shoulders and claimed to not be able to hold a tune, chimed in. The rhythm of the songs seduced me back into walking, and my tired legs lifted once again to carry me home.

Our most frequent and favorite destination was a small Alpine Club hut called Liegeret Alm. An *Alm* was usually a cluster of huts often high on the mountains where animals were taken for summer grazing. The Liegeret was just a single, small hut that lay in a mountain meadow at the foot of Kehlstein. It was ideally situated, far over to the side where the west face of Hoher Göll (a favorite wall for serious rock climbers) fell straight down to the beautiful green vale of the Scharitzkehl Alm, a beloved tourist attraction. It was owned by a man who successfully resisted its sale to Martin Bormann. The Liegeret had a shingled, overhanging roof held down by large stones, shuttered windows, and a bunk room with mattresses and wool blankets for climbers. On the two-hour hike from our house Mutti carried a backpack filled with food, and my father carried Ingrid and the tools he had brought to make repairs to the hut, fix a wooden rail in the cow fence, and help keep the stack of firewood high.

The same clique of Alpine Club members gathered here most weekends. The women's role was to wash the blue-and-white-checked curtains, sew checked pillows and tablecloths, and keep the common room and the bunk rooms *gemütlich* (cozy) and clean. When a fine wood smoke rose from the cookstove through the chimney, we children knew it was lunchtime. We helped bring in the icy water from the wooden trough that captured a brook before it moved on down through the buttercups on the meadow, and we helped set the table between the long benches in front of the hut. I was glad that the talk was focused on the food, the sunshine, and us, the children. On one of these occasions Hans Richter, a colleague of my father's, who had a bushy beard and two children about our age, proposed that they drink to the future of Germany, and everybody, including the children, grabbed what was in front of them and clinked their glasses.

By the spring of 1939, however, the mood of the Liegeret friends had changed, and the hut and its meadows were no longer the carefree and pleasurable places they had been for far too short a time. The hut now stood just outside the tall fence Martin Bormann had put up around Obersalzberg and directly underneath the Kehlstein Haus—later known as the Eagle's Nest—with its new road that we had watched being blasted and hewn out of the rock leading up to it. Surrounded by all these symbols of Nazi power, the conversation at the Liegeret quickly turned to politics and the probability of war. Poland, Russia, Italy, Great Britain, and France were mentioned frequently, and in spite of huge misgivings, the consensus of the men around the picnic table was that they would of course follow the Führer and fight for the fatherland. Most of them had been called in for their *Musterung* (physical exam) over a year ago, and Vati had been declared *tauglich* (able to serve).

My Pöhlmann grandfather had told me about the grimness of World War I in France, and I had seen tears well up in his eyes when he talked of friends and comrades who had died there next to him in the mud. He had instilled in me, even at five, a very deep fear of war. War was worse than any story; it was real, it killed, it was horrible. Would Mutti and Vati allow it to happen? Indeed they would, and at that time I could have counted on my two hands the times we would still be together in peace.

Tante Susi spotted Chamberlain and, on another day, Mussolini driving up the mountain. "Don't be crazy," Onkel Peppi said one evening, "Adolf is not going to sign a treaty with Stalin. He hates Bolsheviks." So close to the seat of power, they knew nothing of what was going on. No one stopped their busy lives; on the contrary, everybody wanted to squeeze as much pleasure into any free time as was possible. Relatives and other visitors came and went, and my mother cooked and baked and cleaned. Except for Vati, who did not drink, the grown-ups frequently drowned any sense of foreboding and trouble in a couple of bottles of Rhine or Moselle wine and sang the old *Volkslieder* (folk songs) mixed with patriotic songs like "Die Wacht am Rhein" (The Watch on the Rhine), which reminded them of the French occupation of the Rhineland and Hitler's defiance of it.

part THREE: 1939–1945

WAR AND SURRENDER

□   □
□   □

SALZBURG

For my birthday treat in May 1939 Vati kept his
promise. We left Ingrid with Tante Susi and Trudi for
the day and went to Salzburg, our beautiful, ancient
neighboring city.

   The border crossing was easy now that Austria
was part of Germany. Vati said Hitler was going to
build a railroad through the gap to ease access to
the Austrian lowlands and Italy. The project had
begun with the short tunnel blasted underneath the
rocks on which Berchtesgaden was built and that
Grossvati had criticized. For now we traveled by
bus, and in less than an hour we arrived in Salzburg.
We got off at the Mozarteum, a somber-looking
institution that, I was told, was a world-renowned
music conservatory. We took a footbridge across the
river Salzach into the Altstadt, the old city. The wide
river had by now absorbed the Ache into its waters,
and the magnificent castle of Salzburg glistened
above it. The plain facades of the old city houses,
their unadorned windows reflecting the noonday sun,
and even the steeples and domes of the churches
seemed to take a backseat to the drama provided
by the juxtaposition of the green river below and the
long, looming castle above.

   A noisy country fair had taken over an old church
square. I asked if I could watch the outdoor Kasperl
Theater, a traditional puppet show in which I knew

that the good guys always won. Mutti said all right, as long as I stayed put while they looked at a church and took a little walk. They would return when the puppet show ended. As the two of them walked away arm in arm, I knew that turning five was a gigantic step in the direction of growing up and being trusted. Along with all the other children, I screamed and screeched as danger for Kasperl, the hero, rose and ebbed, and was greatly relieved when at the end of the play he and his wife, Gretl, were once more saved from their enemies. I looked around but my parents had not returned. The applause had stopped, everyone had left, and I was the only child still seated on one of the hard, backless benches. I dangled my feet, and in spite of being a year older I was about to cry, thinking they had forgotten me. But then I saw them cross the empty square, looking happy as they came toward me, and my relief was beyond words. Vati wiped my tears, they smiled and apologized, and we headed for the road that led up to the Festung Hohensalzburg, the huge, fortified castle I had seen from the river. Tourists from all over the world were strolling through the vast castle grounds and enjoying *Kaffee und Kuchen* in the terrace and garden restaurants. We ordered lemonade, and Vati lifted me up so I could see over the stone balustrade down onto the roofs of houses, the graveyard of Saint Peter's, and the towers and cupolas of the city's churches. It all seemed so peaceful, toylike, and beautiful, with the mountains luminous in the distance. It was the way I would always remember Salzburg.

Back down in the old town we stepped into the

Dom, the baroque cathedral on the main square, and listened as the organist practiced. "It's by Wolfgang Amadeus Mozart," Mutti whispered. "He was born here in Salzburg." When we got back to Berchtesgaden, I was so tired that I actually fell asleep as I walked. Vati carried me the last stretch and put me straight to bed, where I dreamt about the splendid day. When I woke up the next morning, I thought that I would wish for another outing to Salzburg on my next birthday and the next and perhaps always. I knew then that there were three things I would never get tired of: our mountains, Mozart's music, and Salzburg.

But the shadows were lengthening and the clouds were losing their light. The Nazis had taken over our mountains, and soon most of Europe's ancient cities would be in ashes. Bombs would fall on the great dome of the Salzburg cathedral, and to this day the sound of Mozart's music breaks my heart.

□   □

□   □

8 EARLY SACRIFICE

ON SEPTEMBER 1, 1939, THREE MONTHS AFTER my birthday trip to Salzburg, Hitler sent fifty German divisions into Poland, and Stalin attacked that country from the east. The night before we had witnessed the wild and bright display of northern lights above Untersberg—a phenomenon hardly ever seen at our latitude. We joined a crowd of neighbors who stood silently at the edge of a cow field staring at the shooting colors and wafting pale pink to deep purple curtains rising and waning across the sky. "This means war," mumbled our old landlord—wise in the lore of these parts—through his bushy, snuff-stained mustache. I pulled on the sleeves of his wife's black wool sweater and asked whether she thought he was right, but she said not to mind him. I did not know that Hitler and his guests were observing the same ominous celestial display from the terrace of the Berghof and that, according to Albert Speer, Hitler said: "Looks like a great deal of blood. This time we won't bring it off without violence."

The Führer left Obersalzberg in his car the next morning to begin the invasion of Poland. Neither the press nor gossip had informed us of any of the debates, intrigues, or shenanigans on the mountain that preceded this tremendous step. It was only much later that we'd learn of the intense rivalry between Hitler's top man, Hermann Göring, and the warmongering foreign minister, Joachim von Ribbentrop. For now, though, shrill news reports, propaganda speeches, and rhetoric about the necessity of the invasion increasingly filled the radio waves. Mutti and Vati clung to every word and based their somber, resigned discussions of

Hitler's move on what they were told. Public protest and open debate were far too dangerous to contemplate—what could one do but stand with the swastika and march with the firebrands?

Hitler forecast personal sacrifice for everyone, and it came as no surprise that among the first waves of young men drafted were most of the dozen painters from the Adler workshop. Their wives

The city of Salzburg in Austria, showing the Hohensalzburg Castle and the Salzach River.

and children were left behind to carry on and to begin the ritual of waiting for mail from their men, just as my grandmother had in 1914.

Eight months after the invasion, I saw Mutti's face fall as she read the official letter that called my father, now thirty-four, to join the army. The reality of war and the inevitability of our personal involvement suddenly became clear to her in a way it had not before. She said quietly, "Vati has to leave for the war soon, and we must be very brave." Just how brave she did not say. Two-year-old Ingrid asked if he would come back from the war soon and bring her a present. I did not want him to leave at all, but I understood already that he had to do what the Führer wanted. Mutti had a measure of certainty in her voice when she promised us that he would not be gone long and life would be just the same when he came back.

Trudi, who liked my father very much, told me again and again how much he hated to leave us. But of course he had no choice but to don the gray-green uniform of the infantry and the boat-shaped cap indicating his rank as a private in the Deutsche Wehrmacht and make ready to leave. He was assigned to a Nachrichten Ersatz Korps (Infantry Communications Relief Corps) that would train for a few months within Germany before being sent to the front.

At the age of five, I felt it was only fair that I should be allowed to come along to see Vati off at the oversized *Hauptbahnhof* (main rail station) in Berchtesgaden, built by Hitler only a few years before. We had little time, inclination, or room to look at the giant wall paintings in the great hall. The station was jammed with hundreds of uniformed young men, their pink faces scrubbed and clean-shaven, surrounded by families, brides, and friends whose good wishes and confident cries of "We'll see you back soon!" filled the air. The young men looked expectant; if they had any anxieties, they hid them well behind the smoke of their cigarettes and the casual way they flicked their ashes and slapped one another on the shoulder. Most of them were *Gebirgsjäger* (mountain troops), with the silver edelweiss insignia on their shoulders and upturned caps, the rims of which were studded with farewell gifts of cigarettes.

Mutti and I stood on the platform outside the third-class train compartments, searching for some final words. I watched the minute hand on the big clock moving from number to number until, after ten, I could not read them anymore, and suddenly a voice boomed, "Alles einsteigen!" (All aboard). Vati held Mutti in his arms for what seemed a long time, and then it was my turn to be lifted up for a hug and a kiss on both cheeks. In a sudden, decisive move Vati put me down, and as the train was beginning to move almost imperceptibly, he jumped onto the metal grate of the steps and up into the carriage just before the conductor slammed the door shut behind him. Everyone tried to stay as close as possible to the edge of the platform, and a cloud of white handkerchiefs fluttered from the train windows. I stood on tiptoe and waved mine but quickly lost track of which handkerchief belonged to my father. His image melted into the sea of faces of soldiers going off to war. Five years later most of those young men would be dead, wounded, or prisoners of war scattered from Siberia—a most horrible fate—to Morocco, the United Kingdom, or the United States (if they were lucky).

My father *(second from left)* with his infantry unit at the Loire River in France in 1940.

Looking up, I saw tears streaming down Mutti's young face— we had just celebrated her thirty-second birthday—as she used the white embroidered handkerchief she had been waving to wipe her eyes. With a long, dissonant whistle blow the train disappeared along the curves of the river Ache. There had been no jubilation among those on the train or those left behind. A mostly silent crowd, with barely a nod for a friend or an acquaintance, left the station. With downcast eyes Mutti and I began a slow, thoughtful walk home, soothed first by the rushing sound of the Ache and then by the familiar feel of the steep hill under our feet.

Berchtesgaden was rapidly becoming a community of women, except for a few much older men, invalids, young boys, assorted party hacks, others who were able to avoid the military, and of course the S.S. men stationed on Obersalzberg. Our home felt lonely and empty with just the three of us left in it and with Vati's shoes standing untouched on the small shoe shelf in the hallway and his jacket and tweed cap hanging unused on the hooks. Mutti, of course, took over efficiently and seamlessly as head of household, just like millions of women in warring countries all over the world. But she missed my father, and "If Vati were home" became a daily refrain, along with her assurances that he would of course be home soon. She evoked his image and his name when she needed to discipline us, which she did more frequently and severely now that she had to make up for his absent authority. Aside from that, nothing much changed in our home or in our daily routine initially, and even doubters like the Reitlechners were amazed at the speed of German victories in the west. In fact, by the spring, a few months after Hitler had opened the western front and overrun Belgium, the Netherlands, Luxembourg, and France, stopping short of Dunkirk, it looked as if it would indeed be a very short, victorious war.

Encouraging our optimism, Vati came home for a week's furlough in October 1940 after about six months of service in France. Mutti had marked the day of his homecoming on the fat calendar that hung on the kitchen wall, allowing us to tear off a sheet every day to count down to his arrival. I felt my face turn red as a beet when he opened the door, while Ingrid cried big tears of joy. I thought my little sister a crybaby and was slightly annoyed that she did not want to let go of him and give me my turn in his strong arms. For the entire week the two of us vied for his attention, and I resented visits from friends who came by to discuss the war situation with him and wish him well. He seemed more serious and preoccupied than I remembered, telling Mutti that he simply did not have the temperament for the army; besides, the army fare aggravated his chronic stomach ailment. "I wish I could cook for you," Mutti said sadly.

I had started first grade, and this visit was my first chance to show off my brand-new reading and writing skills to Vati. Every first-grader had a *Setzkasten,* a flat wooden case, about the size of a cigar box, containing tiny cardboard rectangles depicting upper- and lowercase letters stashed in small individual compartments. We chose letters and slipped them into slots along the box's stand-up lid, eventually putting together syllables, words, and, finally, sentences. I had inherited my *Setzkasten* from an older child and was constantly frustrated by the shortage or complete absence of certain crucial letters. Vati saw my problem immediately, sat down, and with his calm, skilled hand drew me a whole supply of beautiful, black Gothic letters that were just as good as the printed ones. A black slate with a wooden frame replaced the *Setzkasten* in second grade, but I kept a few of Vati's letters before passing it on to another child. The small paper rectangles became dirty and wrinkled and eventually disappeared. But I did not need them to remind me of the time Vati helped me with my schoolwork, a memory that had to do for a whole childhood.

Each moment of that enchanted week of Vati's leave gained significance way beyond the actual events. Ingrid and I took turns standing on Vati's feet while he danced us around the living room to the waltzes, fox trots, tangos, and polkas that, just like Hitler's speeches, miraculously came to us across the mountains from either the Munich or Salzburg radio station. Our large, boxy, wooden Siemens radio, its fabric front interwoven with shimmering metallic threads, had one knob for volume and one that moved an indicator across an illuminated window, sweeping by dozens of names of cities with radio stations that sent us nothing but static. But if, as Vati had taught me, I placed it carefully just in the center of Munich

My father with us in front of Haus Linden during his furlough in 1940.

or Salzburg, we suddenly heard words or music clearly. For many years those stations would be the only ones to reach us in the mountains with news controlled by the Nazis and then, after a period of total silence, by the victorious Allies.

We did not play all the time. Like all soldiers on leave, Vati wanted to make sure that our woodshed was well stocked; with his small, sharp ax—during his absence it had become Mutti's— he chopped a mountain of stove-size pieces from large logs every day, praising us for helping him stack them neatly. That done, he would often initiate a noisy, fast, late-afternoon soccer game on the road with neighborhood youngsters, Onkel Peppi, Tante Susi, Mutti, and Trudi. During one game a long, dark brown snake slithered across the road in front of me. I screamed in terror. Without hesitation, Vati took the ax from the chopping block and, while Trudi and Mutti tried to calm me, stepped into the brush to track down the snake. Part of me hoped he wouldn't find and kill it, but another part of me wanted him to be a serpent slayer for my sake. The snake, meanwhile, had obviously found a hiding place, forcing Vati to give up the search and reassure me that it was gone for good. The snake hunt made me admire Vati even more, and I felt reassured that his love for me was special.

On one of the final days of the furlough Tante Susi looked after Ingrid and me until Mutti and Vati returned happy from a daylong hike across Hoher Göll and Brett. Mutti had a lovely suntan; Vati's fair skin was as red as a boiled lobster. Much as we tried to ignore the looming departure, it came closer with each sheet we tore off the calendar. I asked if Hitler would allow Vati another leave soon, partly because I knew that after he left, my mother would once again not have enough time or be in the mood to play and laugh with us the way she did while he was here. It was as if after having regained two parents I was about to lose at least one and a half. To still my worry and sadness at bedtime I made myself a round nest from my white, puffy feather bed and sat by my window listening to the last, sweet song of the blackbird that perched every night high on the tip of a spruce. As I drifted into sleep I could still hear Vati's muffled voice from the living room.

□　□

Too soon Vati put his uniform back on, said his good-byes, and started down the road with Mutti to catch his train. A few minutes later—I had just begun to play with Ingrid on Tante Susi's balcony—he came running back through the flower garden, arousing for a short moment my hope that he had changed his mind after all and would stay with us. It turned out that he had forgotten to take his gas mask, a green canister still hanging on the coatrack in the corridor. We waved to him through the heart-shaped cutouts in the balcony, and he waved back before he disappeared again into the woods. A little later the wind carried that long, disconcerting whistle of the departing train up the mountain, and Tante Susi said, "That's your father's train."

When Mutti learned in the early spring of 1941 that Vati was hospitalized with ulcers in a *Lazarett* (army hospital) in Ingolstadt in Niederbayern (Lower Bavaria), she went alone to visit him, making me very upset and angry at being left behind. The excuse that I had to go to school seemed flimsy, since some of my classmates were excused all summer to herd the cows on the mountains. I was somewhat consoled when Tante Susi made *Dampfnudeln mit Zwetschgenmus* (steamed dumplings with stewed, puréed prunes) especially for Ingrid and me, a dish that Mutti, who cooked in the style of Franconia, never even attempted.

Mutti returned from the hospital wrapped up in her own sadness and hardly talked about the visit. I'm sure she did not bring me a hug or a kiss from my father—and I'm equally sure I did not expect or even want it. As I had outgrown my toddler years Mutti and I had acquired a shyness with each other, and I felt hugs and kisses to be babyish—the domain of my ever-so-adorable little sister. We loved each other, but Mutti showed it by caring, giving, feeding, guarding, watching, and always being there; whereas I went to great lengths to fill all our many vases with wildflowers on her birthday and on Mother's Day (a day that had the full support of the Nazis), warmed her slippers near the stove before she came home from an errand on a cold winter day, and with Trudi's help produced all kinds of crafts objects, from hot pads to coverlets, to surprise her on Christmas. I began to feel, however, that her motherly deeds usually had a condition or requirement attached, one that, if not met, might lead to the loss of her love or at least to a scolding. I was supposed to be on time for her lovingly prepared meals and finish what was on my plate whether I liked it or not; a dress she sewed at night was supposed to stay clean and not get torn; her conscientious hovering over my homework was to result in good grades. When she came back from the hospital I yearned for her to embrace me with a greeting from Vati but knew that neither of us could break the invisible barrier between us and that I would feel smothered and vulnerable if she did. In the long run I easily rationalized our standoffishness by the fact that the Pöhlmanns, perhaps like most Germans, were loath to show affection openly.

Shortly after his hospitalization in the spring of 1941 Vati rejoined his regiment in the Loire Valley in France. Occupied France was not an outright danger zone, but when Hitler declared war on Russia on June 22, 1941, Mutti began to worry that Vati's unit might be called to the eastern front any day. As always, my anxiety rose with hers. Regardless of the propaganda Hitler dished out to the gullible Germans, the mood among the women of Berchtesgaden grew more somber at the news that the war was expanding to the east. It was beginning to dawn on everyone that this war could take longer than they had originally thought.

Mutti's friends whose husbands were away fighting drew closer together and without giving it a name formed a loose but probably helpful support group that shared grief and joy throughout the war. Tante Susi, Marianne, Sophie, or Nanni would drop by in the evenings and, bent over their sewing, knitting, and mending, gossip about the letters they had received announcing transfers, promotions, or well-being of their men. They sighed and shook their heads while trying to second-guess the Führer's war plans and how long it might be until their husbands returned. Onkel Hans too had long since been drafted, and every time the postlady—no longer a postman—brought mail from him or Vati my mother would be in a good mood all day, which of course brightened ours as well.

School vacation had not begun yet, but it was finally summertime in Berchtesgaden and even on the high mountains the snow was disappearing. An invasion of female visitors took advantage of free lodging with us, meaning that I moved into the master bedroom with Mutti and Ingrid while Tante Emma from Selb, Cousin Erna Bieser from Wiesbaden, and our beloved Tante Emilie occupied my small bedroom in turn or else slept on the living room sofa. Paying guests to supplement Vati's military pay were increasingly rare, as travel had become very restricted for the average German who might rent such a room. After a few weeks of constant visits I began to miss the window above the glossy, white, grown-up bed that my grandfather had made for me along with a matching tall white linen closet where I had my own shelves. At the same time I enjoyed the commotion and diversion that our various guests brought, the small presents of sweets, and the telling of their tales.

Tante Emilie, more a stroller than a high-altitude hiker, offered to baby-sit while my mother, her friend Marianne, and Trudi undertook an overnight tour across Göll and Brett. Carrying their rucksacks and wearing their dirndl dresses, the three women gaily left for the Purtscheller Haus, a hut at the Göll trailhead that straddled the Austrian border. The next day, easily overcoming an exposed and tricky spot early in the climb, they made their way over the narrow ridges, steep broad slopes, and a few remaining, soggy snowfields. They were in good physical shape and in great spirits, for a short while forgetting the sorrows of the war and life in the valley as they reveled in the beauty of the mountains. It was the same route Mutti had hiked with Vati during his leave, and she took the lead. She remembered each turn she and Vati had taken, telling her friends where they had stopped and rested and where Vati had sketched a few flowers on a small pad he carried. "It was as if Max was with us that day," Trudi said later. "We didn't talk about politics or the war but sang and laughed and reminded each other of the old days." Naturally there was no bus, no lift, and no car that would shorten the long trip home, and the three women returned quite late, exhausted and ready for bed.

The next day, another one of brilliant summer weather, I woke up to the age-old rhythm of scythes moving through the grass on a slope beyond our house and the strong fragrance of a freshly mowed meadow. I knew that it would be the long-skirted farm women who were doing the men's job of harvesting the hay. Later I heard the dinging of old Rasp Muchei's hammer as he straightened and sharpened the blades of the scythes for the next morning of mowing. These were the familiar, soothing sounds and smells of summer days that gave a deceptive assurance that all was right on our mountain. In the kitchen Mutti talked childish talk to my cuddly little sister and made a quick fire in the stove to cook our *Haferflockenbrei* (oatmeal) for breakfast. She told me, "It's barely spring yet up on the mountains, with the *Schusternagerl* (a spring gentian) blooming right next to the last snow patches." I said, "We should send some flowers to Vati in France." She thought they might not keep on such a long journey through the military mails, a problem for which I had no clever solution.

Just as on any other ordinary morning I put my homework— neat rows of letters written on my wood-rimmed slate—and my *Setzkasten* into my secondhand leather school satchel. Vati would have been pleased with the care I had taken to make the letters line up like soldiers, something the pointed German script almost begged for. My damp sponge for wiping the slate and a crocheted pad for drying it dangled on two strings tied to my satchel. I waited till Trauderl, Walli, and Dori, from further up the mountain, came by the kitchen window to pick me up, and with shining faces, bouncing braids, and outbursts of laughter we skipped into the woods to begin our daily walk down to the bottom of the valley and up the other side to the Salzberg grade school. I made a secret, ritual stop in the steep ditch that we crossed, imagining that I could still see in its clay the imprint of the square nails in the soles of my father's shoes. Some days I traced the imaginary shape with my fingers and was deeply satisfied with the thought that I was the only one who knew about this spot.

Our school day ended at one o'clock, but on the day the Catholic students had religious study at the end of the morning I was able to start home for *Mittagessen,* our main meal, an hour early. First, going downhill, I passed over a set of railroad tracks and the slow, deep millstream that turned the turbines at the local utility. At our stone bridge across the Ache I waved to the S.S. guard outside the guardhouse. He nodded and casually waved me on as I started uphill. Just ahead of me on the first steep part of the road I saw Trudi walking home from the high school with Onkel Peppi, who was taking his two-hour lunch break from his work at the Zechmeister wood-carving studio. A serious heart defect had so far prevented his being drafted into the army. He was a rather cranky man who usually said little but would scowl if Ingrid and I got too noisy during one of our upstairs visits.

I began to chatter, a little out of breath when I caught up with them. "I got a gold star for spelling. And my teacher said summer vacations start in two weeks. She beat Wolfgang Stössl with her thin cane today, not the thick one. She always hits him because of his sloppy homework." I stopped because they did not respond or ask any questions. There was an awkward silence, which puzzled me. They both looked sorrowful and avoided eye contact with me. I stopped my prattle, deciding to also walk quietly and to take their serious looks and exchange of nods as just one of those inexplicable moods adults occasionally fell into.

We continued up the mountain in silence until Haus Linden came into view. And then I saw my mother standing in the doorway. She looked wretched, strangely destroyed. She said, barely audibly, "Der Vati ist tot" (Vati is dead). I did not understand. What did she mean? Not my Vati, not our Vati! Dead? Mutti left me standing there and went into her bedroom, where she remained for seemingly endless days, crying inconsolably. I can't imagine what I did that afternoon, but I remember Tante Emilie telling me that an official messenger on a black motorcycle had come by Haus Linden that morning. He handed Mutti a telegram informing her that my father had died for the Führer in France on July 5, 1941.

Tante Emilie stayed for a few days and helped find some mourning clothes for my mother, while Tante Susi and Trudi looked after our needs. Every time one of them came out of her bedroom with the large ceramic pitcher they used to pour fresh water into the matching washbowl on Mutti's commode I was certain that they were carrying away the tears that Mutti had wept, just as in the story "Das Tränenkrüglein" ("The Little Pitcher of Tears") in my second-grade primer. I was quite certain that Vati's spirit was peacefully floating somewhere nearby, amid the snow- and ice-covered peaks where Mutti would join him someday and

My father's coffin in the funeral chapel before his military burial in an *Ehrenfriedhof* (soldiers' graveyard) in France.

where I would always find him. I wished fervently that Mutti would stop crying now and come out of the bedroom.

When Mutti finally rejoined us she pulled my little sister onto her lap, held her tight, and choked on new tears. I suddenly realized that at seven I had become the "older daughter," the responsible one, the one who was to be my mother's support, the one who should not show weakness. And so I tried not to cry, swallowing hard instead. I succeeded most of the time except when seemingly unrelated things suddenly triggered uncontrollable tears—a song, a cloud over a mountain, most of all flowers that my father had painted and drawn. On the day I learned of Vati's death, my outlook on life changed profoundly. I had discovered that a good day could never be trusted to remain good; indeed, a good day would inevitably lead to disaster, and I must always be prepared for the worst. The glass was now half empty.

□   □

Very few German soldiers had died up to this point in the war, and there was some question about just how my father had lost his life. The official word was that it was a drowning accident—not witnessed by anyone—in the Loire River, but rumors that the French underground had killed him kept resurfacing. At any rate, according to the photo album that his comrades sent to my mother, he received a hero's funeral. People in Berchtesgaden reacted in two different ways to his death—our friends, relatives, and neighbors with sadness and compassion; the Nazi officials in our lives with pompous, irrelevant condolences. My father's boss, Herr Adler, who for unknown reasons was not drafted, came by—in his S.A. uniform, no less—a few days after the news arrived and said in an oily voice to my stricken mother, "Chin up [*Kopf hoch*], Frau Paul, chin up. He died for the Führer."

If I were to name a moment when seeds of doubt about the Nazis and our Führer, already strewn by Tante Emilie, the Reitlechners, and my grandfather, took hold in my rather critical soul, it would be this visit by Herr Adler. He had no right or reason to deny my mother her right to be heartbroken; besides, could he not at least have brought us one of the pieces of porcelain painted by my father that were no doubt still in his atelier? I have hated Herr Adler ever since.

□   □

I too received a lesson in heroism, a lesson in how to bear sacrifice and keep my head up. The morning after we got the death notice, my teacher, Fräulein Stöhr, a fanatical Nazi, ordered me to stand up in front of the class and tell everyone how proud I was that my father had given his life for the Führer. I stood before those hundred children, my face burning, my hurt heart thumping. I clenched my fists and swallowed hard, determined not to cry or otherwise show anyone how I felt. I forced myself to drain all emotion from my voice, even forcing my mouth into a grin, and said, "Yes, we heard yesterday that my father died in France for the Führer. Heil Hitler." My face was flushed, but I made sure to walk calmly back to my seat. No one said a word to me. Trauderl and Else studiously avoided eye contact, meeting my forced indifference with an embarrassed smile. They were relieved when I joined them in a school-yard game during break, hoping that all was back to normal.

Trudi told me—and my mother's diary confirms it—that even years later Mutti, a fiercely loyal woman, secretly cried over the loss of Max, the love of her life. But except for those first weeks of intense pain, she bravely hid her sorrow from us, trying in vain to protect us from much of the daily, omnipresent news of, and later despair over, the war.

□ □

THE EMOTIONAL TOLL OF THE WAR had not yet been equaled by the toll on basic physical needs. Mutti still received enough food stamps to feed our growing appetites. There were still vegetables and fruits at the green-market stalls and meat for the Sunday roast at one of the butchers in town. The lines at the bakery were getting longer, but usually everyone received a loaf in exchange for the correct number of red stamps (those for meat were blue, those for dairy products white). A good deal of my basic arithmetic came from studying the stamps, adding or multiplying the right numbers of grams to make up a pound or a kilo of the items on my shopping list, and making sure that the grocer would not cut one single stamp too many.

In 1941, as it was every year, Heldengedenktag (hero's memorial day) was celebrated on November 9 (the same date that Kristallnacht occurred in 1938). Now that Vati was a fallen hero, Mutti and I were to attend the official ceremony on the *Schlossplatz* (castle square) in front of the war memorial. Widows—a steadily growing group—wore mourning attire for a whole year, and for this occasion Mutti was dressed from head to toe in pitch-black, a

The castle square in Berchtesgaden decorated for a Nazi event.

long black veil falling over the rim of her hat. The garb seemed appropriate for our thoughts on that miserably cold and damp fall day: black and bleak and knowing that our loss was final and infinite. Buried in a grave in enemy country that we could not visit, not even to lay a wreath of mountain pine, Max Paul, the man we both cherished, had become nothing but a name on the lengthening list of the fallen.

I pulled my gray loden coat closer, put up its hood, and began to examine one by one the facades of the buildings that defined the castle square. The most overwhelming sight was the large number of billowing, bright red flags with their white medallions highlighting the black rune of the swastika. I noticed that only the church was free of swastika banners. As my eyes rested momentarily on its roundly arched marble entryway with its peaked embellishments I heard Vati's voice saying quite clearly, "Remember, Gothic arches are always pointed." At that moment the golden hands on the large clocks on the two bell towers moved to the full hour and struck the time. Surely this was Vati sending me a signal that he was with me.

I kept looking at the church, hoping to hear more about the style of this particular arch, but the voice did not come back. Disappointed, I let my eyes move past the plain facade of the L-shaped Royal Castle to the fascinating and strange World War I memorial. It consisted of sharply defined yet chunky—and to me, highly realistic—frescoes of wartime scenes set above a colonnade of ancient arches and fountains; beneath a large crucifix soldiers with helmets and guns were leaving for war, women and children staying sadly and bravely behind. Just like now, I thought.

Vati's name was engraved on the marble plates adorning the Village of Salzberg's war memorial on the side of my school. "I don't like Vati's name on this wall," I always said to Mutti when she wanted to stop there for a moment. "I hate it there." I did not want to see her make that sad face, the face that made me feel ill. Yet I proudly pointed my father's name out to classmates, relatives, and friends to show them that my family had made its sacrifice to the war.

Finally the ceremony began with the singing of the "Deutschland Lied" (national anthem), followed immediately by the "Horst Wessel Lied," to glorify again the march of the S.A. in Munich, on November 9, 1923. We sang both of them heartily with our right arms stretched forward and up in the correct Hitler greeting. My right arm hurt and turned to lead at some point during the second song and only by quickly and surreptitiously shifting to the left arm could I last to the end. Finally we sat down, and the *Gauleiter* (Nazi-appointed administrator of the region) and other Party bigwigs, perhaps even an S.S. officer, made speeches abounding with phrases like "brave German soldiers," "German heroes," "German homeland," "German blood," "German honor," "German women," "our Führer, Adolf Hitler," "your sacrifice," "the grateful fatherland," and "death to the enemy."

The names of the fallen men were read out loud, but if a wreath was laid, I missed it. I became restless and embarrassed by the weeping and sniveling women around me. Finally, the sad, romantic German song that made my grandfather cry when he heard it was played: "Ich hat einen Kameraden, einen bessren findst Du nicht" (I once had a comrade, a better one you could not find). I knew that the song would be my breaking point, and to my great chagrin I began to sob and weep along with the women, even though I tried to stifle my outburst by putting my handkerchief over my mouth. Mutti stroked my head, and after shaking hands with a few women and politicians, we walked back home, up the very mountain from which the Führer continued to dictate and manipulate the spirit, emotions, and fate of millions upon millions of people, including me.

On Christmas Eve that same sad year, before we opened the living room door on the candlelit tree and before the Reitlechners joined us for singing and present opening, Mutti said, "Let's go outside first and think of Vati up there with the stars." It was a clear, bitterly cold night, and a deep, soft layer of powdery snow covered the landscape, rounding any edges and sharp angles. It did not help me to think of Vati up there among those specks of light piercing the black sky; I knew he was much closer by, right here in our mountains. I could only stand stiffly, thinking that if I were to start crying I would never be able to stop. I hated the fruitless sentimentality and extreme pain of this moment and was glad when we went inside. I had begun to hate so many things, even this part of Christmas Eve.

A large and mysterious rectangular brown carton lay under the tree urgently inviting us, it seemed, to finish "Silent Night" so we could open it. To everyone's amazement the box was a present from, of all people, Frau Emmy Göring, the wife of Feldmarschall Hermann Göring, who lived with his family near Hitler's Berghof on Obersalzberg. We gingerly removed the fine, white tissue paper that was hiding two beautiful baby dolls—made in France—in pink dresses, lacy pink bonnets, and silk socks. The dolls' blue eyes opened and closed in their sweet baby faces. The gathered adults could hardly believe their eyes, while Ingrid and I squealed with pleasure and immediately fell in love with the dolls, caring little about what else was in the box. Mutti searched deeper and found a winter coat and a winter dress for each of us girls. They fit perfectly, which meant that someone had researched our birthdays in order to send the right sizes. My coat, made of an incredibly soft, navy blue, pure wool fabric, had a big hem that would be let out year after year until I finally outgrew it in all directions. My dress was a moss green Bleyle knit dress with embroidery across the top and a separate belt to tie at my waist, just as if I were a grown-up. Ingrid's dress was dark blue and hung loosely from an embroidered yoke. She looked very cute in it, and I felt a pang of envy because blue, not green, was my favorite color. Mutti was told upon her inquiries that Frau Göring had decided that all children on Salzberg who had lost their fathers during that first stretch of war should receive a special, neighborly gift from her. I never knew whether the gifts were paid for or simply taken from occupied France as war booty.

We named our *Puppen* (dolls) Emmy in honor of Frau Göring, and Edda, for her little daughter. The gifts assured us that my father's life had indeed been laid down for an important cause, recognized by very important people. It was a peculiar bribe, though. Given the lowly rank my father held in the army and that Ingrid and I were so young, there was no need for any extra effort to capture our loyalty; as children we were automatically indoctrinated day after day. Mutti allowed us to play with the *Göring-Puppen* only on Sundays, carefully putting them back into their box with the white tissue paper before she stashed them on top of her large, flame-colored wardrobe with the star motif. Even now the Göring dolls, in the attic of the house that we moved to after the war, are waiting to be played with again someday—although I have heard that the eyes of Edda, my doll, have fallen into her hollow, celluloid head.

Nineteen forty-one was the year my world shattered. By the end of the Nazi era, millions upon millions had suffered beyond imagination in the camps, in cities, towns, and villages, and on the battlefields; fifty million were dead. How does anyone survive such loss and pain? I only know that for me, a child, and probably for most children, the adult world of terror, sadness, and sacrifice was only a part of the experience of that time. The other part was our capacity and urge to escape into play and fantasy, to hold on to innocence no matter what the adult reality was. The Göring dolls, whether given in recognition of a devastating sacrifice or as a bribe to fortify us for more suffering, were for Ingrid and me simply wonderful, luxurious toys providing hours of happiness and escape.

Years later, in Mutti's diary I found a note addressed to my dead father: "My dear Max, I wish you could see your two little girls playing happily in their secret house under the sewing table. They are children even in these terrible times."

9 LEARNING TO HATE SCHOOL

SCHOOL WAS THE SERIOUS SIDE OF LIFE, NEVER meant to make a child happy. From the day Mutti delivered me into Fräulein Stöhr's clutches it was obvious that this woman was a fanatical Nazi, a true believer. Surely she had become a teacher not because she had an affinity for children but because she wanted to tyrannize them. The Nazi doctrines designed to raise citizens wholly obedient to the Führer's bidding captivated and excited her. I began first grade at Easter 1940, but since Hitler changed the beginning of the school year to the fall shortly afterward, I am not quite sure whether my first year was very short or very long. At any rate, the war had already eaten into resources and materials, as well as the supply of male teachers, most of whom were drafted. As a result, Fräulein Stöhr got to sink her fangs into one hundred children belonging to three different grades. We were huddled together in her stark, whitewashed classroom learning the basics by rote plus a bit of local history, needlework for the girls, and geography.

The curriculum did not include anything like "political education," but Fräulein Stöhr knew how to use occasions like my father's death, Hitler's birthday, good or bad news from the front, or the visit of a prominent local Nazi to indoctrinate us. The leaders from Obersalzberg did not come to speak to us, preferring instead to hold forth on the radio or before gatherings of millions. But if we needed a reminder of their proximity, we had only to look out the window and see atop Kehlstein the oddly angular yet round shape of the Eagle's Nest, Hitler and Bormann's fantasy building.

It stood whitish gray and stark, like a castle against the sky. Its large windows were lit every night, casting a cold glare that was visible even through thick fog. Vati had said that it was a pity I would never see the velvety black of the skyline without that light, but by now hardly anyone noticed the all-too-familiar, unnatural sparkle. When Hitler was in residence, the swastika flag would flutter next to the Eagle's Nest like a thin, dark rag in the wind. Hitler actually visited the Eagle's Nest but a few times—he hated high altitudes—preferring the Berghof even for receiving foreign dignitaries who were supposed to be impressed by the Eagle's Nest.

Every morning at eight o'clock sharp Fräulein Stöhr began to work with one grade while the other two had silent assignments. Usually I could not help paying more attention to the history and geography lessons of the third-graders than to my own assignment of linking perfect letters on my slate, forming a simple sentence on my *Setzkasten,* or solving basic arithmetic problems in neat sets of five. Nevertheless I kept up with my own work so that the grades I took home in my report folder every six months for Mutti's signature were always better than average. The flimsy folder was designated on the cover as a lifetime, official, and unalterable document. It had spaces for eight years' worth of elementary-school grades. My religion was noted as *Gottgläubig,* my nationality of course as German, and, for good measure, it was also stated that I stemmed from German blood.

Hitler despised intellectualism and glorified athletic prowess. There was no danger of the former in the Salzberg grade school, and the latter was not enhanced much either, with only one hour of *Turnen* (physical education) once a week, including the time it took to change into and out of black shorts in a smelly, old public gym near the school. However, our mountainous surroundings provided us with enough exercise to build strength and stamina.

Grades ranged from 1 for "very good" to 6 for "failing" in the subjects of behavior, industry, physical achievement, German language, local geography, music, needlework, and arithmetic—in that order. Those handwritten grades and signatures still have the power to conjure up each and every teacher, classmate, disaster, and victory that made up the experience of my first school years. Prussian obedience, order, and discipline as well as blind submission to Nazi ideology were Fräulein Stöhr's undisputed forte. In these efforts she was aided by two canes cut from a filbert bush, one thin and one thick. She used them freely for slight infractions; we discussed endlessly which one hurt more when it came down on our outstretched hands.

It seemed that a subtle division between two groups of children occurred early on. One—a smaller group—consisted of newcomers like me who, while born here, were not considered *Einheimisch* (locals or homesteaders). Most of us were Protestant and spoke Hochdeutsch (High German) as a first language and Bavarian dialect second. The other, far larger group was the children from the old-time Catholic families of traders, peasants, merchants, laborers, and miners who had lived in the valley for hundreds of years. In Fräulein Stöhr's classroom and classrooms everywhere we were supposed to speak Hochdeutsch, a difficult requirement for local kids who were raised in the distinct Berchtesgaden form of Bavarian, despised by Fräulein Stöhr. Hitler found the brown eyes and dark hair dominant among the valley's people not to his liking, suspecting undesirable Italian or even Slavic influences, and accordingly, Fräulein Stöhr seemed to prefer the Nordic-looking children. (Rumor had it that Hitler encouraged his tall, blond S.S. men to impregnate Berchtesgaden women to create a more Aryan type.)

☐ ☐

STILL, MY LIGHT COLORING, rather good High German, and the fact that I was *Gottgläubig* could not save me entirely from Fräulein Stöhr's wrath. Over the course of two years she used her filbert canes on my hands at least four times, three times for whispering answers to kids she had called on. Each time I had to leave my crowded bench and walk, embarrassed and infuriated, to the front of the classroom and onto the podium to receive a couple of stinging lashes on my outstretched hand. Not surprisingly, my enthusiasm for anything having to do with school vanished quickly. No matter how happy I was running down the mountain with my friends in the morning, by the time we crossed the Ache and started up the other side toward school a sense of dread had come over me. I wanted nothing so much as to turn around and go back home.

It was spine-tingling torture to sit absolutely still for four or five hours, interrupted only by one short midmorning break. The only diversion inside the classroom was the dark brown, shiny crucifix above the teacher's desk on the front wall. The Nazis, ever irritated

In spite of everything, I learn to write.

by the symbols of the church they attacked but did not quite dare dismantle yet, had attempted to remove the crosses, only to be foiled by several fearless and pious farm women. Word of this resistance spread like wildfire, and sensing a public relations flap the Nazis backed off and the crosses remained. Mutti and Tante Susi, being nonreligious, were ambivalent about the outcome, saying that they would not have minded if the crucifixes had been removed.

Accuracy and *Ordnung* (orderliness) were the key virtues in which we were drilled under Fräulein Stöhr's tutelage. The proudest achievement of the day would be a word of praise for a row of perfect letters that held strictly to the limits of the three lines defining their lower, middle, and upper spaces. *Schönschrift* (penmanship, literally "beautiful script") was an exacting art requiring rigorous training. We wrote our numbers neatly in blocks of five or six problems each on paper with a square grid like a bookkeeper's. After all, "Ordnung muss sein" (There must be order). That was what we heard when disorderliness and worse, loss of control and chaos, threatened, especially on a piece of paper, on forms, receipts, accounts, and in any dealings with bureaucrats or officials. I did not know it then, but this basic compulsion for order and a fear of diverging from the norm must have lain behind the careful and cynical accounting of gold teeth and all other items taken from the victims of the concentration camps.

One seemingly typical day, as my longing to go outside grew with the ringing of the church bells every quarter hour, I was startled by Fräulein Stöhr's voice signaling the beginning of midmorning break. She told the third-graders to shut their reading books—they had been reading out loud in unison with her—and, limping slightly in her low-heeled, simple black shoes, opened the classroom door. We stepped, bench by dark green bench, into the aisle and headed in orderly pairs outside into the already tightly packed school yard. The noise and screams and movement made me wolf down my rye sandwich with its thin layer of homemade jam, the sooner to join the crowd. I belonged to a large group that played circle games, and we frantically tried to get in one more round after the whistle had sounded, calling us back to the class-room two by two.

On this day, after the break, Fräulein Stöhr barked, "Alle auf-passen!" (Attention everyone) in her usual grumpy tone. We were, she added, in a great war against the enemies of Germany and should expect our foes to use poison gas in future attacks in order to kill us. We would therefore have to know how to put on a gas mask and breathe through it. We welcomed this diversion, sinister though it was. The idea of an invisible killer gas in the air seemed unreal and unimaginable. But, I thought, perhaps it would be sim-ilar to the white, chemical fog that S.S. men had begun to release from iron barrels located all over Salzberg in order to hide the mountain—including Haus Linden—from approaching enemy planes. The chemicals were obviously kept under pressure, and on contact with air they turned rapidly into a billowing, spreading cloud of acrid fog that made any of us who were caught in it cough and our eyes water. The chemicals burned a large circle of grass around the barrels and changed the green of nearby trees into charcoal black.

Fräulein Stöhr asked a couple of boys to hand out the army-green, cylindrical tins with the gas masks and commanded the children in the outer rows to put them on, breathe calmly through them a few times, stuff them back into the tin, and pass them on. Interrupted every few minutes by her shout of "Ruhe!" (Silence), we took our turns with suppressed laughter and whispers about the bug-eyed and pig-snouted faces of the gas-mask wearers. We were told to help the little first-graders, who could barely handle the tin, let alone pull on the mask. I felt somewhat blasé because Vati had shown me his gas mask when he came home on his fur-lough, even though I had refused to try it on then. I pulled the tightly fitting, black rubber bands over my head. There was no choice but to try and breathe through the round filter covering my nose and mouth. It immediately felt as if I was stuck in a tight, air-less place. It was hard to imagine that I could run or do anything else with that mask over my face. Ripping it off as soon as I thought permissible, I took a few deep breaths of the classroom air that suddenly seemed sweet instead of sweaty and chalky.

□   □

THE NEXT DAY FRÄULEIN STÖHR continued our preparedness training, explaining that if we had no gas mask handy, we should wet a handkerchief and hold it over our mouth and nose. If we were not near water, she said, we should simply pee on the handkerchief. The girls giggled and blushed. I had a quick vision of having to crouch over my handkerchief while the boys would be standing up to accomplish the goal. And then to put it on my face! It seemed against all the rules of hygiene and decency that I had absorbed so far in my civilized and prudish German life. Our squeals and sounds of disgust were quickly cut off with a stern "Ruhe!" After a few more words about the ruthless, cruel enemy and our great leader, Fräulein Stöhr began the morning lesson.

On one of those precious, early-off days on which Catholic children received religious instructions by a Franciscan monk, I had started to walk home when I saw the friar coming down the dusty road from the *Markt*. He was a slender man with a long stride that made his flowing, brown monk's garb swing like a bell and the knots at the ends of the white rope around his waist bounce. A long, pointed hood reached far down his back, and a circle had been shaven on the top of his head. I had stopped for a minute in front of the marble plaques on the ivy-covered school wall to look at the gold inscription of MAX PAUL, the name that I did not want to be there. The friar walked up to me and with a warm smile put his hand on my head. He asked me to join his *Religionsstunde* (hour of religious instruction), saying that I might really like it. For a moment I was tempted, but the thought of spending another hour sitting still in that classroom made me shudder and shake my head. As politely as I knew how, I told the friar that my mother was waiting for me with lunch. He kept smiling and mumbled a bless-

ing while crossing my forehead with his thumb. I shook his outstretched hand, curtsied, and ran down toward the S.S. guardhouse at the bridge.

□　□

THE NAZI INFLUENCE AND ENCROACHMENT on the life of our
small family did not stop with just one fanatical teacher in a classroom. No two women on Salzberg were more notoriously engaged
with the Party and more ardent followers of Hitler than Frau Penzig and Frau Deil. They were both middle-aged widows of independent income who had migrated here to be near their Führer. Both
were officially engaged in Party and youth programs. They dressed
similarly, in handsome, long city dresses or slim skirts, with gold
chains and medallions dangling from their necks. They spoke, always with fervor, in a High German that Mutti told me had an accent typical of people from Saxony. Frau Penzig lived up toward the
Grafllehen, a mountain farm, and Frau Deil rented two whole
floors of Haus Pfeilbrand—a handsome place that would one day
be our home. Frau Penzig walked past Haus Linden on the way to
her house, usually stopping at our window with some request for
my mother. There was the Frauenschaft (German Women's Organization) meeting on Wednesday, and the speech by the *Gauleiter*
of the region on Thursday, and some other official event on Saturday, and certainly Mutti would not want to miss the honoring of
mothers on yet another day.

Along with hundreds of thousands of women, Mutti had joined
the Frauenschaft not just because she was ideologically drawn to it
but, as she said to Tante Susi, because they offered courses on
child rearing, first aid, gardening, and other things she wanted to
learn about. Tante Susi, never a joiner herself, added that it was
just plain good for my mother to get out of the house once in a
while. Frau Penzig was always on the lookout for smart, energetic
women who might rise through the ranks, no matter how put-
upon they might feel in the face of her constant requests. Mutti

took to making herself invisible if she saw Frau Penzig coming our way. That woman's authority apparently did not allow a simple, face-to-face refusal.

Frau Deil was the more likable of the two women, but she too had her eyes on my mother. One day she came by and asked Mutti to help her with running the *Kindergruppe,* since she herself was getting too old to deal with it alone at a time when it needed to be energized and expanded. The *Kindergruppe* was a voluntary, once-a-week after-school program for Salzberg children who were too young to join the Hitler Youth, including Ingrid and me. Since Mutti loved children, she agreed to make herself available one afternoon a week after taking some training courses in appropriate, Nazi-oriented children's activities. Around twenty to thirty children showed up at those Wednesday sessions throughout the school year; during our six-week summer vacation the program closed down. Mutti grumbled that on cold days her duties included starting a coal fire in the iron stove in the morning to preheat the *Kinderheim* (children's home), a wooden shack— amazingly primitive for such a program here on Hitler's mountain.

The afternoon always began with Frau Deil giving a short report on the war along with the Führer's latest pronouncements. Sitting around a table under Hitler's photo portrait, we listened silently. Frau Deil did not encourage us to ask questions. We then sang a cappella. Some songs were new and patriotic, some plain old children's favorites. Crafts and games took up the rest of the time. As our supplies for crafts became more and more limited, we used whatever was around, making animals and people from chestnuts and acorns and building whole villages from small squares of construction paper. When we could no longer get glue we tried to make it from flour and water or used the white of an egg that Mutti sacrificed. Neither approach worked; our paper houses just came apart. A course that Mutti took in the art of fold all kinds of shapes—helmets, boats, and baskets—allowed us to switch to a kind of primitive origami to fill a portion of the afternoon.

We, Hitler's children, where captivated by the games that took us outdoors. My favorite, most memorable outdoor activity was a war game we played in the damp meadow behind the *Kinderheim*. Frau Deil, back from a training session in Traunstein, a town outside the mountains, explained the roles we were to play. Else, Trauderl, and I immediately shouted that we wanted to be nurses. The boys wanted to be German or enemy soldiers—it did not matter which, as long as they could fight one another. Some girls were soldiers too, crawling on their bellies to surprise their enemies behind trees and inside a dirty concrete pipe lying in the field, using sticks or fingers for guns, and making shooting noises. Frau Deil had ripped apart an old sheet to provide us nurses with white headbands marked with a red cross, as well as bandages that we stuffed into the pockets of our pinafores. There were some rules as to who was dead and who had won, but to me the game was a glorified hide-and-seek with more noise and a couple of wrestling matches. I loved bandaging the wounded, and I don't think we were made to differentiate between our and the enemy soldiers, except that Germans were sent to the pretend army hospital and the enemies to a camp for prisoners of war.

There was nothing like seeing the real wounded to drive home the reality of war. In the spring of 1943 the Salzberg *Kindergruppe* was invited to put on a play for wounded officers recovering at the Hotel Platterhof within the Hitler terrain on Obersalzberg. There was even the possibility that we would perform for the Führer on his birthday. Just before April 20, the Berghof withdrew that invitation, much to Frau Deil's and our disappointment. Only Mutti was relieved, as she was not convinced that she could shape us up to sing well enough for the Führer.

Overflowing army hospitals had made it necessary to convert the Hotel Platterhof into a hospital for wounded officers. The men welcomed our enthusiastic performance of *Sleeping Beauty* with loud, gracious applause. They had saved some candy for each of us, and we were served vanilla and strawberry ice cream in pretty glass bowls. That alone was worth the effort we had put into rehearsals and making our pink-and-light-blue paper costumes with dozens of folded paper roses.

Though she was satisfied with our overall performance, Mutti found that our singing left much to be desired. My attention had certainly wandered during the songs. I could not take my eyes off the young men with their thick, white head bandages, moving along slowly on crutches, arms in slings and legs in casts or missing entire limbs. I felt slightly sick and hoped fervently they would all get well, but wondered what on earth they would do with only one arm, one leg, or no legs. Frau Deil, looking elegant with her silvery hair and Party button on her white lace collar, made a little speech, saying that she hoped they would not get hurt again once they were back out at the front fighting for our Führer. She thanked them for their sacrifice and for protecting us. We were invited back a few times to entertain the soldiers, and Mutti was always unhappy with the way we sang.

□   □

A HUGE CHANGE FOR THE BETTER took place in my third year of school. For the sake of efficiency, our third grade merged with that of the *Marktschule* (town school), which was located near the *Schlossplatz* in the center of Berchtesgaden. This meant a longer walk but also an escape from Fräulein Stöhr's tyranny. I was to encounter her at her very worst one last time.

□   □

OLD OBERLEHRER (HEAD TEACHER) SCHRAMM, our new teacher, took attendance on the first day and realized that he had an extra student. Wolfgang Stössl had tried to get into third grade to escape repeating second grade back down the hill with Fräulein Stöhr. The *Oberlehrer* pointed to me and to my horror asked me to take him back to her. The two of us walked silently along the high wooden fence that surrounded the park of the Royal Castle. Wolfgang's head with its unevenly cut, bushy blond hair was hanging low. He seemed resigned to his fate of spending another year with a teacher who clearly hated him and made his life miserable every day.

The moment we entered the classroom Fräulein Stöhr grabbed her cane and came toward us. She began to beat Wolfgang hard, on his arms, his shoulders, and his head, until his nose began to bleed, at which time she dragged him into the entry hall and held him by the neck under the cold-water faucet. Then she pushed him roughly back into the classroom and closed the door. I was terrified and enraged. The moment I got home I told Mutti what I had witnessed and begged her to take Fräulein Stöhr to task, to get the other parents, especially Wolfgang's, to protest. But I hoped in vain. No one, not even my mother, dared stand up to Fräulein Stöhr. Mutti said that the teacher was the authority and it was not up to parents to interfere. I was very disappointed and perhaps frightened by what I thought was contemptible cowardice on her part. Would she stand up for me if I needed her to, or would she give in to any authority and become paralyzed in the face of official injustice? The only revenge I could think of was to walk past Fräulein Stöhr silently, without a greeting, whenever we passed each other by chance on the street.

Oberlehrer Schramm had been called back from retirement. His silvery gray hair matched his mustache; he walked with a slight stoop and had a wrinkled face that did not scare me. He was an old-timer but much less of a disciplinarian than Fräulein Stöhr. Instead of the militaristic "Ruhe!" we had become accustomed to, he used the mild-mannered "Bitte seid jetzt still" (Please be quiet now). His title indicated that he had made a fine career of teaching, but he was clearly old and often tired. He tapped our knuckles with a square ruler or rapped them on the desk when we became too disorderly, but the penalty did not seem malicious.

Mutti, concerned over my very small amount of homework but endless preparation for show-and-tell, wondered if we were learning anything from the old man. I, of course, did not share that concern. In his class we never talked about the heroic deeds of the Führer, the death of our enemies, our endless victories, or the need to sacrifice for the fatherland. Oberlehrer Schramm seemed not to be a Nazi fanatic, if he was a Nazi at all. When I met him on the street after school, I went up to him and said "Gruess Gott, Herr Oberlehrer," with a curtsy, and not "Heil Hitler." Maybe he had not noticed the change of times or maybe he had a special courage, but even with many children of the Obersalzberg Nazi elite in his classroom, he left indoctrination out of his teaching.

The most prominent of the Nazi children in my class was little Albert Speer, son of the all-important Albert Speer, Hitler's minister of armament and war production and the architect of pompous Nazi buildings in Munich and Berlin. He was a friendly boy with a square jaw and a head full of thick ash-blond hair parted neatly on the side. His freckled face still seemed to have some baby fat. We were quite in awe of Albert, knowing that he came from the inner circle of Nazi leadership, and we hoped, of course, that he would divulge some real secrets of life up there behind the fence and the big gate. But during show-and-tell—the *Oberlehrer*'s way of filling hours without adequate teaching materials and in between ever-increasing air alarms—his stories were just like ours, about a cat or a dog, climbing a high tree or a mountain, or getting away with some minor mischief like reading past bedtime under the covers with a flashlight. I wanted to know whether he was invited to the Berghof or whether Hitler came to his birthday parties. Did they talk about us? What might he know about the war that we did not?

It would have been unthinkable and far too forward to ask any of those intrusive questions of little Albert Speer even though he sat just a few seats away from me. He had a shy smile and made nothing special of himself, something I instinctively respected. In fact, most of the Nazi elite up on the mountain, including the Bormanns, sent their children to the local schools. It seemed very egalitarian, except that these particular children arrived at school in black, sparkling clean Mercedes-Benzes driven by S.S. chauffeurs, just as Hitler himself would have, and whenever sirens announced an air raid they were picked up and whisked away to safety in luxurious bunkers on the mountain.

One time my new best friend, Gertraud Oberndörfer, the daughter of our family doctor, was invited to play with one of the many Bormann children at their villa. Frau Bormann was an un-pretentious mother, she told me, but Gertraud had not been sure how to greet the group of officers who sat at lunch with them. So she went around the table, shook their hands, curtsied, and said, "Gruess Gott." I could imagine that the officers too did not quite know what to do with a ten-year-old who greeted them one by one the old-fashioned way.

By 1943 the hours we spent in the town shelter had increased dramatically, due mostly to overflights by Allied bombers going after strategic targets to the south. By ten o'clock every morning I began to listen for the shuffle of feet in the classroom above ours, a sign that they had received their warning. On hearing the familiar noise, I tapped my neighbor with my elbow and whispered that it was time to get ready for the shelter. Unobtrusively we began to pack our satchels and made ready to leave as soon as the kid who ran from class to class screamed through the door, "Voralarm!" (early warning), or "Hauptalarm!" (priority warning), or even "Akuter Alarm!" (immediate warning), meaning that planes were already directly overhead. The surreal wail of the sirens would begin, making my heart flutter and beat faster. We could tell from the rhythm of the up-and-down howl how fast we had to get to a shelter. On "early warning"—three long ups and downs of the sirens—it was assumed that we could get home before the planes were overhead and seek refuge in our own cellars, but as time went on, this option diminished because enemy planes arrived faster and with little advance warning.

Most of the time, though, we were quickly herded into the school yard and marched along with Oberlehrer Schramm in his worn, gray loden knickers and jacket toward the wooden gate at the jagged, rocky entrance to the town shelter. From all sides children arrived with their teachers, and civilians with their suitcases. Air-raid wardens oversaw our entry into the dank, rough tunnel that had been blasted into Lockstein, a small, steep mountain rising from the center of town. In better times tourists had walked the trails to the top of Lockstein to enjoy homemade *Torte* and the lovely view directly down into the streets of Berchtesgaden and onto the high mountains. Now the run-down, no longer hospitable Café Lockstein housed children from the Kinderlandverschickung (K.L.V., the program for children's evacuation to the country).

Deep inside Lockstein we sat on crude, backless wooden benches lined up along the dirty, raw walls. The air-raid warden was impatient with our shuffling and cries of "I want to sit next to Marianne and Anneliese!" or "Save me a place, Annemarie," and shouted repeatedly, "Alles setzen!" (Everyone sit down). We planted our feet on wooden planks to avoid the deep puddles formed by the constant drip of water from the porous rock. Every ten meters a bare bulb illuminated the tunnel, but it was too dark to read. I don't remember what the boys did, but we girls played endless word games and cat's cradle. I admired Lisi's or Linde's new tricks with their strings, and we whispered, gossiped, giggled, and tried to change places without falling into the puddles. "Let's sing," someone said, beginning a folk song. We joined in for a while, until Hansi or another boy said, "I know a joke." Someone else knew a riddle that we passed from bench to bench until it faded into the darkness of the tunnel.

At last, when I had just about come to the brink of my tolerance for sitting still, a loud shout from the warden signaled the end of yet another two, three, or four hours spent in the shelter. We were apprehensive about what we would find when we emerged into the light of day. I held my breath as I stepped out half blind and, thanks to some undeserved fortune—and so unlike thousands of other European children—saw no fires, dust, smoke, or ruins. The ancient houses still lined the streets and squares, the steeples of the churches pushed toward the sky, and peaceful silence reigned. I walked home yet again through an undisturbed, familiar landscape that relaxed me and restored my sense of balance. I felt an almost overwhelming love for this mountain land and gave no thought, at least for a while, to the next wave of enemy planes that might already be flying in our direction.

When the year with Oberlehrer Schramm drew to an end, I probably was not much smarter, but school felt a little safer, air raids notwithstanding. We did not know who our next teacher might be, but as Mutti kept reminding me, it would be my last year in elementary school if I passed the entrance exam to the *Oberschule* (high school). And at ten, I would be old enough to join the Hitler Youth.

10 LESSONS FROM A WARTIME FRIENDSHIP

ALL OF MY FRIENDS ATTENDED *KINDERGRUPPE,*
the prelude to joining the Hitler Youth, except for Wiebke Molsen
and her younger sister, Bärbel. From the day in 1942 that Fräulein
Stöhr had introduced Wiebke as a new student into our classroom
in a grade below mine, I sensed that something was different
about her. The first inkling came when Fräulein Stöhr pointed out
that Wiebke was a Dutch, not a German, name. Moreover, new
children—most of them here under the evacuation program for
children from cities that were being bombed—usually did not
merit an introduction from our teacher. The new girl seemed shy
and with her uncertain smile made me wonder why she seemed
special.

For one, Wiebke looked different from the rest of us. Her sand-
colored, wavy hair was cut in a short bob, held off her face on one
side by a tortoiseshell clip that gave her an air of refinement that
the rest of us lacked. We wore the inevitable long, tidy braids, tied
with a ribbon or a rubber band, hanging down our backs or dangling over our books. Wiebke's skin was pale, almost pasty, and
you could tell that it would freckle, not tan, in the sun. A fine, dark
blue wool cardigan with white mother-of-pearl buttons topped her
pretty, light blue dress, and on her feet she wore white socks and
obviously new brown leather shoes. We all went barefoot during
the summer months to save our shoes and by this time had developed calluses that served us as well as leather soles. It would not be
until winter, when we had to squeeze once more into last year's
leaky boots, that we envied Wiebke her shoes.

The moment I learned that the Molsens had rented the summer cottage on the grounds of the Stadlerlehen next to our house, I determined to become Wiebke's friend. When school finally ended at one o'clock, I overcame my shyness, telling her that I lived next door and offering to show her the steep shortcut home. I intended to learn all there was to know about Wiebke and her family before we got home. But Wiebke had no intention of telling me. It was as if she had been carefully briefed about what she could and could not reveal. All I found out was that she had moved here with her mother, grandmother, and younger sister, Bärbel, and I learned nothing about why they had come to Berchtesgaden or where her father was—except that he was not in the army and seemed to live in Holland. She said, yes, they were German but also Dutch and that her mother and father were divorced. I didn't know what to make of that.

The summer cottage in the Stadlerlehen was a simply furnished, comfortable one-story wooden guesthouse, not built to be lived in year-round. Wiebke and Bärbel (short for Barbara)—who was about Ingrid's age and became her friend—shared the master bedroom. Frau Molsen and her mother, Frau Glauert, slept in the two small bedrooms off a large, wood-paneled living room. French doors opened from the living room onto a veranda bordered by a gravel yard, a lawn, and beyond it the white-fenced, sloping cow meadows of Frau Villnow's farm. The kitchen and bathroom—with a wondrous full-size, white enameled bathtub and a hand-held shower (at Haus Linden we bathed in an oval tin tub in the kitchen on Saturdays)—faced the shady north side. From Frau Molsen's bedroom the fragrance of lavender and fine perfume filtered into the living room, and while they never said a word about the modesty of the cottage, they probably had lived in far more luxurious quarters before.

Being North German, the Molsen ladies had about them a certain formality, or rather an upper-class restraint. However, just like the rest of us they worked in their assigned slice of wartime garden in a stony meadow of the Stadlerlehen. Slim and elegant

Frau Molsen, dressed in a pretty, pastel, long-skirted dirndl dress and a broad-brimmed straw hat, would even help to bring in the hay when a thunderstorm threatened the winter fodder of Frau Villnow's few cows. The stable was otherwise empty, as early in the war Frau Villnow's two strong, handsome horses had been drafted into the army. The black lacquered horse carriage that in peacetime had taken her to town stood unused and covered with spiderwebs in the woodshed that doubled as a carriage house. Its only function now was as a marvelous prop for our games.

Frau Glauert was, in spite of her increasing deafness, the more outgoing of the two women. She overcame her impediment with an ear trumpet—when she chose to, that is. Her affliction seemed to be of a selective nature, and Wiebke and I had convincing evidence that she heard and understood perfectly well, even without her horn. Whenever the two of us shared a deep secret about our games in her presence or worked on a venomous poem about someone in the neighborhood, Frau Molsen somehow found out about it. Frau Glauert wore long, dark silk or wool skirts and dresses with discreet patterns and always a black velvet choker with a beautiful silver-and-pearl clasp. Nanni, our stout and jolly landlady, a woman with little education but a great sense of humor, also wore a black velvet choker with a clasp, no doubt of lesser value, every single day. The two women had little else in common, but they agreed that they both felt naked until their chokers were fastened around their necks. That confession was the most intimate conversation I remember Frau Glauert having with anyone.

With the war it had become customary for visitors and children to leave a friend's house before a meal was served. Food was too scarce to share, and no one wanted to shame the woman of the house into an invitation to join a meal. On one occasion—it must have been later in the war—I was waiting on the lawn in front of the Molsens' dining porch for Wiebke to finish lunch. All of a sudden Frau Glauert exclaimed in a raised, angry voice, "Why, after we have not had meat for ten days, did Zenzi [the maid and cook] just today not set the table with *Messerbänkchen?*" *Messerbänkchen,* it turned out, were little silver gadgets for resting the knife after cutting one's meat, I assumed to prevent it from dirtying the tablecloth. With a certain amount of wonderment I felt sorry for Frau Glauert because her so infrequent meat dinner had been spoiled by not having a *Messerbänkchen*. No such gadget existed in Haus Linden, but I liked the sound of that word and never forgot it.

I was awed by the fact that Wiebke's mother and grandmother took a nap every afternoon in their sweet-scented bedrooms; during this time we were asked to play very quietly. Mutti had never in her life even heard of such a thing as an afternoon nap. I also pointed out to Mutti that Wiebke and Bärbel never got yelled at, and that Frau Molsen did not spank them with a wooden spoon or slap their faces if they got their dresses dirty or lost something. Mutti was unimpressed. My compassionate little sister would cry when Mutti slapped me with her quick hand, while I felt simply infuriated by the red marks her fingers left on my cheeks.

In hundreds of ways Wiebke led a different life from the rest of us. Trudi practiced her zither—the favorite Bavarian folk instrument, which she played beautifully—and I was supposed to learn to play an old accordion whose buttons stuck hopelessly the moment I touched them. Wiebke, however, practiced on the grand piano the Molsens had brought with them. It took up almost half of their living room. Trudi and I schlepped our instruments in clumsy, heavy black boxes down and up the mountains to group lessons. Wiebke received private piano lessons from Fräulein Werner—a skinny spinster with washed-out straight hair that ended in a few meager curls—who walked all the way up to the Molsens' house. My parents of course loved German art and German artists, but there were no shelves filled with large, beautifully bound and printed art books in my home. Wiebke and I borrowed Frau Molsen's art books mostly to giggle over the small but highly visible penis of the baby Jesus in a nativity scene or over a breast-feeding Mary. But it was not just for these titillating and surely forbidden images that I wanted more than anything else to own a real, beautiful art book after the war. I would then be able to look

for as long as I wanted at the wonderful faces, flowers, and land-
scapes created by Dürer, Grünewald, and Cranach, and the Italians
Botticelli and Da Vinci. I fantasized that if Vati had lived, he might
one day have painted pictures like these. He might have painted a
portrait of me.

□   □

THE MOLSENS SOCIALIZED WITH FRAU VILLNOW and her rare
guests but otherwise kept to themselves. Neither S.S. officers nor
any of the other Nazi elite came and went in their cottage. They did
not engage in any of the many activities or affiliations the Nazis organized for people of every class and age. On the contrary, I felt
Frau Molsen and Frau Glauert were contemptuous of the Nazis. I
noticed a disparaging smile and secret eye rolling when, for in-
stance, they saw the painter Hans Schuster, who, old as he was,
strutted around in his S.A. uniform and made us greet him with
"Heil Hitler!" They were blasé over my excited accounts of this or
that Nazi leader I had seen driving up or down the mountain, and
they seemed uninterested in battle reports and the progress of the
war. It annoyed me to see them thumb their noses at so much in
which we had a stake and a belief. It was not as if they stood up in
protest, rather it was a passive negativism, an attitude of "we can
wait this out," that was probably common among those who could
afford it.

Most middle-class people I knew gave at least lip service to sup-
porting the Third Reich and the war. Many were actually forced to
sign up for a duty, such as collecting money door-to-door for Nazi
charities like the Winterhilfswerk (W.H.W., Winter Assistance), or
Eintopf Sonntag. The latter was a contribution of savings supposedly derived from eating stew on Sundays instead of other, more
costly dishes. Mutti, whose assignment to collect donations to the
Winterhilfswerk involved several days of walking from house to
house, resented both: gathering and making these contributions
that cut into her scarce time and small widow's pension. Yet right
here under Hitler's nose the Molsens lived their completely pri-

vate lives with no apparent interference, warnings, demands, or snooping from the authorities that might have included the Gestapo. What was the secret of their safety? Gossips conjectured that because they came from an old Düsseldorf banking family they may have paid the Nazis off, or that the Dutch father or the separation from him somehow protected them. It seemed that no one really knew or cared.

Every day Zenzi set the lunch table with fresh linens and matching napkins. I asked Mutti why we did not have a nice tablecloth and napkins every day like the Molsens. Mutti's starched hand-embroidered tablecloths and napkins came out of the linen cupboard only for special visitors or on holidays. But one evening after I had mentioned our lack of style once again, she sat down at her sewing machine and made napkins from some leftover cotton fabric and embroidered the hems with a pretty stitch to make me feel better. I was terribly pleased that she had done this and told her that it made all the difference sitting down at the table with napkins. She did not budge on the daily tablecloth, however, and we continued to set our plates on the speckled, light-brown linoleum that my grandfather had carefully worked into the top of our white kitchen table. Mutti pointed out that the Molsens had Zenzi, a local woman who took their laundry home and brought it back washed, starched, and ironed. She, Mutti, had to do ours herself on Mondays in the Haus Linden tenants' washhouse. And besides, where would the soap for washing the extra load come from?

Normal soap had indeed become an item for which the ersatz never seemed to do the job. We had *Schwimmseife* (very light floating soap that developed a little foam), *Lehmseife* (a sandy-feeling clay soap with no foam that sank like a rock), and *Knochenseife* (bone soap that the women made from animal bones and lye in a process that stank to high heaven). Every other Monday was wash day. An unbelievable number of steps kept Mutti in the large, clean communal washhouse all day. Sorting, scrubbing, boiling, rinsing, and finally hanging the clean laundry on the outdoor lines made her hands red and rough but apparently also gave her a sense of accomplishment. She said that it was good to get away from all the sewing for customers who paid in butter, milk, eggs, or money—all scarce in our small family. Besides, for as long as she was by herself in that steamy, damp washhouse she did not have to pretend enthusiasm for the sake of her children but could weep freely as she sang sad German songs that evoked memories and *Weltschmerz* (weariness of the world). On wash-day Mondays Ingrid and I coped on our own, except for lunch. I resolved, along with many other resolutions about how I would lead my life "after the war" or as a grown-up, that I would never do my own laundry in a washhouse or hang it up outside in rain, snow, sleet, and bitter frost.

Unexpectedly, Frau Molsen offered to teach Mutti how to embroider a child's dress with stitches that formed fine pleats and patterns, and for my ninth birthday Mutti, much to her own pleasure, was able to make a bright aquamarine-colored dress just like those Wiebke wore, with a big sash to tie in back. Wiebke and I wore our dresses of clashing blues always on the same day, prompting Bärbel and Ingrid to call us *die blauen Weiber* (the blue women). This remained our nickname until long after my blue dress was let down for the last time and, slightly faded, finally passed on to Ingrid.

With increasing scarcities, especially of fruit, we children took things into our own hands, making secret excursions to the steep old plum orchard of the Angererlehen to taste the ripeness of the *Baunken,* a special kind of round plum, or the apples in another farmer's small and meager orchard. We not only ran but tunneled on our bellies through the high, off-limits grass that was about to be mowed to the huge lilac bush below Frau Villnow's terrace to pick some of its fresh, fragrant blossoms for Mother's Day, knowing full well that this was a fraudulent gift. The difference between mine and thine and other moral imperatives was wearing thin, what with shortages and mounting desires. Wiebke and Bärbel, though they were our playmates, did not take part in our worst transgressions and rambunctious behavior; they were different in that regard too, always seeming to keep their dresses clean effortlessly.

After I moved from the Salzbergschule to the Marktschule into Oberlehrer Schramm's class, it became more difficult for Wiebke, a grade below me and still with Fräulein Stöhr, and me to walk home together; also, new friends entered our lives. Still, we remained close through the remaining years of the war, sharing confidences, dreams, and fantasies that greatly influenced my transition from child to teenager. They helped us to keep up hope that the war would end with both of us alive, and imbued some of the most frightening and terrible days with a sense of normality, even laughter, and a childish gaiety so lacking in the adult world.

I never did find out much more about the private life of Wiebke's family. Knowing her, however, allowed me to live a part of my war years on the edge of a different world, a world with an unspoken, subtle, but obvious contempt for the Nazis, and of determined noninvolvement in their activities. Under the influence of the Molsens, I became more aware and critical of the individual Nazi fanatics—Fräulein Stöhr, Herr Adler, Hans Schuster, Frau Deil, and Frau Penzig—who surrounded me and whose total, crazy commitment at one point or another infringed on my life. I also learned what holding power over someone felt like from a game I had played with Wiebke a few days after we met. Irritated by her secretiveness, I had suggested that we play dog and owner on our way home through the woods. She agreed to be the dog and fetch wooden sticks for me and to sit in the woods until I called her. I walked far away from her, and she obediently stayed crouched under a tree, surely frightened by this to-her-unknown deep and mossy mountain forest. I felt the thrill of my dominance and later felt guilt whenever I thought of the game.

11 A WEARY INTERLUDE IN SELB

EVERY SUMMER MUTTI TOOK US TO VISIT OUR grandparents. In 1943 too we said good-bye to our friends on Salzberg and embarked on the increasingly difficult and haphazard journey to Selb. Mutti felt demoralized by the constant bombing of our cities. It seemed that with every attack she hated the Allies more and found renewed strength to bear up under hardship, hoping that our armies would prevail. A report from Hamburg said that after one attack 800,000 homeless were wandering that destroyed city's streets in search of food, clothing, and shelter. What if, Mutti worried, our overcrowded train had to stop in the middle of the night to wait out an air raid, or worse, what if the train was bombed while stopped at a station?

We really had no choice but to go. Tante Emma had written that my gravely ill grandmother needed Mutti's care, adding ominously that my grandfather had been called in by the Gestapo for his public anti-Nazi declarations—most likely made during a meeting of his guild. After being held overnight he had received a warning that next time he would be considered an enemy of the people and face the consequences, meaning concentration camp. I began to suspect that this vacation would not be much fun. Luckily I had no foreboding about the length and the stress of our stay in Selb. We caught the train, as always with seconds to spare, and began the trip that in normal times took about six hours but now took close to two days.

By the time of our third train change in the town of Landshut, Mutti realized that the easiest way for children to get in and out of the hopelessly crowded train was through the windows. Travelers who stayed on the train simply handed Ingrid and me through the opening into the outstretched hands of people on the platform who knew the routine. I was mortified at the thought that my skirt would slip up and they would see my underwear, but no one even noticed that it was me who came down; I was just one small body among dozens.

Mutti, fighting her way out through the train corridor, had called out, "Watch the suitcases!" as our luggage followed us through the window, disappearing from her sight. I pulled our bags to one spot and told Ingrid to sit down on my father's large brown suitcase with the yellow wooden braces encircling it. Mutti was nowhere to be seen and for a very long moment I wondered if I would have to continue on alone with Ingrid. I was nine and thought I could handle it as long as Ingrid cooperated; in fact, everybody in Selb would think how brave and smart I was if I did make the trip without Mutti. To my enormous relief, however, Mutti showed up, straightening out her dress and ruffled hair. The three of us ate our sandwiches and drank from our thermos of peppermint tea in the small, smoky waiting room while we listened to garbled announcements, anxious not to miss our train. Suddenly late, we ran down the wrong steps to the wrong platform and then in a panic to the next, hoping it was the right one.

Women, children, old people, and groups of soldiers stood guarding their baggage. When the train pulled in, the disorderly crowd pressed forward, fighting to get on with awkward bundles and large packs and suitcases that poked and pressed against us. Helpful hands again lifted Ingrid and me in through the window, and even Mutti followed with a helpful push and heave from the rear. Ingrid and I were lucky enough to find seats, squeezing ourselves between two adults onto the coveted, hard wooden benches of the third-class compartment. Years earlier the benches had been painted with a yellowish varnish that was now old and scratched. Across from my seat hung a broken mirror in a metal frame, and the sliding door of the compartment had a poster showing a dark, shadowy spy figure with the caption "Feind hoert mit" (The enemy listens in). We could not have cared less if this was a *Raucher* or *Nichtraucher* (smoking or no smoking) car as long as we had a seat instead of sitting on our suitcases in the drafty hallway with its open doors, rattling wheels, and clanking chains.

One old lady complained about the draft from the open window, while another insisted on fresh air. The fresh-air fan won and I was allowed to stand up between them holding my face into the wind, knowing that black specks of soot from the engine would land on it, fly into my eyes and my nostrils, or, as Mutti warned, settle irrevocably in my lungs.

We ate Mutti's last sandwiches as night fell and the train moved through the darkness without lights, in order to be shielded from any enemy pilot who might be overhead. I was awakened once by the silence of the stopped train and heard explosions that seemed quite close. No one said a word until we moved again; then someone stated the obvious, that we had luckily not been hit. I thought how mysterious trains were at night and remembered a scary conversation I had overheard a short while before. My mother's friend Sophie and her husband, who was home on leave, stopped by Haus Linden one evening and Mutti and Sophie quizzed him about his experiences on the eastern front. Reluctantly—no soldier was supposed to reveal anything about the front—he began to tell a story of trainloads of women rolling through a railroad station guarded by his unit, in Poland perhaps. The women on the train were so desperate to relieve themselves that they actually did so out of the train windows, regardless of the armed onlookers or the bitter cold. He said that thousands of people came through in cattle cars, but at least this one offered a sight that made the soldiers laugh. That was all he said about the secret trains except that he would make any sacrifice to spare Mutti and Sophie such a sight, let alone such a fate.

Very disturbed by his account, I threw caution to the wind, asking Mutti what he had meant. Who sent the trains? Why were the women shipped this way, and where were they going? She had been unsettled too but became more so for not having prevented me from overhearing. She didn't answer my questions, and eavesdropping on grown-up conversations—my secret hobby—became even harder after that.

In the early morning of a luminous summer day we finally arrived in the city of Regensburg on the Danube. The waiting room stank and offered no food, so Mutti decided that we would walk into the city and try to reach the famous ancient cathedral that she had admired years before. The luggage storage was open and functional, and so we set off unencumbered by suitcases. But where we expected to see lovely streets of an ancient city we saw devastation. Barely believing my eyes, I stared at a whole street turned to rubble by bombs. Gaping holes where rooms should have been opened onto the pale morning sky. I felt I was walking through a nightmare and realized how sheltered we were from all this in our mountains. When we finally stood before the large, looming Gothic cathedral, we had run out of time and had to turn around without setting foot into it. With Mutti urging me to move faster, my anxiety rose by the minute and Ingrid began to cry for fear of missing our train—the only one that would get us to Selb that day.

Both sets of grandparents, my godmother, Frieda, Tante Emma, and little cousin Uschi were eagerly awaiting us at the old, rust-colored brick *Hauptbahnhof* at Selb. We exchanged handshakes and said "Gruess Gott" in a Franconian dialect, sparing my Pöhlmann grandfather the irritation of "Heil Hitler." Ingrid and I curtsied to the elders, but not being a family that showed emotion in public, we neither hugged nor kissed one another—except for Frieda, who, slightly embarrassed, gave Ingrid and me a soft, welcoming hug and a wet kiss. The two grandfathers lifted their hats in greeting. Both wore their old, gray summer suits, immaculately cleaned and ironed by the grandmothers, and each of them sported a polished brown walking cane.

The luggage was loaded onto the same kind of wooden pull cart that we used at home, allowing a very tired little Ingrid to ride on top of the suitcases. Our party started down the Bahnhofstrasse, where Tante Emma pointed to an old, unadorned brick building that now housed the "Polish women" who were brought here—no doubt by force—to work in factories. These women were part and parcel of wartime Selb, but even though I encountered them on a few occasions, I learned nothing about them except that they were not German but in our service. Amid travel stories the grown-ups talked about our troops and the bombings—luckily without getting into arguments—before the Paul grandparents peeled off at their apartment building on what was now Adolf Hitler Strasse. The Pöhlmann contingent continued up the Hutschenreutherstrasse, a cobblestone street that led to the turnoff of the Birkengasse (Birch Alley), a gravel road shaded by white birches. My grandfather's house at Birkengasse 7 was one of the oldest houses in Selb. Along with only a few other isolated buildings, it had survived the great fire of 1856, an infamous date memorized early by every child in town.

Unfortunately, the venerable age of my grandfather's house did not translate into a very comfortable or pretty setting for even modest contemporary living. From the outside I thought the house looked naked, with its steep slate roof, its plain casement windows without green shutters or balconies to break up the height of the yellow walls, which were dirty with age-old soot from the porcelain factories. But under the gable facing the street was a large white sign announcing in tall black letters BAU UND MÖBELSCHREINEREI—ALBIN PÖHLMANN (Carpentry for Buildings and Furniture); the sign made me proud that my grandfather was a *Schreinermeister* (master carpenter) with his own, obviously important business.

The peculiar, rich smell of glue, varnish, and sawn wood greeted us from the carpentry area, and across from it a few steps led into a storage room for coffins and furniture waiting for customer pickup. I loved the coffins with their shiny wood veneer and ornate gold decorations; sometimes I wistfully ran my finger over their smooth finish and wondered who would lie in them eventually. I planned to try one out as soon as I got a chance and found someone who would help me lift the lid. Behind the storage room was the washhouse with its cold-water faucet and tin and wooden washtubs. A damp, dark cellar blasted into the rock at the back of the house held barrels of homemade sauerkraut, shelves with more empty than filled jars for preserves, compotes, jams, and jellies, and in one corner my uncle's long-unused winemaking equipment. Before he was drafted, he would make red-currant wine when the berries were ripe in Grossvati's garden. On a special occasion a long time ago, he had opened a bottle of the deceptively sweet and highly alcoholic ruby red liquid he called Finkenstich Riesling, after the local name for the area, and poured us children a sipful in our own small glasses.

□ □

WE ENTERED THE LARGE LIVING ROOM—KITCHEN with its big cast-iron cookstove. Grossvati had made the simple, sturdy oak furniture, and a flat, hard ottoman stood against the wall with the dining table pulled up against it. My grandmother's lush pink and red geraniums on the deep, shiny windowsills along with her snow-white crocheted curtains made the room look friendly and crisp. There must have been a side to my grandmother that I did not know, for how else could she grow such splendor? The windows overlooked the sloping berry garden and the stand of birches. When a breeze moved the branches, you could see the glitter of the Selbach, a small meandering stream.

The first thing I did was to check if the yellow, woody fungus in our bedroom had grown again between the floorboards. I shouted that I had found the yellow mushroom, and Mutti removed it with disgust. The windows to the backyard seemed lower this year—I had of course grown—and would serve nicely as an exit when I wanted to avoid my grandmother's questioning looks on my way out through the living room.

Right now, though, my grandmother was exhausted from the trip to and from the station. By the time we had reached Birkengasse 7, Mutti's concern for her mother was obvious. Grossmutti, always petite, seemed still smaller this year. Her stern, wrinkled face bore traces of pain around her eyes and her mouth. She removed her dentures, saying that they hurt her. Without them, her pointed nose collapsed toward her pointed chin, so that she reminded me of a real witch. She sat without speaking on her hard, upright chair, making no effort to hide her impatience with the two rambunctious children who had invaded her home. Even Ingrid, who made friends with most anyone, gave up trying to engage her. Mutti said sadly that her mother was worn out from her hard life and very ill. Patiently and without question she assumed the role of obedient daughter and caregiver.

Tante Emma warned us that Grossmutti refused to go down to the dank cellar when there was an air raid. Only a few nights after we arrived I was awakened from a deep sleep by the howl of the sirens. I panicked when I realized that Mutti was not in her bed and all I could think of was to escape through the open window and hide in the yard. In the dark I misjudged the amount of space available next to my grandmother's large Christmas cactus; it fell to the floor and broke in half. Now I faced two horrors: the air raid without my mother, and my grandmother's wrath over the broken flowerpot. Mutti arrived out of breath a few minutes later. She had run home from a friend's as soon as the alarm sounded. She lectured me on the foolishness of trying to go out into the yard instead of waking my grandparents or Tante Emma, all of whom lived on the same floor as us. It took me a while to go back to sleep even after the all-clear sirens signaled the end of the air raid. I knew then that my fear of my grandmother was unfounded but that the terror I felt in the still, strange bedroom when the sirens sent their spooky cry into the night was all too real. Ingrid had slept through the whole commotion but could not refrain from saying the next morning that she was sorry I broke Grossmutti's cactus pot, earning her a withering look from me.

That night's adventure caused the first quarrel of this visit between my grandfather and my mother. The next day she told him how awful it was of the enemy to threaten even small towns like Selb and that "they" were hunting down and harassing the civilian population of Germany like wounded animals. Grossvati answered her as he had many times before: "What do you expect? This is all Hitler's doing. I told you a long time ago that this war is madness. Mark my word, we will see worse." They raised their voices, but then Mutti stopped the dispute in fear that someone might over-hear them. Having seen the streets in Regensburg, I thought my mother was right about the crimes of the enemy. I wondered, as I had when I was very small and had my encounter with Hitler, what to make of my otherwise trustworthy grandfather's opinion. Was there a similarity between the Molsens' ineffective silent contempt and his loud, dangerous, but equally ineffective criticism?

□ □

ON THE LANDING BETWEEN MY grandparents' quarters and Tante Emma's small apartment were two smelly, fly-ridden toilets that worked through gravity rather than water. There had never been enough money to modernize the old building so that one faucet and a chipped, enameled sink on the landing were the only source of indoor water. Compared with this, our apartment in Haus Linden was downright luxurious with its flush toilet and running water in the kitchen. However, Tante Emma's kitchen had a gas range in addition to her wood-burning stove, and whenever the gas flame began to sputter, she drew a five-reichsmark coin from a small china bowl, moving as fast as she could to feed the gas meter.

One of the great annoyances of summer in Selb was my grand-parents' insistence on taking us to church every Sunday, provided my grandmother was well enough to go. Since we had adopted the Nazi religion, *Gottgläubigkeit,* I couldn't understand why Mutti went along with my grandparents' wishes. In contrast to the Catholic churches in Berchtesgaden, the plain, neo-Gothic parish church of Selb had no images of saints to study on stained-glass windows, no Holy Mary with an infant to wonder about. It was almost impossible for me to sit still through the long sermon. After a while I began to wiggle on the hard bench, fiddle with the songbook, look around, try to talk and gesture to Ingrid or, worse, make her giggle. The old couple simply could not understand what was wrong with us, and my grandfather only half jokingly called us *die Wilden von Bayern* (the savages from Bavaria). They insisted that the only way to cure us was with more church. In the end, just to stop the bickering, it was agreed that we only had to go to church on high holidays, which were rare indeed during the summer.

The Lutheran church in Selb, where my grandparents worshipped and my mother was married.

If bathrooms or lack of them and Sunday church were the worst parts of being in Selb, the best part was having more food. The chickens, rabbits, ducks, and geese that lived in my grandfather's yard provided a Sunday roast every so often; conditions in Berchtesgaden and Haus Linden were far less suitable for keeping such animals. The grain for chicken feed did not grow in the mountains, and our small woodshed next to Haus Linden had not yet been converted to hold a roost for hens or rabbit cages. The meat from a fat rabbit would be served Sunday and Monday, while the gravy would flavor the Franconian potato dishes on Tuesdays and Wednesdays. In my grandfather and Tante Emma's kitchen garden the cabbages actually formed solid red or white heads; ours barely developed a few leaves. Carrots, which remained the size of a child's finger on

Salzberg, grew long and thick here. Most wonderful of all, toma-
toes ripened on the vine, while ours—still green at the first frost—
were supposed to ripen inside a paper bag on the windowsill but
always turned black before they turned red. In addition to protein,
the ducks and geese provided feathers for pillows and bedcovers;
the hens, eggs for cooking and fat for rendering; and the rabbits,
pelts for coat collars, bedroom slippers, and warm muffs. I knew
that to fall in love with a rabbit or a fluffy yellow chick was a foolish
luxury that would only make me sad, even sometimes tearful,
when it was time to kill and eat the animal. After a few weeks in
Selb, Mutti noted with pleasure that I had put on a little weight
where I had been skin and bones before. She chalked the gain up to
the food but also to the fact that we did not have to climb up and
down mountains for school and daily errands.

□   □

I LIKED SELB MOSTLY BECAUSE of Tante Emma. She was my con-
fidante, a kind of replacement for Trudi and Tante Susi, saving me
from my mother's scolding by washing a pair of socks I had soiled
or fixing a hem I had ripped. She fretted if the postwoman brought
no letter from Onkel Hans; Grossmutti had to remind her that no
letter was better than receiving a message of death or even worse,
news that her loved one was missing in action. The young, very
pregnant baker's daughter who had married the year before in a
wartime ceremony had just learned of her husband's death. Clad
in black, her face pale and her eyes rimmed red, she continued to
sell bread every morning until it ran out. Waiting my turn in line, I
wondered how it would feel for the baby never to have a father at all.
The deaths of the young men he knew threw my grandfather into a
rage. Mutti and Tante Emma kept the windows closed and said as
little as possible while they themselves contemplated the carnage
in resignation, yet still in opposition to my grandfather's stand.

I knew Onkel Hans mostly from a photo on my aunt's living
room wall that showed him in his infantry uniform indicating the
rank of a *Feldwebel* (sergeant). When the longed-for letter from

him finally arrived, it came from Spitsbergen in occupied Norway, a place that seemed to be at the cold end of the world. A few weeks later Tante Emma received a medium-size wooden barrel filled to the brim with Norwegian salt herring that Onkel Hans had managed to send. The silvery fish in their brine were a treasure to behold. Immediately the women set about soaking a few of them, and then we feasted—half a fish per grown-up and slightly less per child. The barrel was rolled into the cellar, and once in a while—we thought not often enough—Tante Emma would ask if we wanted a herring. She knew that after an initial polite "Ach nein, danke" (Oh no, thank you), the answer would be a resounding yes. My mother pickled herring in milk and vinegar, or my grandfather wrapped it in a piece of newspaper, put a hook through its head, hung it from a wire in the attic, and lit the paper to smoke the fish. Every time he did this I foresaw that he would set all of Selb on fire once again, but he said with a laugh not to worry because he had done it before. Ignorant of carcinogens, we enjoyed our share of the wonderful, fatty, smoked delicacy for lunch. One herring made five portions. My grandmother always said, "The piece with the head is for Grandfather; he needs it most," while she insisted on the small tail piece for herself. My grandfather ate every smidgen, including the eyes. Ingrid and I rolled our eyes in revulsion, but we understood his hunger and remained silent.

The mood that summer was somber. We tried to focus on the smallest, meanest everyday chores as the catastrophe around us gathered momentum and impinged on our lives in a thousand ways. My grandfather's two young apprentices had recently been drafted, leaving him sad and angry. His refusal to join the Nazi Party to curry favors and contracts had left him with barely enough customers. Yet we were welcome to play alongside my grandfather in the carpentry shop, looking for scrap wood, sweeping up piles of fragrant shavings and sawdust, hammering and watching Grossvati handle his saws, planes, chisels, pliers, hammers, levels, rectangles, and rulers with calm efficiency. He taught me to hammer a nail in straight and to measure a piece of wood. In the background was the whine of the scary monster machines with their huge horizontal and vertical leather belts driving the saws through the boards. Before our very eyes and in a multitude of patient steps Albin Pöhlmann transformed the raw boards from the yard into a shiny wardrobe, a chest of drawers, and, of course, coffins. The only time we were banned from the carpentry was during the painting process—the dust we might stir up would ruin the glossy coats that had the smoothness of Japanese lacquer.

In early August the adults took a break from the tension over politics for the berry harvest. There was a flurry of activity, for it was crucial to pick every last ripe currant and gooseberry at the peak of sweetness. For many days Mutti and Tante Emma sat under the huge old currant bushes in the garden and filled bowl after bowl with clusters of the shiny red berries with black caps the size of pinheads. Ingrid, our cousin Uschi, and I helped intermittently, but mostly we ate berries until our faces and hands were stained a deep red. The currants, stems and all, were cooked briefly in a very large pot and the crimson mass poured into the cheesecloth that hung like a red udder between the legs of upside-down kitchen chairs. As the ruby syrup dripped into the bowls below, a delicious, sweet, and slightly acid fragrance filled the kitchen and seeped into the hallway. Finally the thick, sugary syrup was poured into sterilized jam jars that were then sealed with wax and stored in the cellar. I dreaded having to struggle with a basketful of these jars on the trains back to Berchtesgaden, but I couldn't deny the value of having our own currant jelly for school sandwiches during the winter.

□　□

AS THE END OF OUR VACATION approached we realized that my grandmother was going to die. Emphysema had turned her legs into swollen, bluish white sacks of fluid. They could no longer carry her, and if the fluid rose to her heart, the doctor said, she would die. Horrified and scared by that prospect, I tried not to look at her ankles when she sat there resting her neatly combed head on her folded hands. She no longer frowned at us, too absorbed by the stabbing pain in her heart, her lack of breath, and making peace with her God. A Protestant sister came daily to help bathe her, to pray with her, and to read to her from the New Testament.

Mutti needed to remain by her mother's side. She traveled alone to Berchtesgaden to collect our fall and winter clothing and arranged with the landlord to hold the apartment for us. He was concerned that the authorities would not allow an apartment to stand empty but promised to do his best. Ingrid and I missed our friends, our home, the mountains, and even the feeling of importance that came from living on Salzberg near the Nazi elite. But when school began that fall of 1943, Ingrid, now six years old, started out cheerily enough in first grade and I, at nine, entered Fräulein Hofmann's fourth grade at the very large and intimidating Luitpoldschule, a city school within easy walking distance. Ingrid proudly carried her *Schultuete*, the traditional shiny paper cone that Mutti had managed to fill with apples, a few candies, and a pencil box meant to sweeten a first-grader's first day of school. Her teacher, an older man, asked the mothers to leave right away and led his charges—often crying and sobbing—to their seats. Real life began with a vengeance.

Shyly I walked into my classroom, looking around for a familiar face. Fräulein Hofmann, my new teacher, a slender, short woman of indeterminate age, welcomed me and assigned me a seat. After the first morning I knew that she was not the ogre that Fräulein Stöhr had been but that she too was a Nazi fanatic, more dangerous, it turned out, than Stöhr. On the first day, as if we did not know it, we once again practiced a loud and clear "Heil Hitler." My impatient sigh prompted my neighbor to whisper that the training would help me to avoid the wrath of Herr Hetz, the school principal, who loathed a mumbled version of the sacred German greeting. I made his acquaintance all too soon when Fräulein Hofmann asked me to carry some documents to his office. I walked through the dimly lit, silent, and bare corridors past endless rows of shut classroom doors and up a flight of stone steps until with a

beating heart and sweaty palms I stood before the principal's office. I knocked timidly and on entering raised my arm shouting,
"Heil Hitler!" Herr Hetz glanced at me and said that I should go
back outside the door to try again and do a better job with our
Führer's name. He made me do this three times, and I was close to
tears when he finally sent me away in disgust. I never found out
what it was that I did wrong or why this greeting was such an obsession. I began to hate saying it, for it always sounded wrong and
more and more stupid.

The moment people heard that I was from Berchtesgaden and
actually lived on Hitler's mountain they became fascinated, showing an almost feverish interest in anything I might know about the
Führer. Fräulein Hofmann asked immediately if I had seen him.
When I told her of my personal encounter before the war she was
more impressed than a good Catholic hearing of an audience with
the pope. She paid special attention to me, inquired about my family, and asked one day what my grandmother talked about with the
Diakonisse (Protestant sister) who took care of her. Puzzled, I
truthfully told her that they prayed and read the Bible together. She
looked doubtful, making me wonder what she had expected me to
say. Even so, she made me her reluctant pet. I wanted nothing as
much as to belong to a clique of girls that lived in the neighborhood, something Fräulein Hofmann did nothing to prevent but in
my mind hindered. She had made me the unfortunate present of a
little black pillbox cap with an embroidered rim and a tassel to one
side. Fearing ridicule by my classmates, I wore the cap only for the
last few steps into the classroom. I was tremendously relieved
when the first winter frost arrived and Mutti insisted I wear my
knitted wool hat.

Monday mornings each pupil had to weigh in with at least two
pounds of used paper and a ball of smoothed-out silver aluminum
foil to help with the war effort. Ingrid and I were in fierce competition for the few scraps of foil and paper we could get our hands
on in both grandparents' households and had difficulty meeting
our quotas. Mutti reused every available paper bag until it was torn

to bits; the scanty newspapers were cut for toilet paper, and grocers would put everything unwrapped into our string bags. One rainy day I had a brainstorm. We were playing in my grandfather's large, dusky attic, looking through the trade magazines that he had saved over the years. Suddenly I realized that here, right in front of us, were pounds and pounds of paper gathering dust. Certainly now in 1943 Grossvati would no longer need journals showing tools, machinery, and furniture fashion from the twenties and thirties. I told Ingrid that I had found the answer to our problem, and she immediately understood.

I had no doubt that Grossvati would say yes if I asked and hurried as fast as I could down the three flights of stairs into the workshop where he stood bent, intently focused on the tall circular saw that was slicing through a long, thick board. He looked up when the blades had run through the wood and asked me to collect some scraps for Grossmutti's kitchen. I said I would, but first I wanted his permission to take his old journals to school for the recycling collection. He looked at me as if he had not quite understood my question and then said in a calm, icy tone that not a sliver of any of his magazines would go to support the war of that scoundrel Hitler. Disappointment and something akin to hatred must have shown on my face. How dare he not support the war that we were told every day was a life-and-death struggle for the German people? Was support for our soldiers not more important than saving the old journals? I left the workshop without wood scraps but with what I felt would be a permanent resentment against my grandfather.

Meanwhile Fräulein Hofmann continued to single me out. "Heil Hitler, Irmgard, come on in," she said the day I accepted her invitation to have a special treat of hot chocolate and cookies at her house. She was dressed in her usual straight skirt and dull beige blouse and wore no jewelry. I wondered why she had invited me. After a few *Höflichkeiten*—polite words—she asked point-blank what my grandfather thought about Adolf Hitler and what he said about the war. I was still angry with my grandfather but stalled, sitting uncomfortably on the moss green, upholstered chair in

Fräulein Hofmann's living room, weighing my feelings against my answer. On the one hand, Grossvati was withholding paper for the war effort, and Mutti and Tante Emma had a job closing all the windows and checking the landing for listeners when he started his loud badmouthing of Hitler. Perhaps I should tell Fräulein Hofmann about that. On the other hand, he was my grandfather. I knew the twinkle in his eyes when he was amused and had seen tears running down his face when one after another the messages arrived that both his apprentices had been killed on the eastern front. On those terrible days he had not thrown a fit, just gone quietly into his workshop and looked around as if he was lost in this, his own space.

After much too long a pause I came to the decision that I liked this nosy teacher less than my grandfather. "Well," she said with just an edge of impatience, offering me another cookie, "is he on our Führer's side and the fight for Germany's future or not? You must tell me. I am sure you are on the Führer's side."

I said, my heart beating so hard she must have heard it, that I did not know what he thought and that he never said much anyway. Just saying that gave me the courage to lie further, and I assured her that he said nothing about the Führer. I stopped fumbling for more lies when I realized that she didn't believe one word I said. I felt my face turning red and had no idea what I would say if she pressed further. But after a pause she let it go, saying that we would talk again after I had listened to my grandfather more carefully. Shaken and relieved, I finished my chocolate and she led me to the door.

The bracing air felt good on my cheeks as I walked and tried to figure out what had happened inside that room. Had I done the right thing by not telling her the truth? I was not at all sure. I was, after all, a good German girl and deeply under the influence of the Nazi regime. Of course there was no risk involved in my lying, but in my confusion I might easily have blurted out all that I witnessed at home. Although I did not know it that day, Fräulein Hofmann was a Nazi informer, and my telling the truth would have sent Grossvati to a concentration camp. Something had made me protect my grandfather, but it took a long time before I realized how lucky I (and he) had been in making that decision. On that particular day, though, I felt thoroughly sick of these conflicts forced on me by adults. It would be best, I decided, not to tell anyone about this conversation. It would only create more fighting. And so I tried to bury the whole encounter, hoping that Fräulein Hofmann would not question me again. She did not, though she continued to try to influence my life in another, significant way.

After I failed her as an informant, Fräulein Hofmann's goal became to send me off to an Adolf Hitler Schule even though I was not yet ten. These schools were Spartan and rigorous training grounds for the future leaders and Party elite of the Nazi state. Mutti never once mentioned Fräulein Hofmann's recruiting campaign to me but wrote in her diary that she was highly conflicted about such a decision and finally told Fräulein Hofmann in no uncertain terms to forget about the Adolf Hitler school, since she wanted me at home for a few more years. I don't know if her decision was based on increasing doubts about the regime or simply the wish to keep her oldest daughter by her side. The battle for my ideological future was not entirely one-sided. According to Mutti's diary, the Protestant teacher of religion had also approached her and tried to talk her into letting me attend the increasingly limited *Religionsunterricht* (religious instructions) she was holding for my age group. Mutti debated the idea vigorously with her but stood fast not to send me.

□   □

OUR HOME BASE IN SELB was at Birkengasse 7, but there was, of course, the second set of grandparents, Heinrich and Maria Paul. The Pauls lived in the center of town in a renovated apartment building on the Adolf Hitler Strasse. The ground floor still housed a smoky old pub that reeked of beer and cigars and that was handy for my Paul grandfather's weekly *Stammtisch* (a regular gathering of friends at the same table of a pub). Sometimes I went there to say hello to him and the innkeeper. Paul Grossvati showed me off to his cronies, hardly visible through the smoke, as his fallen son's daughter. But he would quickly bid me to go upstairs because Paul Grossmutti was waiting for me.

To my delight and wonder my grandmother could activate the automatic lock from the second floor when I pushed the "Heinrich Paul" bell. Two flights of carpeted steps led to where she stood, greeting me with her bright, open smile and holding a frosted, decorated glass door open with the back of her heel. I loved the modern look of the furnishings in the three rooms of the apartment, even though my Pöhlmann grandfather had pointed out that the Pauls' furniture was factory-made and surely one could see the difference. I had indicated to my mother that it looked just as nice as Grandfather Pöhlmann's furniture, but she shushed me, saying pointedly, "It is not made by hand." It was one of the rare times she agreed with her father, both feeling that a self-respecting family would consider only handmade furniture.

The Pauls, however, had cold running water, a sink inside their living room–kitchen, and a gas range just like Tante Emma. Showers or fancy bathtubs with hot water were undreamed-of conveniences at the time, and it was only years after the war that most middle-class Germans acquired them.

The big event that fall was my Paul grandfather's fiftieth jubilee at the Heinrich porcelain factory. Mutti had ironed our white hair ribbons and Sunday dresses, and when the whole family arrived at the factory for the ceremony his colleagues and bosses congratulated my slightly embarrassed grandfather, whose bald head seemed more polished than usual. Swastika flags decorated the auditorium, creating an appropriate setting for the speeches by important-looking men who assured the audience of the Führer's personal interest in German workers and his confidence that they would help him win the *Endsieg* (final victory). The hall resounded with the national anthems and solemn shouts of "Heil Hitler!" A framed document given to my grandfather testified to his faithful service. After the speechmaking he passed around the box of fine cigars he had received. Glasses were filled with champagne, but food, the one thing that really would have made my day, was lacking, as were the faces of young men among the audience.

As Mutti's doubts about the outcome of the war grew, she increasingly hung on to public assurances and pronouncements that Germany would prevail. On the way to a jubilee party at the Pauls' apartment she shared her renewed optimism with Tante Emma, who agreed. Quite predictably, Grossvati began his litany of gripes against the regime. With sarcasm in his voice, he began to sing, "Wir wollen weiter marschieren, wenn alles in Scherben faellt, denn heute gehört uns Deutschland und morgen die ganze Welt" (We will march on, even when everything turns to shards, for today we own Germany and tomorrow the world). We all knew this song—no other so clearly laid out the aims of the Nazis—and sang it on many occasions with great enthusiasm as indeed everything turned to shards around us. Ingrid and I traipsed nervously behind the adults, relieved when Mutti called a halt to the debate, worried that a passerby might overhear her father. My Pöhlmann grandmother was too ill to attend the celebration and Mutti had asked the third-floor tenant of Birkengasse 7 to look in on her occasionally until we got home.

Paul Grossmutti had somehow managed to obtain real coffee and the ingredients for a fine tart. Two tables were set with her best, hand-embroidered tablecloths and, of course, the best Heinrich china, inspiring Ingrid and me to be on our best behavior. The conversation was light until my grandmother signaled to my mother to take a look at Ingrid. My little sister was very quietly moving her own almost empty cake plate over to my grandmother with one small hand and with the other carefully moving my grandmother's plate with a much larger slice of apple tart over to her side. Deeply absorbed in her deed, she did not notice that everyone at the table had grown silent, watching her and barely able to contain their laughter. With my grandmother's cake squarely in front of her she looked up, pleased with herself. We burst out in hilarity, but Ingrid, embarrassed that she had been caught, put her head in my mother's lap and cried. I was sorry she had been caught, but when she recovered and started enjoying being the center of attention with a full plate of cake to boot, my half-empty stomach left me with pure envy of her ill-gotten gains.

Mutti had begun to make sparse, daily entries in her narrow, light green calendar for 1943. The notes mostly told of endless chores: standing in line, tending the garden, gleaning potatoes on harvested fields, plucking the geese, clearing the stovepipes, washing, ironing, mending, cooking, and amazingly often cleaning—a passion of German housewives in war and peace. But on September 9 she wrote: "The Italians have once again betrayed us and our soldiers now have to fight against the Italians as well." The following day Hitler gave one of his increasingly rare radio addresses from his headquarters in Berlin. To me his long presentation sounded like a bout of shouting, but it kept the grown-ups spellbound. Mutti summed up the speech in three words: "Eine harte Kampfansage" (an announcement of hard fighting).

Luise Pöhlmann, my stern and upright grandmother, died in the middle of a clear October night. Mutti was with her when her heart gave out, ending her suffering at the age of sixty-nine. "After so much hardship and work your grandmother has finally found peace," Mutti said, her voice choking. Onkel Hans came home on family leave a day too late to see his mother alive. At the funeral Ingrid cried bitterly when the coffin disappeared into the furnace, and for a moment you could see the red flames as the door opened and shut on it. I did not cry because of my recurring fear that once I began I would never be able to stop. At a family gathering after the funeral I felt guilty and annoyed at one of my distant aunts who praised the softheartedness of my sister. A few times that day I thought of Vati and how he too had found peace, but what kind of peace was it, willfully inflicted on him and leaving us out?

From the Pauls' window we could see the Polish women walking up and down Adolf Hitler Street after work. We knew them by the purple-and-yellow diamond-shaped *P* they had to wear on their flimsy clothes. During the day they worked by the hundreds in factories, and in the evening they walked in tight groups of threes and fours, linking arms, seeking comfort in one another's touch. A gang of kids, including me, made a sport of standing on a wooden fence rail along the black cinder-covered road that the workers used from the factory into town and shouting *"Polakin!"* and other derogatory terms for Poles. Mutti saw us taunting the women one day and told us to stop. We dispersed, and from then on I did not join in the harassment. I was slightly embarrassed about it but really did not give it much thought. They were, after all, not Germans, and their fate here in this German factory town meant nothing. I heard a neighbor remark once that it was a shame that we had to feed these women and diminish our own rations, a complaint that seemed perfectly reasonable to me. This callousness, or complete silence, was part and parcel of the world in which I grew up.

"What book do you have there?" Mutti asked when she saw me reading a large picture book that Else Puchka, a neighborhood friend, had loaned me. It was a children's book with page after page showing the physical differences between Jews and Germans in grotesque drawings of "Jewish" noses, lips, and eyes. The book encouraged every child to note these differences and to bring any-one who bore Jewish features to the attention of our parents or teachers. I was horrified by the crimes Jewish people were being accused of—killing babies, loan-sharking, basic dishonesty, and conspiring to destroy Germany and rule the world. The description of the Jewish people would convince any child that these were monsters, not people with sorrows and joys like ours. Mutti asked me to return the book and not to believe all it said. Our family disputes always focused on Hitler's war and what it would do to Germany and not on the fate of Jews. However, I had absorbed enough of the pervasive anti-Semitic attitude that surrounded me that I was surprised that Mutti drew a line with this disgusting publication and did not want me to dwell on it. The images in the book lingered with me for some time and then I forgot them until after the war, when the accounting began.

□   □

IF GROSSVATI WAS UPSET about his wife's death, he didn't show it much, but he looked very thin and at lunch he usually asked Mutti for more potatoes than she had boiled. One day he received two burlap sacks of wheat grain for some work he had done, and he loaded them on the wooden pull cart to take them to a miller he knew and ask if he would grind them into flour. I was glad to come along, helping to pull the wagon up and down the rolling fields on frozen, grassy foot trails until an hour later we arrived at the mill. My grandfather introduced himself, then asked the miller if he could grind these two sacks of grain. He promised to pay well and leave some flour too. The miller looked sullen and said, "I am not allowed to mill more than my daily allotment, and they are controlling all my records very strictly. I'm sorry I can't oblige you." Grandfather tried a few more times to convince the man that it would be worth his while but without success. Finally he told the miller that he understood. He lifted his hat in farewell, and we turned around to pull the two sacks of grain back home. I felt humiliated and embarrassed to see my grandfather, Herr Albin Pöhlmann, the master carpenter, reduced to not much more than an unsuccessful beggar. But he did not share my sense of humiliation, joking instead about the fat chickens we would eat as the grain was fed to them. My grandfather's equanimity and undiminished sense of self, attributes that were rare during the war, made me see him in a different light. I could not hate him forever for keeping his magazines, and as I remembered the day when Fräulein Hofmann questioned me, I felt very satisfied that I had not turned him in.

Late that fall Onkel Hans lifted our spirits with a letter from Norway in which he said he could buy and send silver-fox stoles for very little money. The three women he had included in his offer, Tante Emma, her best friend, Erna Schöffel, and my mother, debated back and forth whether they could afford to pay for the luxury from their marginal household money or their savings. Finally their desire for this elegant piece of neckwear won the upper hand

and they asked him to "please send the three best silver foxes you can find." The furs arrived in a large box that we unpacked with great anticipation in Tante Emma's kitchen. The women shook the stoles—each lined with elegantly embroidered gray silk fabric—and I stroked the thick blackness of the pelts with their lovely silvery tips. I marveled at the four little legs with claws dangling from the long animal body that ended in a thick, bushy tail with a snow-white point. The head on the other end had a pair of pitch-black beads for eyes, small, pointed ears, and a snout that was fashioned into a clip that closed on the tail after the stole was put around a woman's shoulders. We were so used to utilizing animals that this bizarre fashion statement did not bother us in the least. Mutti said that having the fur close to her face made her feel warm and protected and that she could see why rich people wore fur. The three had paid for their stoles and therefore never considered them unrightful possessions or war booty.

We spent Christmas Eve that year without much enthusiasm except for our Göring dolls, which Mutti had brought back with our winter clothes. The dolls showed up under the tree, and we were allowed to play with them way beyond midnight. On New Year's Day, Mutti wrote in her new memento book for the year 1944: "We all look with a heavy heart to the future."

The family fully expected that my mother would move back home to Selb for good to look after her father's household. This would mean a final farewell to all Berchtesgaden and Haus Linden had been to her and Max, and she postponed a final decision from week to week and month to month. Finally our landlord forced her hand. He wrote that unless she returned by the beginning of March he would be obliged to give our apartment to a family who had lost their home to a bomb. Deeply conflicted about leaving her father and Tante Emma with her two small children—Uschi and baby Gerhard, Mutti's godson—she decided to move back to the mountains. Ingrid and I were jubilant. We had taken to going up every so often into the dusky attic—still filled with the old magazines—to cry together with homesickness.

Only my grandmother was missing from the entourage that came to see us off. We leaned out the window of the moving train, and I saw my tall Pöhlmann grandfather wave his hat, never suspecting how close his own granddaughter had come to betraying him.

That night an air attack on Berlin and Essen delayed our departure from the city of Marktredwitz by many hours, forcing us to sit shivering and hungry on our suitcases until early morning. Mutti assured us that we would be safe once we came closer to the mountains even as we heard the roar of planes low overhead. As we did so often during these scary times, Ingrid and I took comfort in her assurances.

I woke from my sleep when the conductor announced the village of Bischofswiesen. From here on we would begin to see Watzmann, Göll, Brett, and Kehlstein topped with the Eagle's Nest. A dusty rose light began to dim on the snow-covered peaks while Ingrid and I happily called out their names and were once more awed by their steep, white flanks. The snow was too deep for us to take our luggage; we would pick it up with a sled the next day. Miraculously we had held on to all five pieces including a basket of jams. The main roads wound like canyons between snow walls three times as high as Ingrid, while on the sidewalks the giant footprints of grown-ups had frozen, making us slip up and down them like crazed puppets.

We almost cried with joy when finally the snow-quilted roof of little Haus Linden peeked out between the white spruces. Exhausted as we were, we had to shovel the snow from the door before we could go in. The place was ice cold and smelled stale and empty. But as soon as a fire in the stove began to warm the room, the old familiar fragrance of our home, of us, surfaced. The walls in my bedroom at the end of the hall were coated with ice crystals. Mutti put the dented hot-water bottle onto the mattress before I crawled under the duvet. As I fell into a dreamless sleep, Selb—its pleasures and its trials—was already receding into the past.

12 HARDSHIP AND DISINTEGRATION

It never stopped snowing in Berchtesgaden that March of 1944. Mutti skied or waded through the fresh powder to register our return with the police, to reapply for food stamps, to try and order coal, to carry a rucksack of potatoes into the cellar. Her ski tracks were snowed over before she came back from the Schiedlehen, the farm where we had been getting our milk. Mutti was upset because the farmer's wife had told her to look elsewhere for milk. Several cows had gone dry, and she did not have enough to sell, a major setback in our eyes.

My old friends, including Wiebke, picked me up for school as before, and every morning we forged a new trail down the mountain, arriving hot and wet in a cold classroom. My new teacher, Fräulein Röhrle—a calm, totally apolitical woman—had to prepare at least a few of her 110 students for the *Oberschule* (high school) entrance exam given at the end of fourth grade. One of the first things Mutti did was traipse to the school's director to ask for a stipend should I pass the exam. The monthly tuition of twenty-five reichsmarks would have taken a large slice of the forty-reichsmark orphan support she received for me, but she was determined that I go. The director granted her request, and I promised to work hard toward that feared exam.

Tante Susi caught us up on the major changes her family had gone through. Onkel Peppi, in spite of his bad heart and constant shortness of breath, had been drafted to repair fighter planes in Fürstenfeldbruck, a small town about twenty miles west of Munich. Trudi too had left Berchtesgaden for her year of mandatory labor service with a farm family in the Rhineland. Tante Susi was alone, doing her war duty as a housekeeper at the Hotel Platterhof, now absolutely overflowing with wounded officers. I missed Trudi terribly. On my first visit upstairs I noticed the carving of a Madonna emerging from a block of oak clamped tightly to Onkel Peppi's workbench by the window and realized that I even missed her cranky father.

My father's good friend Schego, the sculptor who had created the wax relief of Hitler that hung in our living room, dropped by one evening with a bottle of French wine. His hunchback— the result of spinal injuries sustained during a childhood fall from a ladder—notwithstanding, he too had been drafted for

Ingrid and I outside Haus Linden during the bitterly cold and snowy war winter of 1943–44. Ingrid wears a scarf of rabbit fur.

military-equipment maintenance work. Tante Susi came downstairs, and I listened— pretending to read—to her rather disrespectful report from the rumor mill of the Platterhof. She said we were fools to think that the upper-crust Nazis on the mountain were sharing our shortages. On the contrary, she insisted, most of them, especially Hermann Göring, lived in great luxury. They gave fancy parties with plenty of food and extravagant delicacies that we had never known. Also there was talk of luxury goods being stockpiled in the opulent underground bunkers being built—at great expense, she stressed— beneath the Nazi villas. Nazi officials of high rank would be connected directly with the Berghof, causing a great deal of rivalry among Hitler's favorites. She had also heard, and this was top secret, that weapons for a big counteroffensive were to be located on Obersalzberg. A chill came over us, but Schego, still optimistic about the outcome of the war, said that although there would certainly be a secret weapon, there was no way of knowing from where it would be launched. In any case, this was our first hint that Hitler wanted to make a last stand here in Berchtesgaden.

The people living in far-flung hamlets in the valley of Berchtesgaden communicated either on foot or by getting a letter to a mailbox, which also involved much walking. No one, not even the Molsens, had a telephone. Thus visitors usually arrived unannounced. One afternoon a handsome, blond soldier with a bandaged arm in a sling appeared at our door, thoroughly surprising Mutti. Ossi Eidmann, she told me later, had been my father's rival for her hand in marriage. I was stunned that she had ever considered anyone but my father. Ossi was recuperating from a gunshot wound at a medical facility in the Strub, a part of Berchtesgaden. They sat down for a cup of tea and talked about their youth in Selb, the people they had known, and inevitably, the war. Ossi admitted that it was anybody's guess how long it would last but that in the end we simply must prevail or perish. I did not like this idea of perishing and immediately wished nothing but final victory for our soldiers. Before he left he invited the three of us to an Open Day at which the public would be invited to watch mountain-troop exercises at their barracks in the Strub.

The following Sunday we set out for the long, tedious walk, shortened only a little by use of our toboggans on the downhill stretches. Happily Ossi greeted us with a plate of cookies and hot chocolate in his stark, clean room. Then we joined a multitude of soldiers and civilians walking toward the huge hall where we would watch target shooting. We found standing room on the straw that was spread over mud and puddles and waited impatiently for the show to begin. A sudden deafening blast of gunfire sent me into a complete panic. I began to scream, covering my ears as the shooting continued. Mutti and Ossi, quite startled, grabbed Ingrid and me by the hand to hurry us out of the hall, away from the noise and the shocked expressions of people wondering what on earth had happened. Nothing had, except that the sudden sharp sounds of shots that I could only associate with war and death had triggered an attack of hysteria, as Mutti would say. Ossi understood that she wanted to take me home, and I was still shaking with sobs when we said *auf Wiedersehen*. A few days later he sent Mutti a postcard with the news that he was being sent back to the front. I could not imagine how he could face the terror of those guns again.

Leaving her family, especially her father back in Selb, and being all on her own again was more wrenching for Mutti than she had expected. I too missed Tante Emma, my little cousins, my Paul grandparents, and my school friends. We took to writing long letters in the evenings, venting our frustrations much the same way Grossmutti had done in World War I. On one miserable day Mutti had walked into town twice to buy a piece of fish but each time for naught as she competed with two hundred other people standing in line. I knew that she would write to Tante Emma that night about how easy it was, compared with this ordeal, to get a carp from a local fishpond in Selb.

I wondered if Mutti would also write to Tante Emma about the day I ate half a loaf of bread that I had waited in line for as I walked home. When I realized what I had done, cold terror seized me; I expected a mighty thrashing and eternal shame. Mutti would never believe that the mere smell of bread, not sheer selfish greed, had seduced me to rip the crust and tear the soft inside apart with my fingers little piece by little piece—each time thinking, Now I'll stop—until I had eaten everyone's three-day ration. Better get it over with, I thought as I opened our door. I pushed the half-collapsed brown bag across the table to Mutti and waited. She understood at once, thought for a moment with a sad look on her face, and then said, "You must have been very hungry." I nodded and cried with relief.

Mutti avoided meeting Frau Deil and Frau Penzig, who wanted

to engage her again in Nazi activities. On Frau Penzig's suggestion that she take more of a leading role in the countywide after-school children's programs, Mutti wrote in her daybook, "That's all I need," and eventually fended her off with all the diplomacy she could muster. However, she did agree to run the Salzberg *Kindergruppe* once more.

The prevailing attitude toward women working outside the home was changing, judging by speeches and the fact that Mutti and her friends were given so-called war-duty I.D. cards. Nevertheless, Hitler supposedly still wanted women at home as mothers and keepers of the hearth. Mutti was not taking any chances, reasoning that it would be easier to stay home with three children than with two, she resolved to take in a foster child. She and Tante Emma traveled to Berlin to fetch little Hardi Schulz to the safety of our mountain home. Bombings had already severely damaged the city, and Hardi's mother, a single woman who worked as a radio technician, was relieved to see her son leave Berlin in Mutti's care. Ingrid and I looked Hardi over carefully and did not quite know what to do with him. But we soon discovered that he just liked to tag along and laugh when we were silly; on the whole he was not much of a bother.

Hardi had the longest brown eyelashes I had ever seen, and large, sad dark brown eyes. When they glistened with tears in the morning I felt sad too, because I knew he had wet his bed, infuriating Mutti. She spanked him, exclaiming loudly that she simply could not keep up with constantly washing and drying the sheets and the mattress of our old crib, now his bed. Mutti tried all kinds of home remedies, advice from neighbors and teas from the apothecary, to stop his bedwetting, but to no avail. Hardi was a little younger than Ingrid, but I thought that he was a terrible crybaby. When the nightly wail of air-raid sirens startled us out of sleep and we stumbled down the outside steps into the potato cellar, Hardi would cry frantically and call for his mother. Usually Tante Susi helped calm him down and with some deep, last sobs he would finally fall asleep on a cot alongside Ingrid, while I slept leaning against Mutti on a makeshift bench. When the sirens sounded the end of the alarm, we woke the little ones and went upstairs. I knew it would scare me, but I could not resist looking up at the bloodred sky above the black silhouettes of the mountain ranges. Mutti said the redness came from the burning cities—Traunstein, Freilassing, Rosenheim, Munich—to the north of us in the flatland. I couldn't fall asleep again and was just as scared as Hardi, although I did not cry.

Those were the troubles of the night; during daytime I was now completely focused on joining the Hitler Youth (Hitlerjugend, or H.J.). I would be ten in May—far too old for *Kindergruppe,* I felt—and began to badger Mutti to ask Frau Deil if I could join the Jungmädel, the junior division of the female H.J. that would lead me, at age fourteen, to enrollment in the BDM (Bund Deutscher Mädchen), the next level of a girl's training and indoctrination. Yes, I knew I was the youngest in my grade, and yes, we were late with the application, but how could I tolerate it if all my friends were strutting around in their uniforms every Friday afternoon and I was left out? Mutti should know what it meant to belong to a youth group. Had she not been a member of the Turnverein (gym club), the Gesangverein (singing club), the Wandervögel, a hiking club, even a swim club, all of them subsumed by Hitler into the only youth organization allowed in Nazi Germany, the Hitler Youth? Indeed, Frau Deil arranged for my entry.

On a rainy afternoon in April the new H.J. members were *verpflichtet* (inducted, or sworn in), and Mutti and Ingrid came to watch in the drizzle. I was very happy that I had all the parts of my uniform together, except for a cap, which was not to be found anywhere. The slim dark blue skirt, the white blouse with white buttons already impressed with BDM, and the black kerchief fastened at the neck by a brown leather knot were hand-me-downs from Trudi.

At our first *Appell* (drill and meeting) we were lined up by size four rows deep and called to order for learning how to march in place. The group leader, Hedi Seiberl, daughter of one of the local clothing-and-fabric merchants, called out as loud as she could, "Links, rechts, links, rechts" (left, right), and when we got that she reduced the command to "Links—, links—, links—, und links." The boys were already marching past us, their steps sounding firm and the commands loud, better perhaps than our walking shoes and girls' voices ever would. Their red-haired leader, an arrogant fellow I had disliked even from a distance, marched alongside the troop giving commands, while a couple of boys beat drums ahead of the marchers. Finally we too marched through town from one end to the other, under the old arches along the castle square, past the Gasthof Neuhaus restau-

rant past the marble fountain in the center of the market square, and past the Francis-can church and former clois-ter. Then we turned around in Luitpold Park just beyond the Four Seasons Hotel.

Marching was a mindless exercise. We sang and giggled and skipped a step once in a while to catch up with the *links, links, links* rhythm that we had lost. I was completely seduced by a feeling of be-longing, of being united with all young Germans wearing this uniform that, if nothing else, certified my age and au-

Trudi in the uniform of the Bund Deutscher Mädchen (B.D.M.), the girls' unit of the Hitler Youth.

thority, especially with my little sister and Hardi. "Irmgard came home from her *Appell* with great enthusiasm in spite of an air raid in the middle of the afternoon," Mutti wrote in her book, along with the news that our troops were retreating rapidly in Russia but that they had been able, with huge sacrifices, to hold a place called

Casino. She closed with the note that the Tommies, the British air force, were over Nuremberg and had lost 134 airplanes. "How many must there have been?" she asked. Whether she was despairing or hopeful that day was hard to tell.

We had *Appell* one afternoon a week. My *Schaft*, the smallest unit of the Jungmädel, was led by Gabi Kerschbaumer, the pretty, soft-spoken daughter of the other fabric-and-clothing merchant in town. Like Hedi Seiberl and quite a few of the H.J. leaders, she was a good Catholic who might emerge through the heavy doors of the *Stiftskirche* from a service to change into an H.J. uniform in time for *Appell*. No one was bothered by this seeming contradiction that was, however, indicative of the complicated, uneasy accommodations that Hitler and the Catholic church had made for each other. While the Nazis had dismantled the Franciscan cloister in town to some protest, Hitler recognized that a frontal assault on the institution of the Catholic or Protestant churches, the backbone of German culture, would be ill-advised until, he thought, after the war. On the other side, the leadership of the Catholic church from the pope on down had hardly been active in any resistance, fearing bolshevism more than nazism, and was not particularly keen to speak up for Jews. Prayers for Hitler were routinely included in services.

My pleasure in being a Jungmädel was greatly enhanced by the fact that for that one afternoon a week I was free from homework, chopping or gathering wood, weeding or watering our two stony gardens, fetching the milk, or, most often, standing in line in response to rumors of available food. Mutti, Ingrid, and Hardi just have to cope without me, I thought gleefully.

In addition to marching drills we Jungmädel trained for sports competitions, hiked, sang a great deal, and listened to many lectures and speeches by senior leaders. They always said that every boy and girl had to do his or her share to win the war and that we must believe that the Führer was invincible and Germany's only salvation. No one asked a question; it was not called for and we

Meeting of the Jungmädchen, the under-fourteen girls' group of the Hitler Youth.

were much too well indoctrinated to do so. After every track competition Mutti was hopeful that I had won a prize, but I always disappointed her. So far the Hitler Youth, at least for us girls, seemed to be no more than an afternoon of orderly, fun activities that I

could hardly associate, except for the marching perhaps, with military training.

The Jungmädel sent packages filled with mittens and wrist warmers that we had knitted in rainbow colors from unraveled wool, some food, and tobacco to soldiers in the field. The packages were small, since we hadn't much to give, but we were told that what made them special were our personal notes to the soldiers. I found it difficult to think of something cheery, let alone meaningful, to write to a soldier I did not know and who might die soon. All my notes were the same: "Greetings from Berchtesgaden. I hope you are well and thank you for protecting us. Heil Hitler." I only hoped that none of the soldiers would compare their greetings from the homeland and find that they were so terribly similar, not really personal at all.

We sent the packages to randomly assigned military addresses at one or another of our far-flung but increasingly closer fronts.

My friend Gertraud Oberndörfer had one day been given the address of someone she knew from the village of Ramsau, and she had taken very special care with this package and written a whole letter. A couple of weeks later a farm woman came up to her and said, "I don't know why you sent a package to my son. We are sending him food and anything he might want and he surely does not need your help." Gertraud was shocked that her parcel had caused offense and wondered if the woman was upset with her personally or because it came from the H.J. She concluded that it must have been she who had offended in an unknown way.

□   □

THE ARRIVAL OF THE HORSE-FACED, tall, and skinny mail carrier with the heavy black leather pouch over her shoulder had become the defining moment of the day for Mutti, making it either bleak or bearable. She had developed the habit of sighing deeply and saying, "Ach Gott, ach Gott" (Oh God, oh God) after she looked at the mail. Every time she sighed like that I thought that something terrible had happened. I figured out, however, that her sighs were just an expression of general *Weltschmerz* and despair caused by these dismal times. Tante Susi would briefly cheer her up with her irreverent sense of humor and biting comments about her bosses—important or not—on Obersalzberg, but openly or secretly Mutti was sad a great deal. I would catch her with an absent look on her face that probably meant she was thinking of springtime with Vati, tours to the Liegeret Alm, and the vanished promise of good times.

On my tenth birthday Mutti wrote in her journal, "Irmgard has been with us for ten years now. What a happy day it was when she was born and how Max adored our baby." I had gone overboard with invitations for my birthday party. Mutti could not believe her eyes when her tiny, long, thin pound cake had to be divided into a dozen or more slivers. We ate them sitting on the bench in front of the house and on wooden crates we had found. We wove wreaths for our hair from daisies and made the party, modest as it was, a celebration after all.

Mutti was exhausted, but work distracted her and probably prevented a deeper depression, although the following week several letters came that worsened her mood. One brought the news from Ossi's parents that he was missing in action. This in turn made me morose and more embarrassed about the way I had behaved at the barracks. The worst news was that my eighteen-year-old cousin, Horst Bieser from Wiesbaden, had been killed—I don't know where. It was simply incomprehensible that this handsome, black-haired young man on whom I had a crush and who so admired our mountains was dead too. I felt listless one moment and ready to explode in fury another. Was he not my Aunt and Uncle Bieser's favorite son? Was he not too young to die? This was only the beginning of a string of messages like that one. Vati's former colleague, the handsome, tall painter Walter Höfig, whose daughters were our friends, was missing in the east; Helmut Puff, the only son of Herr Puff, had last been seen seriously wounded and left to be captured by the Russians, a fate considered worse than death. I wondered how much longer we could bear to go on collecting the dead in our lives.

For a while in June I was distracted by a much discussed H.J. field exercise, an elaborate game of opposing groups called *Geländespiel* (game in open territory). On the day of the game we were allowed to walk at a normal gait—not in marching steps—to the Hintergern, an isolated valley of steep farm and forest land running up toward the walls of Untersberg. The game was organized like a treasure hunt except that we were to capture members of an advance enemy group, following them on twisted, misleading trails marked with white powder and misleading messages. At the end of the game, much to Gabi's disappointment, our *Schaft* had not made one single capture. We were reprimanded for lacking team spirit and the will to win. On the two-hour walk home I had time enough to contemplate whether I had caused our team to lose. I had misread a note and led everyone in the wrong direction for a while. I admitted to myself that my heart had really not been in the game and I had indeed not cared much about the goal. At home Mutti looked at my blisters and told me that once again the shoemaker had no shoes for me.

While we were playing games and trying to deal with our grief the war was inexorably moving closer, speeding up, so to say, in the wrong direction. On June 5 Mutti noted in her journal that our soldiers had given up Rome and on June 6, that British troops had begun the invasion at the Orne and the Seine at 1:30 A.M. "It was almost a relief after months of suspense," she wrote. Once more we were glued to the radio when Dr. Goebbels announced on June 20 that the *Vergeltung* (revenge) against England had begun with constant bombardment of the British Isles with unmanned, so-far secret V-1 missiles. Goebbels promised that the V-2, an even more lethal weapon, and other top secret arms would follow, ensuring our final victory.

That night Tante Susi, ever suspicious of the minister of propaganda's claims, told the joke of the old woman who asked to see a globe and then asked to be shown Germany on it. Then she asked to see the United Kingdom, Russia, the United States, and all the other countries we were fighting. She looked at them thoughtfully and inquired, "Has anyone ever shown this globe to Hitler?" Mutti, still wedded to her dream of victory, was quite annoyed with Tante Susi, even accusing her of listening to the enemy radio, which for a while seemed to dampen their friendship. Much troubled by a possible rift between the upstairs and downstairs of Haus Linden, I resolved that I would simply ignore it, and pointedly waited every evening on the wooden outside steps for Tante Susi to come home from Obersalzberg.

On Thursday, July 20, 1944, a group of German generals and other conspirators led by Count von Stauffenberg attempted to assassinate Hitler at the Wolfsschanze (Wolf's Lair), his East Prussian headquarters. We had gotten up at six that day and an hour later started out for the Silberg, a low, rather flat mountain that we reached in about two hours. It was beautiful up on the plateau, and the wild strawberries were so plentiful that we could already envision large numbers of jars filled with jam for the winter. By noon, much to Mutti's annoyance and worry, we could see that across the valley the S.S. had begun to release the chemical fog that quickly wrapped itself around Obersalzberg, signaling an impending air raid. She knew that several flak units were located on the Silberg, poised to shoot at approaching enemy planes. With little cover on the high, rolling upland to protect us, she decided that all we could do was to listen and lie down flat if we heard planes or the *tack, tack, tack* of the antiaircraft fire. We continued to harvest the strawberries, and after a while the fog over Salzberg lifted, which indicated that for now we were safe from planes and antiaircraft guns.

That evening Mutti gasped at the news of the assassination attempt and seemed tremendously relieved to hear that as if by a miracle the Führer was alive and well. He addressed the nation over the radio the following day, promising revenge on his would-be assassins. Mutti did not recognize many of the names of the conspirators but was deeply shaken by the fact that they were insiders, many of them German generals, who had already formed a new government. For some reason—perhaps to look for an omen—she noted in her daybook that the government in Japan had also changed, adding the usual unanswerable question, "What on earth will happen next?"

The following day Mutti and the Nazi painter Hans Schuster had a short conversation that I will never forget. He stopped at our living room window to talk with Mutti about the shocking news while I was sitting with my homework on the sun-bleached, wooden bench in front of the house. Mutti leaned out the window to listen to Schuster's tirade against the traitors. Suddenly she interrupted him and said, "You know what I wish? I wish they had killed Hitler and then there would be a chance to end the war." There was a dead silence, and then Hans began to scream in his high, excited, and now furious voice, "You are a traitor too! I am going to the Gestapo right now and tell them about you!" His polished, black S.A. boots pounded on the gravel path as he headed for the shortcut to town. Mutti said nothing and closed the window. I could not tell what, if anything, she was doing inside.

I sat frozen. I knew that the Gestapo was in charge of enemies of the state, traitors and troublemakers; I knew that they sent you to the *Konzentrationslager,* the worst of all jails. I was stunned by Mutti's remark. Did she really mean it, or was she just trying to annoy Hans Schuster? A suffocating fear rose within me, and I knew that I had never hated anyone as I now hated Hans Schuster. Mutti and I never talked about the incident or what motivated her outburst, but for days afterward we both were jumpy as cats. When nothing happened, we began to relax. Most likely Hans had changed his mind on the way to town; he had, after all, been my father's friend. I told Wiebke about the incident and we both declared him our number one enemy. We secretly called him "Nazishaha," implying that he was a crazed Nazi who said "Heil Hitler" all day long. But once again, moral decisions were neither simple nor straightforward. Schuster had a very sweet, much older wife, whom we called Mother Schuster. She always had an apple or a few dried prunes for us when we dropped by for a visit. I now worried how I could best show my affection for her while also showing my contempt for him.

On July 28, 1944, Goebbels announced in an end-of-the-day speech that the *totale Krieg* (all-out war) had begun. "Well, here is another surprise," said Tante Susi, her voice thick with sarcasm. "What did we have till now, fun and games?" With one of her sighs Mutti turned to Ingrid and me and said that she had so wished that our lives would be different. Then she shrugged in resignation. The women of Berchtesgaden were called to a public meeting at which a Herr Seitz spoke about war duties for women. They could be called on to do any job now still held by old or very young men who might be drafted, to sew garments, to help in the *Lazaretts* (army hospitals) or the K.L.V. homes. Yet nothing happened. I champed at the bit to roam the neighborhood unsupervised, the way Mutti had in the Rheingauerstrasse in Wiesbaden when her mother had worked. But at the same time I realized I disliked coming home to find that Mutti was out even for a short time. So I joined her in hoping that she would not have to go to work.

◦ ◦

SCHOOL WAS OUT NOW FOR THE SUMMER. I had taken the entrance exam for the *Oberschule* and had been so nervous I could barely hold my pencil. Before the results came back we left for two weeks in Selb, while Hardi's mother came from Berlin to spend that time with him in Berchtesgaden. In Selb, Mutti helped with the red-currant harvest, mended Grossvati's shirts, and cleaned his place, including as always the windows of the workshop and the innards of the kitchen stove. I was as shocked as Mutti to find Grossvati so terribly thin, drawn, and without a twinkle in his eyes. He had received no orders for window frames or doors for any of the restoration or construction work that was part of the war effort and crucial for securing allocations of lumber. He was told that he was no longer eligible for this work, since he was not a member of the Nazi Party. Once again he was worried about the survival of his business and, of course, how to make a living. Tante Emma too was pale and exhausted from looking after my two little cousins, Uschi and Gerhard, Grossvati, the house, and the garden. In addition she worried about Onkel Hans if she did not hear from him for a couple of weeks.

To our great surprise Schego showed up in Selb unannounced, providing a brief respite from the monotony of our daily routine. With great perseverance and talent Schego had overcome his physical handicap and become a highly respected sculptor and alpinist. Like most members of the Berchtesgaden artists' club, he was a Nazi sympathizer. His visits with us in Berchtesgaden had been more frequent as of late, which made me mean-spirited and jealous. I thought him very nice, but I told Mutti that I did not want her to date a hunchback with a head that seemed too big for his short body. Actually, as Mutti revealed in her diary, she was not interested in being courted by Schego—she had not yet put her mourning for Vati behind her. Still, much wine was consumed during Schego's visit in Selb, and his optimism about the war cheered Mutti for a few days.

Just before we left, Ossi's parents gave Mutti the good news that they had at last heard from him. He had lost a leg and was a prisoner of war in the state of Washington in the United States. We looked it up in my Paul grandparents' old atlas and were much amazed to find it on the Pacific Ocean side of North America.

There were few soldiers in Selb compared with Berchtesgaden, which was teeming with healthy and wounded men in uniform. I tried hard not to stare when passing a wounded soldier, but sometimes it was impossible not to look at a mangled man on crutches or a group of two or three with their pant legs and arm sleeves pinned back revealing the void where a limb had been. The very young still wore their casts as if they were badges of honor, and we regarded them with great respect and compassion. Sometimes I worked up my courage, smiled, and nodded a greeting to one of them, and once a soldier with a bandaged head, moving slowly on his crutches, smiled back and said, "Good-bye and good luck, little girl." I said, "Good luck," and later realized that we both had neglected to say "Heil Hitler."

A wet and rainy summer brought nothing but bad news. Mutti was often in low spirits, bent over her purring sewing machine day after day. She was convinced that she was doing most of the work, and I thought I was doing most of it, so that the daily requests for additional help that she piled on me made us quarrel and I sulked. Once she made a big deal out of the fact that not-quite-seven-year-old Ingrid had stood in line at the fish store and actually gotten a piece of fish, as if I had not accomplished similar feats many times.

Way behind with chopping our winter wood, Mutti was looking for a couple of soldiers who would be willing to saw our allotment of large logs into stove-size pieces in exchange for tobacco. She had never even tried a cigarette, believing that German women should not smoke, but she claimed her tobacco rations anyway for barter and presents. On a whim she invited a couple of the S.S. *Nebelsoldaten* (fog soldiers) housed in a private home up the road for a lunch of potato soup. They loved the home-cooked meal, and Herr Schulz, the tallest of the soldiers, asked how much wood we needed to get through the winter. On hearing the amount he wondered aloud whether we had to chop all of that ourselves. "Well, yes," I remember my mother saying, and looking at me she added, "The girls are a big help," which made me blush and turn away because she so rarely handed out praise. The truth was that when it came to piling up wood, I called in my chits with Wiebke, Else, Anderl, and any other neighborhood kid who owed me a favor. To make sure they would help I developed a series of competitive games making the work fun. It turned out that the fog soldiers, especially Herr Schulz, were willing to chop quite a bit of wood for us that fall in return for Mutti's cigarettes. In response to my asking him if he was perhaps Hardi's uncle, Herr Schulz laughed and said that Schulz was as common a name as Hans, and no, he was no relation of our Hardi Schulz from Berlin.

With all the soldiers and the S.S. in town, drunken feasts in the local pubs were no rarity. One Monday evening Mutti took the shortcut to get to her weekly gymnastics class in the old town gym. Directly in front of her, blocking the narrow, stony trail, she made out a pile of three or four totally drunk, sleeping storm troopers. She came to a full stop but decided that she would not turn around like a coward. She walked backward a few steps, picked up speed, and took a long jump over the drunkards. "I admit," she said, "my heart was pounding when I landed on some stones that started to roll out from under me, but before the men knew what was happening I was gone." She laughed as she told us the tale. For a short time the animated, adventurous, courageous Mutti I had known and come to miss had returned, although Tante Susi thought Mutti had taken a big risk. The S.S. man Schulz, who heard the story when he stopped by that afternoon, apologized for the behavior of the soldiers and gallantly offered to accompany her down to the gym on Mondays.

Mutti and I continued our tug-of-war over who was doing the majority of the chores. She nagged me constantly, or so it seemed, about my impatience with Ingrid and Hardi, my sloppy home-work, spilling milk on my way home from the farmer, and, of all things, carelessness with my weekly dusting of the curlicues on the iron stand of her Singer sewing machine. We blamed each other for mishaps that at other times we wouldn't even have no-ticed but that now mattered a great deal. I wanted to show her how clever I was when Ingrid and I stood in line for bread on one of those tense days. I told Ingrid to stay way back behind me in line and also buy a loaf, contrary to the rule of one family, one loaf. Sep-arated from me by a crowd of pushy grown-ups, Ingrid got scared and sidled up to me at the last minute. The sales help of course rec-ognized us as the Paul sisters and began to scold Ingrid for trying to cheat. My little sister began to weep big tears, but I could not contain myself and scolded her severely for foiling my plan. When Ingrid told on me, Mutti made a federal case out of it. I swore I would never talk to her again. Before my vow of silence com-menced I told her that she complained if we stood in the wrong line or weren't swift enough to run to the next store said to have food. I said that she had changed from a mother who tried to bring some fun into our lives to one who was always agitated over some-thing or other. And for good measure I reminded her that accord-ing to her own stories as a young girl she had secretly hidden books under the furniture to read while she was supposed to scrub the floor for Grossmutti. And yet she herself did not allow me to finish a book that I needed to return to a friend and even had torn up, *Die Rosenkette* (The Chain of Roses), my absolute favorite book of all. "I will never forgive you!" I cried, slamming the kitchen door and running to my bedroom to seek solace.

Even so, life was not always all work. Hitler himself provided us with a chance to see free weekly movies in his theater up on Obersalzberg. And Dr. Goebbels—a lover of movies and movie stars—allowed a variety of old and new films—love stories, family dramas, operas, and operettas—to be shown, all of course by non-

Jewish filmmakers. On Saturday afternoons the movie house was open to the public, and if Mutti thought a film suitable for us, we made the excursion up the mountain. We walked past the depressing quarters of foreign laborers—now probably working on construction of the underground bunkers—and filed past S.S. guards into the dimly lit, simple hall. Preceding every show was *Die Deutsche Wochenschau,* a weekly newsreel, which always began with a short, punctuated melody that I remember today and that brings up—though much faded—images of soldiers and ravaged battlefields. By the fall of 1944 *Die Wochenschau* had become an endless series of images of explosions, burning cities, fierce-faced soldiers in steel helmets fighting, ducking, or running, and fighter planes taking off or streaking through the sky on the way to hit enemy targets. I often closed my eyes and covered my ears until the noise subsided and was followed by a lighthearted, fluffy feature film with a very happy ending.

Every evening Tante Susi faithfully dropped by after dinner bringing news and rumors that provoked waves of anxiety. The U.S. Army had advanced to Germany's western border, the Russians were coming ever closer, and we had sustained heavy losses in Italy. She said that the best information about the Russian advance came from the grapevine and networks of Russian prisoners of war working in German factories. Mutti thought it a sad state of affairs if we could not rely on the German intelligence to know and tell us the facts.

Later that fall the potato-and-apple cellar underneath Haus Linden was deemed too flimsy to serve as a shelter, forcing the landlord to build a real bunker into the steeply sloping meadow behind his house about a hundred yards up the road from us. Roughly hewn, round logs held up the ceiling, which consisted of a thickness of mud, sand, and soil built according to official instructions. The low, damp, and moldy-smelling bunker repulsed me; the black spiders I saw scurrying along the wall sent me into fits of hysterics that made Mutti pronounce me either high-strung or babyish. With the sirens going off most nights at least once, my relentless protests against going to the bunker finally broke down my poor mother's resistance and we would often just duck into our dry cellar with its pungent smell of apples and potatoes.

Obersalzberg might be a tempting symbolic target for enemy planes—and it eventually was—but except for overflights Berchtesgaden was strategically unimportant and, thanks to the mountains, not easy to approach. The whole valley had become *Deutschland's Luftschutzkeller* (Germany's air-raid shelter), with thousands of evacuated children from the bombed-out cities crowded into every suitable accommodation. Countless boys and girls of all ages and backgrounds and from many different cities were housed in former villas, sanatoriums, hotels, youth hostels, summer camps, and homes of local families. Most of the new arrivals shared our schools, and our classes were forever getting larger in number and tighter in space. Nonetheless, every time we emerged from our cellar following an air raid, and I saw the red haze from burning cities rise over the mountains, I suddenly felt glad that the city children had been brought here and were safe.

The relationship between displaced city children and us local kids was at best uneasy, at worst outright hostile. At night, after an air raid, or when I was by myself or with our foster brother, Hardi, I thought about their plight and felt sorry for them, here alone and not knowing what was happening to their parents. But with my crowd—the boys spoiling for a fight—I shared the disdain for the evacuees. They all wore the same ill-fitting navy-blue sweatsuits that immediately identified them as "foreigners," prompting our boys to call them—no matter where they came from—*Saupreussen* (Prussian pigs). This quickly started fistfights or, in the winter, merciless snowball fights that always ended with the losers having their faces harshly rubbed in the snow. We girls stood at the sidelines watching and cheering, surprised at how tough some of these skinny city kids were and how even with tears running down their faces they would stand up to the local bullies with fierce determination and great anger.

Bombed-out, fatherless families from the big cities arrived in droves, clinging to their bundles of salvaged clothing, looking numb and disoriented, waiting for their accommodations to be assigned. Frau Brummer, a petite woman from the city of Aachen, and her three small children were to occupy a room in the home of our neighbor Frau Daibler, a highly eccentric, well-to-do widow living on her half of the Angerer farm. Frau Daibler maintained a deeply mysterious garden with exotic Italian plants. Ever since her husband's death she had worn layers of long white dresses, a white turban, and exotic bead necklaces down to her waist. She told everyone in a croaking voice that her outfit was in honor of her dead husband, who had fancied Egyptian customs. She hated children, noise, and disturbances of any kind, which caused us to both fear her and try to get on her nerves whenever we could. She also hated refugees and was jailed for a few months when she refused to open her door to a family assigned to her.

On her release Frau Daibler was ordered to take in Frau Brummer and her kids, but rather than making amends she was as hostile as a scorpion. She denied the family access to the kitchen, forcing Frau Brummer to ask my mother if she could use our stove to warm milk and food for her children. It was a ten-minute walk between Haus Linden and Frau Daibler's, but of course Mutti immediately offered Frau Brummer the use of our kitchen. The only condition was that the Brummer kids would help collect kindling, a job that lately took us farther and farther afield. The nearby woods looked as though they had been swept clean.

Oblivious to evacuee and refugee debacles, scarcity, dark moods, and criminal warlords ruling from Obersalzberg, autumn once again put on its glorious, gaudy show. Maple, ash, birch, and larch trees turned into a flaming medley of colors. The brown-and-white-spotted cows came home before the frost from their grazing meadows on the high mountains, each animal decorated with colorful garlands and chiming bells to signify a summer without an accident. Hundreds of pale lilac autumn crocuses bloomed in the fields, while the air took on that peculiar smell of frost and early snow.

Pöhlmann Grossvati paid us a surprise visit, bringing a small, rust-brown hen in a wooden cage that he had carried as hand luggage on the train. At his suggestion—who knows where it came from?—we called the cute puffy hen Madame Pimpernel and fixed a comfortable rod and ladder for her in the woodshed. Conscientious Mutti told the authorities that we now had a chicken, which meant a deduction of eggs from our rations. Madame Pimpernel was a good sport who ate leftover potato peels, foraged along with the neighbor's hens in the woods all day long, and laid one small brown egg every morning. We kept her for many years. I'm not sure when she ended in the soup pot, but I do know that while she was alive we truly loved her. Life was filled with such disjointed, small, yet magnified events and occurrences, but it had one overarching, cohesive theme: the coming of our sixth wartime winter.

We expected nothing but bad news when Joseph Goebbels spoke on the radio twice in October, and indeed, he lived up to our expectations. All men between the ages of sixteen and sixty were to be drafted into the Volkssturm, the People's Army. That meant that Grossvati and Herr Puff would both have to go. About a week later Goebbels again promised victory, and Mutti wrote in her notebook with barely suppressed cynicism that "all our cities are destroyed and yet we are supposed to win the war!" Demonstrating the order of her priorities, her next sentence goes on to record that cows had gotten into the second garden and trampled on everything that had grown. In spite of her grave doubts, the news of the relentless bombing of German cities and the stories of the maiming, burning, and killing of thousands of German women and children in them rekindled her resolve to support the war with all she had. After an all-out attack on Munich she wrote, "I wish I could go fight myself."

We never talked or heard about the suffering women and children in the countries we had conquered, much less the victims of concentration camps and genocide. Mutti never wrote a word about Jews in her notebook or about children and women in London now targeted by the V-1 rockets. In her ill-conceived patriotism and constantly reinforced nationalism all her pity and compassion were focused on our own people, and in deep sorrow she would often sigh and say, "Die armen, armen Leute" (Those poor, poor people).

By now my enthusiasm for the Hitler Youth was wearing thin. Marching turned out to be a great bore in the long run, and I became more skeptical about the speeches and one-sided discussions. Ever since Mutti's run-in with Hans Schuster I had begun to think that the Nazis were my enemies, not my friends. I voiced none of my rebellion to Mutti or anyone yet, but I was ready for something that would convince me that we were being used and misled.

Attendance at the Hitler Youth drills was diminishing, which persuaded our leaders that peer pressure was needed to solve the problem. They decided that after the *Appell* those of us who showed up had to walk to the homes of absentees to tell the mothers that it was their duty to send their children to the mandatory weekly meeting. A couple of us were assigned to houses and farms in the village of Ilsank. At the first absentee's farm—he had said he was feeling sick—we saw him strong and healthy in the farmyard chopping wood. After taking one look at us he put down the ax and disappeared into the stable. Moments later his brisk, grim-faced mother emerged to see what we wanted. My confidence had vanished, but blushing and keeping my eyes on the ground, I forced myself to speak up. "We are here to tell you that attending the Hitler Youth meetings is mandatory and you must order your son to attend next week." Without a word she turned away.

Discouraged by our failure to make an impression, we went on to the next home and the next. As I finally limped up the Obersalzbergstrasse with my feet hurting I thought that I myself would rather play hooky than attend any longer. But I decided that if Wiebke would join in the spring of 1945, I might reconsider. When I raised the issue with her she took on that shy, reticent look and told me that she would not join the Hitler Youth. In spite of my waning interest, I was shocked and automatically responded by pointing out that every German child must join. When she didn't answer I dropped the topic and resolved to quit. No one sent anyone around when I followed my inclination, and even Mutti did not say a word.

Hardi's mother came from Berlin one day to pick him up, much to my mother's relief. The fast-growing boy had become a bit of a behavior problem, she said, and she had talked Frau Schulz into finding another foster home for him. I don't quite know why Mutti wanted Hardi to leave, except that she was always tired, worn out, and short-tempered. Sadly, I must say that I hardly noticed his departure. On the other hand, Herr Schulz,the fog soldier, had become a fixture in our lives. He, Tante Susi, and Mutti played cards on some evenings or talked over a glass of wine. Sometimes he simply came by after supper to see how we were. He was a tall, to me middle-aged man—at least in his mid-thirties—with a bulbous nose and pockmarked skin, and he seemed kind. When he came to visit, Ingrid and I watched and waited for a present—a piece of smoked bacon or homemade sausage from the care packages that his wife sent from their small farm in East Prussia. The father of three children, he knew how to bounce Ingrid, who could not remember Vati at all, on his knee, sing rhymes, and make her giggle by saying in his East Prussian dialect, "Marielken, slepperd di?" (Are you sleepy, little Mariel?) In a troubled voice he would tell us about life in his small Prussian village, which by then must have been close to the Russian advance or already overrun.

At Christmas, Mutti pulled two nature books from Vati's bookshelf as a present for each of us because she had nothing else. The only novelty was the *Lichtbogen* (arc of lights)—something supposedly Nordic—constructed from fir twigs and lights that Mutti had learned to make in a *Kindergruppen* training course. She had also chopped down a young spruce in the woods and, with help from Herr Schulz, added a few missing branches before she put it into its stand. We had a new supply of shiny tinsel that had simply fallen from the sky after an enemy overflight before we gathered it and saved it for Christmas. (The puzzle of the falling tinsel was solved long after the war when a former American pilot told me that they had used it to scramble radar transmissions.) As was our tradition on Christmas Eve, we stepped outside to remember Vati. I could no longer recall what he looked like without resorting to photographs. The real man was receding into the distant past, and yet I still missed him.

Herr Schulz came by late at night after the obligatory S.S. celebration on Obersalzberg. Mutti reported in her journal that she had managed to cook dumplings, sauerkraut, and a nice roast. "It was very *gemütlich* [cozy]. Only the question of what will be depressed us."

By the end of January the bitter cold of that final war winter closed the schools for lack of coal. Twice a week I tobogganed down the Obersalzbergstrasse to deliver homework and pick up assignments and corrections. The tall, cast-iron stove in the corner of the classroom was stone cold, ice seemed to glitter on the walls, and ice flowers grew in shades of platinum on windows. We blew into our fists, warming them enough to jot down our new homework assignment. I could hardly wait to get outside into the snow so we could warm up by running, dodging snowballs, and pulling our sleds up the mountain. Mutti asked what homework we had to do, and all too often I could not read the writing that my cold fingers had produced. But with a vengeance Mutti made sure that whatever English words or mathematical formulas I had to memorize and practice were embedded in my brain and that any written homework was fulfilled to perfection. She often lost her patience over Ingrid's slowly progressing reading skills. We both cried during the course of those afternoons. I had no other thought than that I hated school, hated homework, and hated, in fact, almost everybody and everything else.

❑ ❑

MUTTI'S JOURNAL ENDS WITH THE ENTRY concerning Christmas 1944. Several pages following it seem to be missing, ripped out perhaps. After that all the pages are filled with the dress measurements of her dozens of customers. Hidden among them is a final note written on January 10, 1946: "We have been under American occupation for over half a year now. Irmgard is in the second grade of *Gymnasium* and so much has happened." Those last four words, "so much has happened," encompassing the spring of 1945 to the winter of 1946, sum up the most cataclysmic events of my life.

13 WAR COMES TO BERCHTESGADEN

ON THE DECEPTIVELY CLEAR SPRING MORNING OF
April 25, 1945, like a final thunderclap after a violent storm, British
warplanes came swooping into the valley. First they tried to bomb
the Eagle's Nest on Kehlstein but then emptied their loads on
Obersalzberg. The warning sirens instructed us—wrongly, as it
turned out—to leave school and go home instead of to the town
bunker where we had sat for hours on end forty-eight times since
January alone. A few moments after we were dismissed, we began
to hear the droning noise of bombers overhead. The S.S. driver
who took the children of the Nazi elite up to their luxurious shelters on Obersalzberg stopped next to us on the bridge and called,
"Hop in quickly, I'll drop you off at your intersection." Else,
Wiebke, Bärbel, and I piled into the black Mercedes one on top
of the other, leaving Ingrid, who had arrived last, to stand on the
car's running board, clinging to the window. A few minutes later
the driver let us out at the head of the sandy road leading to Haus
Linden.

"Let's run to my house, it's the nearest!" I shouted over the
deafening noise of detonations coming from the direction in
which the car had just headed. The hellish explosions were followed by an enormous stormlike wind that would have blown me
off my feet had I not gripped the rough bark of the nearest spruce
and pressed myself against it. We had not been warned that the
detonation of each of the six-hundred-kilogram bombs that were
dropped from an estimated three hundred British planes that day
would cause intense air pressure. We waited for a pause after each

explosion to race to the next tree before the displaced air hit us. Ingrid, whose seven-year-old legs were no match for our ten-year-old ones, called to us to wait for her. Else and I grabbed her hands and pulled her along. The earth shook, and the air was filled with the rumble of airplane motors, the whistle of falling bombs, the detonations, and the wind that followed.

I felt no fear, only absolute determination to fight my way from tree to tree until I was home, where Mutti would be waiting for us. She, meanwhile, had sought refuge in our cellar instead of the landlord's bunker. Assuming that we were safe in the town shelter, she suspected thieves in the apartment when she heard our steps overhead. She was stunned when she saw that it was us, her children, out of breath and still not quite comprehending what was happening outside. As she realized the danger we had just been in, her eyes filled with tears and then with dread. Only at that moment did fear strike me too, and I began to tremble.

It took the pilots a mere forty-five minutes to drop their load. However, given the relatively small size of our valley, and the dreadful sounds that engulfed us even in the cellar, we fully expected that the entire valley had been laid to waste. Where was the *tack, tack, tack* of the antiaircraft guns, and why was Obersalzberg no longer shrouded in the usual acrid fog? The answer was simple: The chemicals for the fog had run out weeks ago; the guns had run out of ammunition and, perhaps, the soldiers to fire them. Yet when it was finally over we found that at least our immediate neighborhood was undamaged. The very lack of fog cover had apparently allowed the enemy pilots to be extremely accurate. The bombs had destroyed most of the Nazi settlement on the mountain but left us and the town untouched. There were those who considered this a miracle; the Lord Himself had protected us, evidenced by the sign of a cross they saw in the sky. I, however, was puzzled, and would be for a long time. Why of all places should He protect Berchtesgaden, when all of Europe was in ashes?

The sirens wailed again that afternoon, sending us to the landlord's bunker. This time the bombs were farther away, in the neighboring spa town of Bad Reichenhall, where, we later learned, they had killed two hundred people. By suppertime we went home and were soundly asleep when around midnight Mutti woke us up, put our coats over our nightshirts, handed me my little emergency suitcase, and marched us downstairs into the cellar. Ingrid cried and said she didn't want to go, but she went right back to sleep on her cot. Mutti and Tante Susi were too exhausted to talk, hoping only that we would stay alive just a little longer as explosions in another small town shook the earth.

The next morning, our faces washed and hair braided as if it was any normal day, Ingrid and I joined our friends for the walk to school, which by now—April—had resumed its regular schedule. Mutti was ready too, with her shopping basket and knapsack. She told us that she would try to gather news about the bombing and get to the bakery lines before the next alarm. We ran down our shortcut to the Ache, crossed the bridge where the S.S. guard waved to us as he did every day, and rushed up the slope on the other side. Then, as Obersalzberg came into view, we saw the devastation. The plateau had become a chaotic brown-and-black mess of tree stumps resembling charred matchsticks, irregular dark craters, and ruins that still smoked. "It's all gone," I said to no one in particular.

Our teachers sent us home until further notice. Suppressing an undercurrent of anxiety, we did what children do when an unexpected catastrophe closes school: We thought ourselves lucky and made plans for the afternoon before we ran home. Still, I sensed that this was more than a temporary closing and that the remnants of a more or less predictable order, in which we had found some comfort, were falling away. I had no sense of the future, knowing only that we no longer had to spend school mornings in the damp, dark town shelters and afternoons on hastily assigned homework.

Even the daily routine of listening to the evening news had become close to impossible. Static drowned the voices on the air, and

The Hitler compound after the bombing on April 25, 1945.

we had difficulty making out the words, no matter how close we pressed our ears to the fabric-covered front of the radio. In a few more days there would be total silence.

But you can't stop rumors. People were bursting with news of the large numbers of bombing victims on Obersalzberg. The Tallehen and a couple of other farms had indeed been destroyed; in the end the death count was about forty, among them local and foreign workers and S.S. men. The Catholic and Protestant clergy buried seventeen or eighteen people in a mass grave, and the Party organization held a memorial service with military honors for all the "fallen heroes."

The next day Tante Susi, still in the burgundy-colored brocade dressing gown she had made from an old hotel curtain, came down the stairs to read us the report of the memorial service in the local newspaper. "We had the hope that there would be a limit to the satanic deeds here in the high and elevated beauty of nature's creation . . . [but] the terror of enemy bombs forced its way into our sacred Alpine world," it editorialized. Herr Schallmoser, the local Party leader, gave a speech—he had always spoken to us on Hitler's birthday—in which he said that these heroes had died so that Germany would live and they had our promise that we would work hard and fight bravely to carry their mandate into the future. The Führer, he promised, was suffering along with each and every German. Tante Susi stopped reading and shook her head. Less than ten days from the end and a few days before Hitler's suicide, we were still expected to tolerate such humbug from an officially sanctioned voice. Mutti, struggling with anger and disappointment, was in a dark, morose mood.

Rumor insisted that "they"—the Nazis—were planning to defend the *Alpenfestung* (alpine fortress) Berchtesgaden and launch a terrible new *Geheimwaffe* (secret weapon) from the mountain. Hitler had been expected to return to the mountain for his birthday, maybe even to personally command the defense to the last, but instead he decided to stay in Berlin. However, there were those who still believed that Hitler's last stand would be launched from here. The pronouncements from Obersalzberg became more bizarre by the day. Were we to believe that the Allies and Germany were on the brink of making common cause against the Soviets? That Hitler wanted all of Germany scorched by our own troops before it fell into enemy hands? That our famous Generals Jodl, Keitel, Kesselring, and Rundstedt were still ordering our troops to stand firm? Or had they ordered them to retreat? Finally, was it true that Göring was a prisoner in his own bunker on Obersalzberg and that Grossadmiral Dönitz was to, after Hitler's "heroic death" in his Berlin bunker, became his successor?

A rare clear voice on the radio confirmed Hitler's death. Profoundly shocked, Mutti absorbed the news, not so much because she mourned Hitler but because she felt so deeply betrayed. Our only hope now was that the Führer's suicide would speed up the end and stop the bloodshed.

The changing tune of the daily chatter made my head spin. My mind was still filled with Nazi propaganda assuring certain death for all of us if the enemy won the war. I was eager to be persuaded otherwise and could have hugged Tante Susi for saying that perhaps we would all survive somehow.

As always, the most personal was the most disturbing. We heard—and this rumor turned out to be true—that two young sons of a neighbor halfway down the road had tried to desert and been summarily shot by their officers so close to the end.

The only real question was whose flag would replace the swastika on Obersalzberg. We tended to lump Soviets, Bolsheviks, Communists, Stalinists, and Marxists into the one phrase, *Die Russen* (the Russians), and we feared them the most. This fear was fed by stories from refugees from the eastern front who arrived in our mountains and valleys by the thousands. My old playmate, the former Ruth, now Ingrid, and her family had been kicked out of Austria and returned to a small makeshift apartment on Salzberg. She joined Wiebke, Else, and me to make a foursome of friends. In her rather stoical way she stopped in the middle of a game one day and told us that fleeing west from Prussia her grandmother had been pinned against a barn door with a pitchfork by a Russian soldier. He had held her there until she was dead. We interrupted our play just long enough to briefly contemplate the horrific story, then tried to banish the image from our mind as fast as possible. But it lingered, as did the almost mythical and terrible word *Stalingrad*. Our fear mounted when we heard that the Russians were approaching from Vienna at about the same rate as the U.S. troops from the northwest.

During the day I managed to shield myself from the horror of our experience, but at night it was almost impossible to keep my fear in check. The nightmare returned, and now the black beast was huge, ready to tear me apart. Wiebke too had nightmares of being hunted down by a Russian soldier who shouted in broken German that it would soon be her turn to be killed. I told no one of my secret daydream in which I helped a Russian prisoner of war escape from the Germans and get back to his people. He would be among the invading troops, and I would be spared because I had saved him.

Young women in Berchtesgaden planned to hide in the mountains in case of a Soviet occupation. Mutti gave me—but not Ingrid, who surely was too small—a tiny, light-yellow paper envelope that contained a teaspoon of ground pepper and told me to carry it in my apron pocket at all times. If any enemy soldier threatened to harm me, I should throw the pepper into his eyes. I said I would try but that I would surely escape anyway because I was a fast runner. Pepper, by the way, was not easy to come by. Tante Susi had an illicit source, and even though my mother disapproved of the black market, she accepted enough of the precious spice for our protection.

A few days after the bombings, in the middle of the night, I was awakened by a quiet knock on the door and the sound of a man's voice. I quickly got up, both to check on who could be coming so late at night and to be near my mother. Because the nights were still cool, I was wearing my orange flannel winter pajamas with a square rear opening fastened with buttons. My Paul grandmother had made these ridiculous—though admittedly practical— pajamas for each of us, telling Mutti that they were from an almost new remnant of material and that she had been lucky to find the buttons. She had also knitted warm, supposedly matching pink bed socks from the wool of an unraveled cardigan that I had outgrown. Dressed in this outfit, I stood behind my mother expecting a neighbor with news. Had the enemy troops arrived?

No, but a young S.S. soldier stood back from the door in the dark and asked my mother if she had any civilian men's clothing. He wanted to shed his uniform and get away. Mutti hushed me back to bed and gave the man a pair of my father's tweed knickers, a shirt, and a jacket. There were more knocks that night and the next, and more jackets and pants disappeared. I heard the transactions with increasing resentment over my mother's largesse with my dead father's clothes. I wondered if she knew that even now helping soldiers desert was treason. I asked Mutti repeatedly and pointedly what she thought would happen to us over the next weeks, the next months, years. Would it be like the twenties she had told me so much about? She sighed and had no answer, no smile, and—worst of all—no song that would cheer us.

Among the soldiers who disappeared into the night was the fog soldier Schulz. The day before his disappearance, a gorgeous, clear May Day—though no one thought of celebrating—Herr Schulz and the three of us had walked together up to the old Alpine Club hut Liegeret, the scene of so much happy play and gaiety before the war. We had not been up there in a long time, but the chalet still stood, quiet, peaceful, and undisturbed in the sun below the Eagle's Nest. The clear, cold stream flowed as always into the trough outside the house and then downhill through the greening meadow and the buttercups. Herr Schulz and Mutti walked slowly together on a road near the hut. They were having a long, serious talk, and I knew they did not want me to listen, but I sidled up to them anyway, curious and suspicious of their intimacy. Mutti frowned and asked Ingrid and me to run and gather pinecones for kindling the fire at home. We always brought our rucksacks for just such an opportunity, and we scurried into the woods to pick up the cones beneath the firs and among the smooth, palmate leaves of the *Schneerosen* (*Hellebores niger*).

That night Herr Schulz vanished. We never saw him again. Mutti did not say one word about his disappearance, but she had a certain thoughtfulness and even gladness about her that I could not fathom. I had been sure that she would miss him.

□ □

OCCASIONALLY THE GERMAN COMPULSION for order would gain
the upper hand, even during these disorderly final days of the
Third Reich in Berchtesgaden. It turned out that the S.S. had
stored up on the mountain thousands of yards of black and gray-
green uniform cloth, white-and-blue-checkered cotton used for
barrack curtains and bedding, and hundreds of pairs of high black
boots. Herr Jakob, the *Landrat* (administrator) of the larger Berchtesgaden area, was often at odds with the Party leadership and had
persuaded the S.S. commandant on Obersalzberg to forgo the pol-
icy of blowing up all the goods and instead give the whole lot to the
mayor of Salzberg for orderly and equitable distribution among
the population. As the Allies' tanks rolled toward Berchtesgaden,
my mother and other women on the war-duty rolls were asked to
report to the yard of the Salzberg grade school to help distribute
fabric and boots to local and refugee families.

On a worn, wooden table the women measured and cut the
cloth off the heavy bales, using scissors they had been asked to
bring. After waiting in line, every family received about six meters
of each fabric, along with one pair of S.S. boots per adult. The
adults were of course all women, and most of them had to stuff
paper into the toes of the large men's boots. That summer and
for years to come everybody had dresses made from the sturdy
blue-and-white curtain and bedding material; for years we wore
coats, suits, ski pants, and parkas of black or grayish green uniform cloth and tall, black boots that were eventually downgraded to
serve for garden, field, and stable work. I sometimes wondered
what the Americans thought of all the women in this town wearing
identical dirndl dresses along with those knee-high boots. Wearing German uniform cloth was actually forbidden, but no one ever
questioned my drab green ski pants and matching parka with the
hood that Mutti had lined with some red checkered flannel fabric.

I'm not sure when during that chaotic time we walked up to the

S.S. barracks on Obersalzberg with Wiebke, Bärbel, and Frau Molsen. Through a rear window S.S. soldiers were handing out champagne, cigars, and specialty foods we had not seen in years, while in the front yard a group of diehards was still practicing goose-stepping to an officer's commands. In another part of the yard, soldiers offered us bread thick with butter. They encouraged us to have seconds, since we all looked so thin. We came home with a rucksack filled with champagne that Mutti buried in the dump that for lack of garbage was never used. She said she did not want to have alcohol in the house when the occupation troops arrived, whoever they might be.

When Mutti heard that the entire Hitler territory on Obersalzberg was no longer off limits and that the S.S. soldiers were about to leave, she called us from the kitchen window in a shaky, urgent voice. We stopped playing at once and sped home through the woods. Mutti was already putting on the heavy brown walking shoes that had belonged to Vati, tying their torn and knotted leather laces over two pairs of socks, lumpy and multihued from darning with different-colored threads of wool. We were going up the mountain, to the Berghof.

The gates to Hitler's compound swung freely on their hinges. We passed the empty, littered guardhouse, and I picked up a shiny black telephone that had been ripped out of the wall and tossed into the woods. We would not have a real telephone for another dozen years.

Haltingly, not quite believing what she was seeing, my mother led us through the gate. We left the main road and took an old trail she remembered through the trees. The path wound up toward the houses of Albert Speer and the feared Martin Bormann, who in a few days would vanish for good from the Hitler bunker in Berlin. On the left, Mutti thought, were the ruined villas of Hermann Göring and Joseph Goebbels.

My mother was crying quietly; it made me feel helpless and uncomfortable. I felt sorry for her and for myself and was saddened by the general weariness of life. All I had ever known was Nazi

Germany, and I was frightened by this visible physical collapse and by not having the vaguest idea what, if anything, would replace it. Yet I could not let myself weep with her, despite the lump in my throat. Instead I tightened my neck muscles and swallowed hard. Mutti finally collected herself. How sad it was, she said, that all of Germany was in ruins and that all the horrendous sacrifices had been made for naught.

We continued walking uphill on a well-kept and undisturbed gravel road, and I became more anxious as we ventured deeper into the quiet of the Nazi terrain. I asked Mutti again what would happen to us when the war was over. She didn't answer—how could she when she didn't know? Suddenly my fear gave way to an intense anger at her ignorance, impotence, and sadness. She should not have let all of this happen. Who started this anyway? Why had she believed in Hitler from the beginning and in his war for so long? I had no idea what she could or should have done about any of it, the deaths and the sacrifices. But she was, after all, the grown-up, the head of the household, the mother of children, and I was only a skinny, not even eleven-year-old, fatherless child. Surrounded by the ruins of Obersalzberg, I felt my wish to blame, to accuse, to assign guilt become overwhelmingly strong. Since Mutti was the person closest at hand, she became my first target. But I said nothing to her, still knowing nothing of the atrocities committed by the Nazi regime. I felt only the pain perpetrated on my country and on myself.

After a few more minutes we reached the completely intact Speer *Kinderheim,* a nursery for the children of the Obersalzberg Nazi elite. The doors to the stark, one-story building with its low, overhanging roof were locked, and the children who had played there until a few days earlier were gone. Had Frau Bormann really disappeared from the *Kinderheim* with a large group of children including some of her own nine? Nothing surprised us anymore. We were but passive onlookers, confused, betrayed, and, as before, powerless.

Mutti, Ingrid, and I walked on, listening to the echo of our footsteps on the hard-surfaced road that led to the Speer villa. Bormann had purchased the old house from the painter Waltenberger, and instead of being torn down it was made available to the Speer family, along with Party funds to refurbish it. It had survived the bombing intact, though not a soul was to be seen there. A curious mixture of fear and lust for adventure came over me and perhaps my mother too. Keeping Ingrid and me behind her, Mutti carefully pushed open the door. We stepped inside hesitantly, listening for the sound of voices or footsteps. All was silent, but I could feel my heart pounding, for the place felt as if at any moment the owners would return, sit down at the kitchen table for lunch or at the piano to play a spring song. I knew I would die from embarrassment should little Albert Speer, my third-grade classmate, walk in and see me and my family rudely invading his home. But no one came. As if in a dream we walked through the bright, untouched rooms with their potted plants still well watered and their woven drapes adjusted to the sunlight of recent days. We stroked and touched this or that but took nothing, not even the few lemons left on a kitchen counter.

After we had walked through the house we looked at a few of the ruins of the other houses. Then my mother had seen enough for one afternoon. Empty-handed, except for my black telephone, we walked silently back to Haus Linden. We were drained from the experience of treading on so recently forbidden and revered grounds, entering uninvited the homes—or what was left of them—of Nazi greats, and witnessing the final disintegration of the very heart of the Third Reich.

I soon came to regret what I thought was my mother's foolish "German honesty," which did not allow her to take advantage of the situation and enrich herself with the property of a Third Reich functionary. This much-touted honesty proved to be highly disposable, both in the general breakdown that followed the end of the war and, later, in facing up to the past. The good citizens of Berchtesgaden who entered the house after us took without a moment's hesitation everything they could possibly carry or move. I was jealous when I saw the furniture we had left behind installed in our neighbors' homes, their walls hung with the paintings, bookshelves filled with the books, and cabinets holding the silver and china from the houses, the hotels, and the bunkers on Obersalzberg. The looters were able to barter many of these items for food and cigarettes for years to come.

Driven by envy, greed, and the wish to own something of value from the mountain, I secretly went back a few days later and poked through the now empty and plundered houses all by myself. The only thing left in the Speer house was a large book lying on the bare floor in the corner of a room. Bound in deep red leather, with blank, gold-edged parchment pages, it was unused, and I thought beautiful. Heavy though it was, I stuck it in my rucksack. Years later we would use it as the first guest book at my mother and stepfather's newly opened bed-and-breakfast on the other side of the Obersalzberg road from Haus Linden. No one else knew where the book had come from, but it always reminded me of those last days of the war, its blank pages a symbol of a new beginning for me. Eventually the pages would fill with names of vacationers who lived in the new West Germany that rose from the rubble of the war.

14 THE END AT LAST

On May 3, 1945, a messenger from the mayor's office walked from house to house. Hang a white sheet over your balconies or out of the windows, he instructed us, stay inside, and open the door without resistance to any foreign soldier who wants to enter. He also told Mutti that as far as he knew the American troops were poised to take Berchtesgaden. Tante Susi promptly fetched several large white bedsheets and draped them from the balcony of Haus Linden, while I stood below to make sure they were hanging straight.

Inside, Mutti slowly took Hitler's portrait—the smallish, dark red wax relief created by Schego—from the wall where it had hung since 1933. That night we melted the portrait down. Hitler's face dissolved like a mirage at the bottom of the hot aluminum pan. Later the wax provided us with some desperately needed candles.

The next morning I lay in bed wondering what kind of day this would be and suddenly realized that the smell of wood smoke from the morning fire was missing. I was surprised that on such a fateful day Mutti would not be up and cooking our oatmeal. Instead she asked me to get a slice of bread for Ingrid and myself. "Don't take too much jam," she remembered to say, even though she seemed in a poor state. She looked pale and somehow defeated in her washed-out, long-sleeved nightshirt and her loose, untidy braids. Her hands, not yet tanned from the summer sun, lay equally pale and limp on the snowy white feather bed. "Run along," she said, and Ingrid and I went upstairs to Tante Susi's and knocked on the door.

Much to my delight, Trudi was there. She had come home from

the clinic in Erlangen where she had begun training as a pediatric nurse. Tante Susi looked worn and tired and said that she had not slept all night and wondered if I had heard them. I told her that I hadn't slept either, but no, I hadn't heard anything. She looked at me skeptically and said something like "You must have slept quite soundly; otherwise you would have heard all the commotion, what with Trudi coming home and your mother not feeling well and us trying to get help." Mutti not feeling well and needing help? What did she mean? Tante Susi tried to calm me, reassuring me that everything would be fine.

Trudi and the other student nurses had been let go from the Erlangen children's clinic to fend for themselves and make their way home. She had borrowed a ramshackle old bike and, without ever coming upon the advancing American army, had ridden for about three days toward Berchtesgaden on country roads and the deserted autobahn. She had gotten lost a few times, pushed her bike for hours because of a flat tire, been helped and fed by villagers, and arrived home during the night, to Tante Susi's vast relief.

But Trudi had found her mother deeply alarmed over Mutti, who was in great pain. They did not, of course, reveal to me that Mutti had been bleeding profusely and was about to miscarry a four- or five-month pregnancy. Trudi had quickly decided to venture again out into the night to find a midwife or a doctor. The midwife in town opened her door hesitantly and, according to Trudi, when she heard of my mother's premature labor, said, "I am going nowhere. Don't you know that the Americans will arrive at any moment?" She closed and locked the door. Trudi promised herself that she would never use this woman as her midwife and ran back up the mountain, trying to remember the little she had learned about childbirth. She and Tante Susi boiled water on the woodstove to sterilize scissors for cutting the umbilical cord. They tried to comfort my mother as well as they could.

Finally Mutti aborted a tiny, fully formed baby. They put it in a cardboard box and buried it in the woods, who knows where—maybe near the champagne. A few days later Dr. Oberndörfer, armed with an emergency permit, walked up to Haus Linden and saw my ill and feverish mother through to safety.

Ingrid and I had slept through these nighttime happenings, and my mother never mentioned one word about the child she lost or that Herr Schulz was its father. When I heard the full story many years later from Trudi, I realized that on some level I had suspected my mother's pregnancy and was suspicious of her warmth and even happiness when Schulz came by. During their walk at the Liegeret they had presumably said good-bye, leaving each other to their fates. I knew nothing about adult love and loneliness then, let alone about sex, but much later I remembered some puzzling remarks that should have tipped me off. Tante Susi, thinking that I was reading, told Trudi that my mother's contractions began when they were on their way home from a looting trip on Obersalzberg—Mutti too had recognized that loyalty to the Nazis, perhaps honesty, was no longer a virtue but that survival was—and Tante Susi had expected her to have her miscarriage right there by the side of the road. Later I heard my mother, in a moment of intimacy, tell a woman friend that she had quite unexpectedly fallen in love with one of the *Nebelsoldaten* who had to leave to save his life—S.S. soldiers were said to have been shot on sight.

We never heard from Schulz again, and my mother never once uttered his name. I have sometimes wondered what became of him and his family in East Prussia. Was he too just an average German caught up in the Nazi tide? Perhaps, I rationalized, he joined the S.S. late in the war in order to swell their diminishing ranks and was not engaged in anything more repellent than blanketing the Nazi mountain with a protective layer of fog. I shall never know.

The morning after my mother's miscarriage, one of those cool, crystal clear mountain days that make one breathe deeply and feel clean and fresh inside, another drama took place. Landrat Jakob drove toward the advancing American 101st Airborne Division in a

Lt. Col. Kenneth Wallace, 3rd Division U.S. Army, tells the mayor and town officials of Berchtesgaden how the civilian population is to behave, May 4, 1945.

car, waving a white flag to signal the surrender of Berchtesgaden. After much difficult negotiation, Jakob, as well as the town's mayor and a few other well-connected intermediaries, had persuaded General Kesselring, commander of the German troops north of the Alps now headquartered in the village of Königssee near Berchtesgaden, to surrender. Even the S.S. commandant on Obersalzberg agreed to leave the mountain in an attempt to avoid a confrontation with the oncoming U.S. forces. Quite consciously Landrat Jakob had throughout the war fought the establishment of ammunition manufacture in the area, saturating it instead with civilian and military hospitals, clinics, children's homes, and *K.L.V. Lager*. The presence of those thousands of evacuated children and patients allowed General Kesselring to save face and give up the defense for "humanitarian reasons," even though he still considered it high treason.

The Führer's cowardly death—a suicide, not exactly a *Heldentod* (hero's death)—on April 30 in Berlin, and the suicide of Giesler,

Soldiers of the 101st Airborne Division enter Berchtesgaden on the heels of the 30th Infantry Regiment, 3rd Division.

the much feared Bavarian district leader, helped to convince the officers to give up their desperate, doomed, and entirely symbolic gesture of defending these last unoccupied remains of Germany. Even the Berchtesgaden newspaper, so long the instrument of Nazi propaganda, engaged at last in an act of defiance before closing down. It purposely delayed the printing of a *Flugblatt* (flier) by Kreisleiter Stredele, a fanatical Party-appointed county executive, in which he encouraged citizens to resist to the bitter end. Instead, the paper printed and distributed Landrat Jakob's appeal to surrender to spare Berchtesgaden a last fight and guaranteed destruction. The boys in the mountain-troop barracks training for the Volkssturm were easily persuaded by their officers to put away their weapons and make their way home. Finally, in the nick of time, the S.S. left Obersalzberg quietly, though they did blow up the remains of the Berghof before they withdrew.

I had sometimes tried to imagine what the U.S. soldiers would be like. My knowledge of Americans came from three sources. One was Nazi propaganda, which held that the United States was an instrument of the Jews who wanted to destroy Germany, and that the country's white inhabitants were uncultured barbarians who ate from tin cans. The second were the books of Karl May, writer of fiction about white men—greenhorns—and Indian braves in North America. Hitler much admired May, who had never traveled to America but portrayed Indians as noble savages and heroes. My third source of information was two much read copies of Mark Twain's *Tom Sawyer* and *The Adventures of Huckleberry Finn* from Tante Susi's bookshelf. I loved those two American boys, especially Huck, and imagined living on the Mississippi River with him as I read my favorite passages again and again. But those images did not help me at all to picture a conquering army. On the afternoon of May 4, 1945, I sat on the white bed in my room, sunk in reverie and furtive daydreams. Suddenly I heard a deep rumbling—I immediately thought of tanks—coming closer, and at this moment my curiosity won out over any apprehension. I decided that I must see the first Americans with my own eyes.

Mutti was asleep and Ingrid upstairs as I quietly left the house. In spite of the sparkling sun, not a single human being was in sight, and except for the ominous drone, all was dead still. I ran quickly from tree to tree to the edge of the Obersalzbergstrasse and selected a hiding place behind the trunk of a wide old spruce in a stand of ferns. Almost before I had time to crouch down, I saw the first U.S. tank slowly moving toward me. My heart beat loud and fast. I swallowed hard and my hands felt clammy. I wished I were at home. The huge armored vehicle or tank lumbered above me, close enough for me to briefly see the faces of the soldiers. They wore helmets and battle fatigues, and in spite of my terror I noted that the camouflage of their gear and uniforms was of a different pattern and less green than that of our army. The soldiers had their hands on mounted machine guns, which they rotated slowly from side to side, intent, watchful, as if expecting an ambush or surprise resistance at any moment. They looked fierce but to my surprise just as young and handsome as our soldiers had been. Fleeting as my impressions were, I found the Americans to look more human than I had thought possible and certainly not like a lot of ruffians. Actually, I could hardly think at all as I sat frozen, pressing my body lower into the ferns and closer to the tree

U.S. soldiers rip down the swastika flag at the burning Berghof. The ruin had been set on fire by the S.S. before they left Obersalzberg, May 4, 1945.

until well after the last tank and armored car had rolled past me up the mountain.

I could not gauge how long I had sat or how many tanks had gone by. I knew that the ground had trembled and that the world had suddenly changed. It dawned on me then that we were no longer at war, the guns and bombs were silenced, and I would grow up in a world totally different from the one that Hitler had so forcefully instructed us to believe in. With the faith of my youth and a basic trust in my mother's survival skills, I felt a glimmer of hope that the demise of Hitler's Germany would not be my own as well. I walked home in a daze and told no one where I had been.

Mutti let us go outside the following day but told us to be careful and come home at once should we see any American soldiers approaching. I shrugged and left the house, longing to tell Wiebke about my secret heroics and figure out what to do on a day like this, the first day of "after the war." We met on the road halfway between our houses and looked at each other; all at once the fact that the end had come hit us both. On an impulse we took each other's crossed-over hands and began to whirl around on the gravel road, singing and shouting, "Der Krieg ist aus! Der Krieg ist aus! Der Krieg ist aus!" (The war is over!) We were giddy with happiness, swirling in a wild dance until we fell to the ground. Our joy was definitely not shared or approved of by several neighbors, who complained to my mother about my unseemly behavior in the hour of Germany's defeat and shame. In their eyes there was nothing to celebrate.

We were not at all certain what to expect from the victorious army, and when we heard that a contingent of French and Moroccan soldiers had arrived in Berchtesgaden almost simultaneously with the U.S. troops, we became alarmed and less optimistic about our personal safety. Because this was Berchtesgaden, the soldiers of both armies were given free rein to plunder the town for several days after the surrender—permission that resulted in many vivid accounts of theft and rape. Most rapes were committed by the French and Moroccan troops, but one eyewitness report held that some U.S. soldiers who occupied several administrative buildings in Stangass, a section of Berchtesgaden, took the rings, watches, and passports of other employees and asked for schnapps and women. How a young woman was found was not said, but Alois Hamm, a civil servant, insisted that a sixteen-year-old girl was "produced" and gang-raped by the American soldiers. Of course my mother tried to shield us from these stories. I overheard Tante Susi say that the few doctors in town, even those opposed to abortions, terminated the pregnancies of young women who had been raped in early May 1945 without asking any questions or telling any secrets.

Over the next few days American GIs searched every house and apartment for weapons. Two soldiers with guns slung over their shoulders entered our home and, much to my mother's disgust, insisted on looking through her dresser drawers. In the broken English that she remembered from her evening classes in the twenties she asked indignantly if they really thought that a widow with two children would be hiding weapons among her underwear. I was scared of the GIs' guns and hoped my mother would not infuriate them with her haughtiness. I felt that if I were an American soldier, I too would search for weapons. Secretly I hoped that they would take away Onkel Peppi's rifles so that when he came home he would no longer be able to practice target shooting from the balcony.

After the initial days of occupation we began to feel safe moving around during noncurfew hours. As soon as the church bells struck the end of the night's curfew, Ingrid and I, being caught up in the chaos that took over, joined in the looting of what remained of the huge amount of food and luxury goods the Nazis had left stored in Berchtesgaden. Most of it was on Obersalzberg in the various storage facilities, in the basements of the S.S. barracks, the

Gutshof (model estate), and the Hotel Platterhof. Rumor had it that there was enough to have defended Berchtesgaden for years.

My mother was still convalescing, so Ingrid and I alone took our knapsacks and—this was a brainstorm of mine—a couple of well-ironed pillowcases from the linen closet to serve as bags. Barefoot, since this was May, we ran up the mountain to compete with friends and neighbors for our share of rice, beans, lentils, flour, and oats. We filled our pillowcases, sneezing as the flour tickled our noses. I was frustrated by the small amount that Ingrid could carry without buckling under the load. The remaining furniture, sacks of grain, and boxes of jarred honey and jam were carted away by farmers who brought their hay wagons pulled by an ox or a cow, while others came with wheelbarrows, pushcarts, laundry baskets, and rucksacks.

The *Gutshof,* a kind of model farm established by Bormann (why here on the mountain, where barely enough grass grew to support a few cows, was a puzzle), stood off the road on the left, just below the destroyed Nazi homes. I saw it close up for the first time that day, and my sister and I entered a cavernous hall in a barnlike building holding huge wooden barrels that seemed two stories high filled with red wine, white wine, and apple cider. An old man opened first one and then another spigot with a hammer and filled one of his glass bottles with red wine and the other with cider. But when he tried to shut off the spigots, neither he nor the women who tried to help him could stop the flow. A few people had brought bottles or milk cans that they filled under the gushing spigots, but the pungent red and golden liquids continued to flow freely, mixing on the concrete floor and running out into the yard where very quickly they formed an intoxicating lake. Ingrid and I sloshed through inches of the brew, loving the feeling on our bare feet, the look of our red-rimmed toenails, and the pleasant, heady sensation that the fumes produced.

For a while we forgot all about looting and filling our pillowcases. I looked up and saw a couple of American soldiers with machine guns patrolling the scene. They shook their heads in surprise and puzzlement, clearly not knowing what to make of these Germans wading in wine and filling their small milk cans at the open spigots of barrels as high as a house. We returned to the clean, whitewashed grain-storage room where strong women picked up whole sacks of the nutritious booty and carried them away on their backs. With our pillowcases filled we ran home to show Mutti our loot and then hurried back up for more. We had no idea how precious each grain and gram of everything we brought home would become over the following months.

Afterward I was often amazed that not once did I or anyone else feel pangs of guilt about looting the goods of our recent masters whom until a few days ago we had still confirmed with our mechanical "Heil Hitler" ("l'itler" for short). Mutti said that the Nazi goods belonged to no one at that point. Most people I knew indulged almost gleefully in this orgy of theft, driven by pent-up hostility, the instinct to survive, and a wish to eliminate whatever was left of the Third Reich.

Obersalzberg was not the only place left to looters. Hermann Göring's private train stood in the unfinished tunnel that Hitler had intended for his train connection to Salzburg, Austria. While we focused on the Obersalzberg bounty, the downtown folks went to plunder that train and found it filled with extravagant luxuries. Supposedly it contained stolen art, but the people we knew talked only about the fine cigars, champagne, cognacs, oils, olives, truffles, chocolates, cacao, and other fancy goods that they would barter with for years.

Some of the heists from Hitler's home became notorious throughout the valley. Maxl Brandner was a neighbor and owner of the bed-and-breakfast Haus Erika. The community had little respect for him because he had managed to avoid military service throughout the war. He was home when the looting began and arrived at the Berghof in time to grab Hitler's table silver. Later that summer Mutti, Ingrid, and I were tending our vegetable garden in the field next to Haus Erika when he came by to talk to my mother.

Suddenly he bent down and picked up a silver fork from the ground. More annoyed than embarrassed, he said that he must have dropped it when he buried Hitler's silverware in an unfinished bunker across the road.

Schiedinger, our shrewd old milk farmer, keeper of the village bull and some strong oxen, used his hay wagon for looting and was said to have at least one of Hitler's dinner sets hidden in his barn. As they tried to restore a semblance of order, the U.S. military authorities announced that looters should turn in these substantial and valuable items. A few barns and homes were searched, but I don't know if anything was ever recovered. In fact, the American soldiers, inveterate souvenir seekers themselves, took whatever they could get their hands on.

It was easy to forget specific events in the helter-skelter of those days, but some memories are indelible: I was sitting idly on my bed watching our sandy road on which even now nothing ever happened when I saw a brown ox clumsily pulling a cart down the hill. A farmer and two women walked alongside the rumbling wagon, and when they saw me one of them said to tell my mother that Frau Penzig had hanged herself from the rafters of her balcony.

I realized that the long, covered form on the flat bed of the wagon was the body of Frau Penzig. I ran outside, wanting to see how death had changed that face with its narrow mouth, sharp nose, and leathery, wrinkled skin. Mutti came out and told me to drop the corner of the blanket I had lifted up from the ghastly white face and go inside. The oxen began to pull again, and the farmer, his expression never changing, moved on. Maybe we all were numbed by six years of war, but aside from noting the fact that Frau Penzig had died, Mutti lost no words over her suicide.

Hitler's legacy had been wrought to a large extent here on our mountain. The wish that it would just go away was of course a pipe dream. The Allies were talking about at least twenty years of occupation; they refused to sign a peace treaty. Mutti and Tante Susi sighed and winced, realizing that this might entail most of the rest of their lives, if indeed we could survive the ordeal of the coming years. But most—and worst—of all, as we and all the world slowly learned about the full extent of Hitler's Final Solution, we realized that all Germans, no matter what they had suffered or whether they had participated in any way in the atrocities, would bear guilt, shame, and dishonor, probably forever.

Yet during that May 1945, instead of dark, gray clouds weeping over millions of shattered lives and bloody deeds, the sun shone brilliantly from a velvety, deep blue sky. The mountain meadows once again gloried in their coats of brightly colored buds and blossoms of an infinite variety, signaling rebirth. But my mother did not sing her spring songs this year. When I tried to sing by myself, I felt sad and empty, for inevitably my father's favorite songs came to me, and before I got to "und auf den Wiesen blühen die Blümlein rot und blau" (and on the meadows bloom the little flowers red and blue), I had to hide and cry. He was buried somewhere in France, and I was sure no one had planted a flower on his resting place. Who would have, for a soldier who had fought for Hitler?

part FOUR: 1945–1948

BITTER JUSTICE,
OR WILL JUSTICE BE DONE?

A HANGING IN NUREMBERG

On October 17, 1946, the day after eleven of the
accused twenty-two top Nazi leaders were hanged in
Nuremberg, Frau Dr. Imma Krumm, our new German
teacher, entered the classroom and, before her usual
"Guten Morgen, bitte setzen," said, "You probably
all know that, thanks to God, justice was done in
Nuremberg yesterday and the Nazi criminals met with
their deserved death." I nodded and then suddenly
saw that Bernhard Sauckel, who sat a few benches
ahead of mine, had fainted. Berndie was the son of
the notorious Gauleiter Bernhard Sauckel, head of
slave labor, and he had returned from Nuremberg the
day before, where, unbeknownst to us, he had said
good-bye to his father. Dr. Krumm saw him sink under
his seat, and, realizing why, went to help him up.

Most of us liked Berndie Sauckel, a funny little guy
with very small eyes and a heavy Saxonian accent.
An awful silence followed the incident, and in utter
confusion we tried in our minds to separate the
Berndie we knew from what his father had done. We
were kind to Berndie, and in return he was stoical
and brave. No other teacher touched on the topic of
Nuremberg and what it meant.

15 SURVIVAL UNDER THE STAR-SPANGLED BANNER

WAKING UP IN A VANQUISHED NATION WAS VERY different from the picture I once had of "after the war," at a time when "after the war" meant that Germany would be victorious and Vati would be back home. The terrain that lay ahead now was dark and unfamiliar; I was not sure there was a path, even the beginning of a path, to take forward. Everything behind us had been wrong, and everything before us was uncharted. What price would I have to pay before regaining a normal childhood? Would it be possible? Ever?

Of course it was not. My childhood was coming to an end, six years of it swallowed up by the war. Lately Wiebke and I noticed that our chests had developed hard knobs that would become our breasts, and we compared them, calling them by our code phrase, New Moon. The frenzy of those final days had subsided almost to the pace of stupor. We had no school, and would not for months. After chores we ambled through the Stadlerlehen remembering our games; miraculously we could play them now if we wanted, without fear of the Russians or air raids.

One sunny afternoon we watched wide-eyed as a couple of American soldiers rode on horseback down a meadow toward Frau Villnow's house. We cautiously moved into the woods to watch them dismount and enter the villa. The following day Frau Villnow was ordered to move out and found shelter in two rooms in a nearby house recently vacated by the fog soldiers. Seven American officers who were part of the Obersalzberg headquarters staff moved in. Within days a whole gang of neighborhood children had seized the chance to observe, at first from a safe distance, real Americans in a postwar setting. Their routine was the same every day. They would drive up in their jeep in the early evening, go inside, change out of their uniforms, and before we knew it come outside with a small white ball with stitched curves and a large leather mitt to play what they called "catch," which meant simply tossing the ball between them. Bewilderment set in when one of them told us that this was part of baseball and tried to explain the game, but we all got a turn with the mitt and the ball.

Aided by gestures as in charades, we overcame both the language barrier and our shyness to converse with the American soldiers, who seemed amused by our attempts to use our six months' worth of high school English. On the day President Roosevelt died the officers told us that they were very sad because "Roosevelt is *kaput,*" *kaput* (broken) being one of the few German words they knew. Intending to be funny, I said that we were not sad about that but that we were sad that Hitler was *kaput.* Everyone understood the joke and laughed except for one of the officers. He was a tall, serious man with black hair and dark eyes who had never exchanged a word with us and never smiled. We had nicknamed him Stalin because he objected angrily when one of the officers gave Ingrid a divine Butterfinger candy bar that she let me taste. A few years later it occurred to me that this soldier may have hated us because he was Jewish and knew what had happened to his people. This was pure conjecture on my part, a sign of the guilt we would carry as Germans, marked and hated. Frau Molsen, who to the irritation of some neighbors, including my mother, hung out a Dutch flag when the Americans arrived, had immediately aroused the interest of the officers. She found at least one of them, the white-blond Captain Bowles, socially acceptable and asked him to

U.S. troops raising the American flag at Haar, near Munich, where the German army's Group G commanded by Field Marshal Kesselring surrendered on May 5, 1945. This force had been poised to defend Berchtesgaden.

coffee. Mutti was of very mixed mind about our "fraternizing" with the victors, but she too was charmed by the Americans and our obvious pleasure in getting to know them.

Unwittingly the officers helped us to a bit of schadenfreude: Frau Villnow had hidden her silver in the ashes in the unused hot-water heater in her bathroom. Of course the Americans immediately ordered a sharp fire to heat the water for their hot shower and baths. Herr Dehmel, after the Volkssturm once again the caretaker, had to tell Frau Villnow that her silverware, made with her coat of arms in Berlin many years before, was now a lump of molten metal mixed with soot. Frau Villnow took the loss with stoic equanimity. People remembered that her demeanor had been the same at the death of her horses on the battlefield, the death of her two beautiful dogs, Goldie and Senta, who were shot by accident at the slaughterhouse, and the death of Hans Jürgen, her only son, who had died of diphtheria at the beginning of the war. "Typical Prussian," my mother said.

I don't recall how we celebrated my eleventh birthday or the deep sighs that would have accompanied my mother's wishes for my future. But to everyone's relief my nightmares seemed to have disappeared around that time. Gratefully we received the news that Selb too had fallen into U.S. hands and had avoided Russian occupation by a few miles. Onkel Hans had narrowly escaped from Norway on one of the troop-evacuation transports and was in a French prison camp. Germany was divided into four independently functioning zones, the American, British, French, and Russian, each under the corresponding military government with its own approach to postwar dealings with Germany and Germans.

The loot from the mountain was long since gone, and we were hungry most of the time. Many a day I would sneak off to our nearby garden to pluck a couple of finger-size carrots or a radish that did little to fill my empty stomach.

Meanwhile the Star-Spangled Banner was flying on Obersalzberg and the jeeps and U.S. Army trucks were parked where the S.S. had parked only a short time ago. The Platterhof was used

as a military headquarters until it became the Hotel General
Walker, an army recreation site. My friends Else and Gisela showed
me the remains of the small Hershey's almond chocolate bar that
one of the soldiers had given them there. The two girls had quickly
and without knowing it latched onto the principle of free enterprise, peddling old postcards of Berchtesgaden to the souvenir-
hungry GIs. Mutti as well as Frau Molsen strictly forbade us to go
up there to beg for candy, Mutti because she thought it humiliating
for German children to beg from the victors, Frau Molsen because
that simply was not done in her circle, an easy stand to take, since
by now the Molsens were receiving care packages from abroad.
Wiebke obeyed her mother, but I did not.

An escape from watching Ingrid and a fast walk once more up
the Obersalzbergstrasse brought me directly to the place where
the army trucks were lined up with American soldiers hanging
out their windows, chewing gum—I had no idea what it was they
chewed—and smoking what would soon be our currency: Lucky
Strike, Camel, or Chesterfield cigarettes. Some of the men busied
themselves with their vehicles, a few of them smiled, and one
waved to me. Not feeling brave at all, I waved back, smiled, moved
a little closer, and said in my best school English with its British-
Bavarian accent, "How do you do?"

The soldier with the cute crew cut grinned and without stopping his chewing said, "Just fine, and how're you?" He sounded
like he had a dumpling in his mouth. I took heart and stepped up
to the truck. He asked me where I lived, and using sign and body
language and all the English I could muster, I explained to him the
location of Haus Linden. After some banter he asked if I would in-
vite him to dinner at my home. I hesitated for a moment but, not
wanting to seem rude, invited him, realizing at that instant that
Mutti would have nothing to serve him. Besides, how would I explain meeting this soldier on the mountain? She would most likely
turn her back and give me a spanking right in front of him. I
glanced around, trying to devise a face-saving retreat, and must
have looked worried because he laughed and said that he really

didn't have time but would I like a Hershey bar and a pack of chewing gum? I blushed, suddenly feeling like a beggar. But then I rationalized that this was a gift from my new American friend, and I could not refuse without seeming very impolite. I reached up, said, "Thank you very much," curtsied, and ran off.

I went up to the parking lot one more time and came away with the pockets of my pinafore filled with caramels that stuck to my teeth and melted into the most delicious sweetness I had ever tasted. But it had been harder this time; my innocence was gone, and I felt embarrassed and manipulative. After that I never went again.

Mutti's list of things to do—existing only in her head of course—grew faster than any of us could move. During our breaks from chores, when I walked with Wiebke, we discussed not only our budding breasts but also the burning question of where babies came from, what rape meant, and what the roles of the man and the woman were in all of this. Nature was not to be stopped whether within our teenage bodies or on the mountain meadow already in full summer bloom and with bees ready to offer explanations. However, there was no way I could approach Mutti or she me on the topic of sex, and if Wiebke knew more than I did, she didn't tell. Another uncharted map spread before me.

The uncertainty over a fall opening of our schools convinced our mothers that unless they took action we would end up illiterate or at the very least unable to catch up to the next grade of high school. They explored the various skills available among themselves and the refugees arriving daily from the east. Before we could launch much of a protest we found ourselves in twice-weekly English lessons with Wiebke's old Tante Paula, who was renting a room in the same house that had taken in Frau Villnow. Else, Wiebke, Ingrid (the former Ruth), and I sat on Tante Paula's bed or the floor, putting our tongue gently between our teeth for a proper English "th," a sound Germans always manage to turn into a sharp "s." Herr Kutzner gave us lessons in arithmetic around the kitchen table in the house where he and his family from Silesia had found two rooms. He had been a high school math teacher before they were expelled from Breslau—now Wroclaw in Poland—and was glad to earn a little money for his efforts to keep our minds active.

Despite the lessons, I felt adrift in the wake of the collapsed Nazi belief system. I needed to belong somewhere, perhaps find a way to investigate why things happened the way they did, or at least find some guidance for the future. Two young clergymen, Pfarrer (Reverend) Kraus and Pfarrer Nauschütz, just back from the war, were newly assigned to the Lutheran community in Berchtesgaden, and after Mutti had taken in some jackets and shirts for both of them they became our friends. Mutti was thrilled when Pfarrer Nauschütz showed up one day with a large brown paper bag full of *Haferflocken* for porridge. Unfortunately the oats had been thrashed but not separated from the chaff. We had to spit out the sharp, spiky hulls while trying to eat the good parts of the hot cereal. It was sheer frustration, simply teasing my stomach rather than filling it, but Mutti kept on cooking the oats. Another time the pastors brought a bag of the new government-issued wood flakes made from the bark of beech trees. Not even Mutti succeeded in turning them into an edible product with either milk or water. Even the most vigorous chewing would result in nothing more than a hard clump that was impossible to swallow much less digest. The government's distribution of wood flakes soon ended.

It was not the occasional weird food they brought that drew me to the two clergymen but their effort to rebuild the Evangelische Jugend (Evangelical Youth) here in the diaspora of Bavaria. The number of Lutherans in each class—high school had started up again in January 1946, and I was in second grade—had dramatically increased due to the influx of the predominantly Lutheran refugees and people expelled from the eastern territories. Along with many of my Lutheran classmates I was eager to join the Evangelische Jugend, but much as the two pastors tried to get my mother back into the fold, she had no intention of rejoining the Protestant church. She would never forgive God for her fate—the two wars, the hardships, most of all the death of her husband—but she agreed to have Ingrid christened and to our attending the *Kindergottesdienst* (children's Sunday service).

Church was a refuge for many, very often for dubious reasons. Immediately after the surrender, conversions back to the Catholic church had become so frequent that Pfarrer Schüller, the Catholic parish priest, had announced a waiting time for returnees. Too many tried to hide their Nazi past beneath the mantle of religion, and highly visible, spectacular conversions of fanatics and those who had betrayed friends and benefactors were the order of the day. Just as some people, like Ruth's parents, had changed their children's names from biblical-sounding ones to Germanic ones, some were now changing them in reverse. Immediately after the war the name of one of my classmates was changed from Gotelinde (probably chosen in admiration of the Goths) to Gottlinde (presumably after a Christian god). In the end we simply called her Linde like the Linden tree that figures large in German romantic songs and myths. Everyone in town knew that Linde's parents had been notorious Nazis, who had denounced a wealthy local man for expressing doubts about the outcome of the war for which crime he was condemned to death. Dr. Kriss survived the end of the war in jail and became the first postwar mayor of Berchtesgaden. His informants, however, had at the same time suddenly become devout Catholics and ardently demonstrated their newfound beliefs. The family's swift conversion repelled many citizens and me as an example of hypocrisy, dishonesty, and immediate denial of an active Nazi past.

Shrewd adults quickly learned to say the politically correct things, but for the little people, like my sister, who had known nothing but childhood in the Third Reich, the change of regime and the difference in slogans were more difficult. On one Sunday morning Ingrid, just seven, and I sat among our friends in the front rows of the small, neo-Gothic evangelical church underneath a large oil painting of Christ rising into a bright blue heaven in a brilliant pink loin-and-shoulder cloth. Pfarrer Nauschütz was explaining that the "bad enemy," namely, the devil, was always trying to lead us into temptation and sin. He asked who could tell him what the bad enemy wanted. Ingrid promptly lifted her small hand and answered in a loud, high voice: "The bad enemy wants that our Führer should be dead." This embarrassment was too much for an older sister, and I wanted to sink into the ground. But Pfarrer Nauschütz simply thanked Ingrid, quickly turned away to hide a smile, and did not expel us from church as I had fully expected. I thanked God and prayed that He might enlighten Ingrid.

My newfound Lutheran belief in God was as deep and moving an experience as any young teenage girl could have. Through many years it brought me solace and hope and served as a beacon by which I tried to navigate the newly opening world. To belong to a large group of young people whose most important moral imperative was "Nie wieder Krieg" (never again war) and who wanted to bring healing after so much destruction was truly a gift. The evening meetings and Sunday services were the highlight and the comfort of my week, especially after the Nuremberg trials.

Every Tuesday evening twenty or thirty of us would sit on a wooden bench around a large square oak table in the community room at the parsonage. We read and discussed biblical texts, sometimes a parable or a contemporary anecdote. Naturally we turned to music to restore our spirits. We sang the chorales, cantatas, and Reformation songs by our beloved *Thomaskantor* Johann Sebastian Bach, the words of Mathias Claudius, Paul Gerhardt, Wolfgang von Goethe, and many nameless poets set to music opened my eyes once more to the beauty of summer and winter in the mountains and the possibility of finding my way.

> *Geh aus mein Herz und suche Freud*
> *in dieser schönen Sommerszeit*
> *an deines Gottes Gaben!*
> *Schau an der schönen Gaerten Zier,*
> *und siehe, wie sie dir und mir*
> *sich ausgeschmücket haben.*

(Go out my heart and seek joy
in this beautiful summertime
in your God's gifts!
Look at the lovely decorated gardens
And see how they have adorned themselves
For you and me.)

We rarely talked about the Nazi years during our meetings—a missed opportunity perhaps—but many in the group, especially the refugee children, were so traumatized and surrounded by so much misery that to provide solace in the Lord and uplift our souls was the most important task at hand. That and trying to actively help those who were suffering most, the refugees in the local camps, took priority. With cities destroyed, many of the twelve to thirteen million Germans who were forcefully expelled from German settlements in the east, including the Baltic, Poland, Czechoslovakia, and East Prussia, and those who had fled west before the Soviet army and from the Russian Zone, sought refuge in rural Bavaria.

The shortest way to school took me through the refugee camp, Lager Anzenbach. When room in private quarters had run out, the camp had been crudely clawed out of the ground and erected on an open place near the entry to the salt mines, and its dreariness depressed me each day. The long, brown one-story wooden buildings teemed with listless, thin, pale people who never smiled and rarely answered my greeting. On rainy days I saw the white faces of women and children pressed against the windowpanes. Our pastors were organizing an assistance project for the camp, and I volunteered immediately, convinced that my actions would have a great impact and bring me much gratitude. I was teamed up with Claudia Hepke, the daughter of refugees from Königsberg in Prussia, now living in a part of the former Speer house, and we were assigned a family. On a wet afternoon we made our way between the deep puddles and mud to the door of "our" refugees. A bent old woman wearing a black babushka around a blank, haggard face unstuck the door and let us in cautiously. Her husband sat on the one chair in the room. One leg of his pants was pinned up, for there was no leg for it to cover. It was dim inside, and it took us a while before we saw a little girl, perhaps four years old, sitting silently on the bare mattress of the lower bunk bed. She stared at us with a look emptier than that of her grandmother.

The two old people looked at us wearily, and when they finally understood that we had come to talk to them and try to help, they nodded and shrugged at the same time. The little girl, her blond hair stringy and unkempt, her dress ragged, sat there in the dim room and rocked her upper body—just like Hildegard—slowly back and forth. The moment we spoke to her she started to wail. She needed a dress and a comb and treatment for lice. The three of them needed everything, but mostly something to get rid of the large cockroaches that plagued them at night. The old man could not make it to the outdoor toilet during the night, and so they needed empty cans or a chamber pot. Once they started to talk it was as if floodgates had been opened. They told us in their heavy Silesian dialect that the mother of the little girl had been raped and killed in front of her by Russian soldiers during their flight west from Poland. The old man had been a coal miner, and he cursed Hitler and the rest of the world and could not understand what he had done to deserve this. Claudia and I left in shock, trying to figure out something, anything at all, we could do to help these people.

Mutti dug up a pretty piece of cotton fabric and helped me sew a dress for the little girl, and we collected a few meager pieces of clothing, an apron, and a pair of well-mended long johns, but no one had any spare clothes. We visited our family a few more times, and then with help from the pastors they were relocated. I had found the squalor and desperation extremely difficult to bear and was overwhelmed by the frustration of being able to do so little. Much to my relief, a glimmer of hope arrived by the next spring: Some of the refugees had begun to string little rag curtains across their windows, a few geranium cuttings in tin cans appeared on their doorsteps, and next to them small beds with vegetable seedlings. The men worked to repair the potholes, the doors, and the leaky roofs, while newer, better camps were under construction.

The endless radio broadcasts reciting a litany of names of lost and missing persons conveyed more despair than hope. The voice of the announcer was droning and monotonous, and the announcements were always the same—a name, age, home, army unit or status, and date last seen. Hundreds of thousands of men, women, and children, refugees, evacuees, former prisoners of the Nazis, POWs, possible concentration-camp victims, and those missing in action were listed and named. Anyone with any information was asked to contact the search service. Whenever we were near the radio we listened, just in case we heard a familiar name and knew something that might help.

In the American Zone the media were under the censorship of the U.S. military government, and most of our radio program was taken up with announcements of rules and regulations and with news reports that left us guessing about what was really going on. The zones were units that were far too small for any economic recovery, and the Allies were not yet certain that they wanted to create a greater German unit and under what conditions.

For the time being our minute domestic economy in the U.S. Zone, household by household, would be driven by American cigarettes. For Tante Susi, a nicotine addict, nothing was more important than a little tobacco to roll into a cigarette between her skilled fingers and then inhale deeply. So from the early days of the occupation I rushed out in the morning when curfew ended to gather the butts that the American soldiers had tossed away, proudly presenting them to a grateful aunt. With the high demand for the commodity, Lucky Strikes, Camels, and Chesterfields became the only viable currency in Germany. You could get almost anything, particularly food, if you paid with American cigarettes on the thriving black market. American soldiers who bought souvenirs were asked to pay in cigarettes instead of the worthless deutsche reichsmark. How many cigarettes one had to pay for edibles fluctuated with demand and supply. One pack might buy two pounds of butter or, if the market was flooded, only one pound. But where was one to get cigarettes? Mutti fretted.

We found the answer by way of our sleazy neighbor Maxl Brandner. He asked Mutti one day if she could paint; after all, her husband, Max, had been a painter. Mutti, by now a rather desperate opportunist herself, said yes, of course, at which Maxl offered her a part-time job in his new enterprise of producing wooden boxes decorated with small, Bavarian folk-art-style flowers for sale in the souvenir shops in town. He said he would pay in cigarettes. Without missing a beat Mutti said that we girls were pretty good at painting too, given that Max had been our father. The next day the three of us and several other women covered in big old aprons sat in Maxl's workroom—the former breakfast room for guests—and with the aid of cardboard stencils painted red, blue, yellow, and orange flowers, each with five petals and a green stem, on colored boxes. In the evening Maxl came to examine our work. Sometimes he looked askance at our output, saying that he doubted some of the boxes would bring more than a few cigarettes. However, at least for a while, everything sold—the GIs could not purchase much else in Berchtesgaden even with their powerful currency. Our access to cigarettes came in the nick of time, as Mutti had already used most of her spare china and the linens left from her dowry as barter and was often at a loss as to what to feed us.

Our prospects for cigarette income increased dramatically and in a way I least expected when, in the early summer of 1946, my mother announced that we would move to Haus Pfeilbrand on the other side of the Obersalzbergstrasse. I was stunned. I knew the beautiful, rather new-looking house she was talking about quite well, since I had at times gone there to drop something off for Frau Deil, who rented the upper two stories. We passed it when we went to work in our garden near the salt mines. If the owner of Haus Pfeilbrand was standing outside with his inevitable rubber-tipped walking stick, Mutti would ask him if we might pick dandelions

Haus Pfeilbrand, my stepfather's house and our new home.

along the fence for the two rabbits that now shared our woodshed with Madame Pimpernel, the hen. He would say, "Of course, help yourselves," and begin to talk a little haltingly about garden moles and the deer that came from the edges of the wood to feast on a few scraggly vegetables and even the roses.

Sebastian Pfnür, or Pfeil Wasti as he was known, coughed a great deal, blaming it on the harsh smoke that his tobacco plants yielded no matter how he dried and cured the leaves. We learned that he was a wood-carver who was just beginning to sell his carved elk, deer, and Bavarian dancers to the Americans for cigarettes. It seemed to me that this was not enough reason to up and leave Haus Linden. But Mutti was under pressure from the landlord, who needed a place for his daughter and her family to live. I don't know if she had an offer of marriage from Wasti when we moved, but there certainly was a new man in our life.

Wasti came from the Pfnür clan, who for hundreds of years had worked their farm the *Pfeillehen*. He had trained at Berchtesgaden School for Woodworking but without a job in the early thirties was recruited to work on Hitler's massive road-building project connecting Munich and Berchtesgaden. One day a large, square block of stone began to slide and crushed his leg. I always cringed when Wasti told us how his coworkers wanted to save his boot. In spite of his excruciating pain they had tried to take it off his bloody, swelling leg without cutting it open. At any rate, after two years of operations that salvaged some of the leg, he came home from a clinic in Munich outfitted with a cane and a clumsy leather-and-metal brace. A few years before the war he and his father had built Haus Pfeilbrand on a piece of the family land, intending to open a *Pension* (bed-and-breakfast). But the fickle nature of this short, seasonal income and a large mortgage had forced them instead to rent the two upper floors to the rich, recently widowed, and ardent Hitler admirer Frau Deil.

His disability had prevented Wasti from marrying, and he was one of the few men who were not even fit for the Volkssturm. He was a few years older than Mutti and lived on the ground floor of Haus Pfeilbrand with his father, Muchci, an alert, stern eighty-six-year-old devoutly Catholic man—then considered ancient. Muchei had farmed the *Pfeillehen* and worked during the day in the salt mines as a master cartwright until his oldest son took over and he moved with Wasti, his younger son, into Haus Pfeilbrand.

I considered my mother's decision to move into Haus Pfeilbrand a major betrayal of my father. Even before a wedding date was set I was sleepless over the questions of whether Wasti would wear my father's clothes, sleep in the same bed as Mutti, and, horror of horrors, ask us to call him Vati. If Mutti had any insight into the reactions that a teenage daughter might have to the news, she did not show it. As usual, we found no way to talk about her feelings or mine, focusing instead on the thousand practical details of the move. I must have been sour-faced most of the time because once she stopped what she was doing and told me that I would be much better off in Haus Pfeilbrand and that Wasti was a very kind man. She might have said that she was very lonely now that a few husbands were coming home; the close-knit community of women she had belonged to had become weaker and less supportive. Each family had to restructure relationships and adjust to new realities, and she too had to get on with her own life.

Moving day came, and since no civilian had a truck, much less gasoline, we moved our furniture and possessions in two trips on a hay wagon pulled by two Haflinger horses. I carried Findele (little foundling), my pretty calico cat, across the Obersalzbergstrasse to our new home. It would have been unthinkable for Mutti not to dig up the champagne in the garbage dump and bring it along in a rucksack hoping that someday in the future there would be cause for celebration.

The most remarkable thing about Haus Pfeilbrand was that the kitchen, pantry, and cellar contained not one bite of food of any kind except for a brown, half-filled *Salzfass* (salt cellar). The housekeeper who looked after the two men in return for a room had moved back to Ludwigshafen, and if she had left any food, it was gone when we got there. Mutti was stunned and searched the house several times in disbelief, but there would be nothing until the next food stamps came due. We were forced to share our loaf of bread, a small ceramic pot half full of rendered chicken fat, and a few eggs that Madame Pimpernel had laid. The next day, under the skeptical, watchful eyes of Grandfather Muchei, we moved the ugly ochre furniture from the Pfnür kitchen into the basement and replaced it with what fit of Mutti's white kitchen set. I could see on Mutti's face that under her charge *Ordnung* (order) would be created in this household. I could also see the slightly worried look on Wasti's face as he realized that asking my mother and her two daughters into his life would indeed change it.

The distance between Haus Linden and Haus Pfeilbrand was minimal, but I felt as uprooted as if I had moved to a different planet. I was sure that Mutti had replaced both Vati and me with this strange man, an invalid, and a Catholic at that, nondevout as it turned out he was. Muchei to the contrary was a devoted Catholic but perhaps because of the times pragmatism won out on all sides. They needed a woman in the house, and if his son had found one he loved, albeit Protestant, so be it. None of this appeased me. I was sure that Trudi, Tante Susi, Onkel Peppi, and even my play-mates on the other side of the road would be lost forever. Over-wrought and feeling deserted, I went back across the road that divided my world many times and, like a small child, hid in the woods behind Haus Linden weeping with self-pity. Waiting for me yet again was another body of uncharted water, the life of a step-daughter.

16 THE CURSE OF THE PAST

THE SUMMER OF 1946 FOUND US GLUED TO THE large black radio in Haus Pfeilbrand, listening to broadcasts of the International High Tribunal for German War Crimes in Nuremberg. Twenty-two of our most important former leaders were on trial. Our everyday worries and family dramas paled before the nearly incredible revelations contained in the daily reports from Nuremberg. I tried to listen to the full proceedings, but they were too lengthy and hard to follow, and so with the rest of my family I caught the daily summaries and, at the end, the final words of the condemned.

Mutti doubted that the men got a fair trial and joined those who said that most of them were "only following orders" and doing what Hitler wanted them to do in the best interest of Germany. This ridiculous position incensed me, and with vehemence and fury—high emotions seemed to be my trademark whenever I differed with my mother—I argued that these men had indeed been tried fairly and deserved nothing less than the death penalty. I even said that I was sorry they had but one life to give. It upset me that Göring escaped his own hanging with a vial of poison. This was the first time that the vast majority of the German public heard about the enormity of the crimes the Nazis, and therefore Germany, had committed. Albert Speer, who curiously received only a jail sentence, hoped that the trial of the "real" criminals might avert wholesale condemnation of the German people. He was not the only one to be so naïve.

The guilt of genocide would be upon all of us for generations.

Nothing could undo what had happened—the victims would n
come back to life, the survivors would never forget and probably
never forgive, and I would never make sense of it. Who had we become under the Nazi regime, and how was it accomplished? There
was no point in asking my mother. She had never contemplated
the danger Hitler posed, never thought beyond the great immediate need at the end of the twenties for someone, anyone, to end inflation, unemployment, and the nationwide disorder and violence
that marked the Weimar Republic.

I asked Mutti if she had read *Mein Kampf*. Not really, she said.
(Neither had I, of course, nor had I ever seen a copy of it in the
households I knew.) But she had readily bought into the myth of
the great German destiny and the right to *Lebensraum* in the east
expounded by the Nazi propaganda machine. Did she know of the
gas chambers? No. And no, she had never denounced anyone,
never hurt anyone, never preached hatred of Jews to us, never even
known any Jews personally. When my father left the Nazi Party
around 1933 (I do not know why), did she start to have doubts about
Hitler? No. She believed in him, his promise of jobs, security, dig-
nity, and purpose for all Germans. Only when the war began did
she and thousands of others have doubts, yet how could they not
support the fatherland in time of war? Patriotism, that misused
word that I began to hate, became the excuse for almost everything
that had transpired. Hadn't it bothered her that she lived in a dictatorship, that all democratic principles espoused by Weimar had
been sacrificed? She said that Hitler was democratically elected
after everyone had seen that a Weimar kind of democracy did not
work—an iron hand was needed. I was angry at her because she
would not be pinned down, admit guilt, admit that my newly found
convictions were better than her old ones. To be honest, it didn't really matter how she answered my questions. I was determined—as
only a fiendish adolescent can be—to blame her, my personal
scapegoat—for all the misery the Nazis had wrought, and for mine
specifically.

I realized only when he fainted in Frau Dr. Krumm's class on that

Fritz Sauckel *(fourth from right),* head of labor procurement, and other Nazi war criminals on trial in Nuremberg, summer 1946.

October day in 1946, after his father was hanged at Nuremberg, that Bernhard Sauckel, a boy I had paid scant attention to, was the son of one of the most notorious killers of the Third Reich. I pitied him but found it difficult to believe that he could have loved his father. We sat two kids to a seat, and more than half of our class consisted of refugees and evacuees. Berndie Sauckel was not the only one with a more-than-average Nazi history. On the girls' side sat the pretty, irrepressible, and funny Gisela Schmundt, daughter of Major General Rudolf Schmundt, one of Hitler's military advisors. Schmundt had been killed in the failed attempt to assassinate Hitler on July 20, 1944. He was not one of the assassins but had served the Führer. A few seats away from Gisela were the pale, quiet, and beautiful Armgard von der Schulenburg and her twin sister, Renate. They were the nieces of

Fritz Dietlof von der Schulenburg, one of the July 1944 conspirators executed by the Nazis after a show trial before the people's court. None of these children talked about their families, and judging by the way Mutti had tried to keep disturbing news from me, they may have been protected from knowing exactly what roles their parents played in the tragedies that occurred. Until the incident with Berndie I did not know or pay attention to a family's connection with Hitler. Every refugee and evacuated child in my class had his or her own history to bury as deep as possible. Claudia Hepke did not talk about her family's flight from East Prussia; Gisela Fiebing, always barefoot and with frostbitten hands, was silent about her past and her present life; Irmgard Koll, my special friend, just said that she and her siblings lived here with an aunt because they were bombed out in Cologne.

The Nuremberg trials had focused on the top Nazi leadership, and several more trials were held there for that purpose. But general *Entnazifizierung* (denazification) in the American Zone (each of the occupation powers developed its own method of dealing with ex-Nazis) cast a wide net intended to catch even the smallest fish—the bystanders, the *Mitläufer* (those who ran along). In the end we were convinced that all too often the really guilty, the big fish, escaped unpunished. Volumes of questionnaires were to be filled out by all twelve million adults in our zone. After a U.S.-controlled review, five categories or degrees of guilt or nonguilt were established. Of the respondents almost three million were to go before German-run denazification committees. Our despair over the endless stream of paper that arrived at our doors finally turned to laughter, and we joked that the first of the 131 questions were always "Are you alive? If yes, why?" Actually, these would have been the pertinent questions. Why indeed were we alive when fifty million human beings had died, six million in the Holocaust alone?

One day out of the blue Mutti said that she remembered hearing about one Jewish woman, the wife of a banker in Selb, who had vanished. The husband was said to be distraught and may have committed suicide. She said that at the time she did not know what to make of the rumors, and anyway no one really wanted to get involved for fear of endangering or merely inconveniencing themselves. It happened at a time, Mutti said, when you could no longer launch a protest on the street, write a letter to the newspaper, or turn to the church for support. I didn't believe her, deciding instead that one of the main sins of my parents' generation was that they *chose* not to look at the dark side, and to whitewash their Führer no matter what. If given further indoctrination, what would I have done in their stead? What would I have done if Germany had won the war? Would I have gone to an Adolf Hitler school and become a Nazi leader, a torturer like Ilse Koch, the notorious wife of the commandant of Buchenwald? Such questions obsessed me. I dared not answer them; I truly did not know.

"It serves me right, fool that I was," said my Pöhlmann grandfather when he heard that he had to undergo the lengthy denazification process before the *Spruchkammer* (German-run denazification committee), which delayed the license to reopen his carpentry shop. He had not told Mutti that after resisting the Nazi regime for so long, he had joined the Nazi Party in the late fall of 1944, about six months before the end. He had been desperate because obtaining work and lumber had become conditional on being a Party member. Now in the aftermath all Party members born before 1919 were automatically brought before the denazification committee. We were shocked that of all people he should be penalized, an irony that was not lost on us. I found myself agreeing that he was a fool and should have stood firm to the end. At the same time he impressed me with his attitude toward his "denazification." He didn't complain or feel unjustly persecuted, as did most of the small-time Nazis, even though it took months before his turn came and he was finally declared *nicht belastet* (not burdened) and could begin to work again.

Wasti, meanwhile, was dealing with a peculiar post-Nazi situation over his motorcycle. He had, toward the end of the war, bought the machine with a sidecar to get around more easily, as even with his lame leg he had been assigned to collect contributions to the Nazi winter assistance fund on Salzberg. After the war the motorbike—unneeded and without gasoline—stood rather in the way on the concrete side porch, where Ingrid and I would pretend to ride it. The original owner of the bike, a Communist, had returned from a concentration camp and begun a vendetta against Wasti. Not only did he want the bike back, he was demanding financial retribution from Wasti, who had bought the bike with his own money from some government agency. After a drawn-out court battle the case was settled. Wasti did not have to pay, but he did have to return the bike.

My future stepfather was definitely unlucky in his quest to become motorized. Just before the war he had paid the final installment on a Volkswagen, which Hitler had promised every German for an affordable price. It was, after all, to be the "car for the people." As soon as war broke out, the Volkswagen factory was converted to war production; nobody ever received a car. After the war Wasti joined a class-action suit against the new Volkswagen Corporation, and years later, after the devaluation of the reichsmark, he received 10 percent of his money minus the costs of participating in the suit. But the Volkswagen affair upset him far less than the personal attack on his integrity over the motorcycle.

Another difficult issue we heard about constantly was *Demontage* (dismantling) of even peaceful German industries in all zones. We came to see this as an act of pure revenge and the death knell to any economic recovery for generations to come. Mutti shook her head in despair when she heard the name of a familiar business, perhaps a watch or shoe manufacturer, being dismantled and shipped abroad. Most of the dismantled industry ended up in Russian hands, since Stalin had insisted that his country had suffered the most. The practice of *Demontage*, especially in the British Zone, continued for years after the war.

□   □

THE SUMMER OF 1946 HAD BEEN relentlessly hot. Forest fires burned on several large, inaccessible mountain slopes, sending acrid smoke wafting through the valley. Aside from picking berries on mountain slopes and in sunny clearings, we had not gone on a single hike all season. When a rapidly approaching autumn broke the heat, Mutti, Ingrid, and I set off early one morning to climb Kehlstein and finally get a close look at the Eagle's Nest. From the old trails we looked down on the ruins of Obersalzberg and up toward the ridges of Hoher Göll and Brett already dusted with snow. Perhaps the huge elevator inside the top of Kehlstein that had taken Hitler and his entourage into the center of the house was not functioning or available to us. At any rate, we walked the final stretch on a narrow, black-topped path. A group of American civilians on their way down stopped to let us pass. They smiled, and one of them, looking exhilarated and very pleased with himself, stated, "Wir sind bis zum Spitz spaziert" (We walked up to the very top). Mutti's face turned from a standoffish frown to a smile, partly because she was amused by the nonidiomatic German sentence, but mostly because here was something very simple we could share: the joy of climbing a mountain. She pointed out into the valley and said in her best English, "It is very beautiful. Yes?" While I tried hard not to be embarrassed by her pronunciation, we smiled some more at one another and said good-bye.

Our smiles faded as we approached the pompous, forbidding facade of the Eagle's Nest. Inside, most movable items had been taken except for a few massive, upholstered chairs and a huge Oriental rug in the large central living room. American soldiers had used their pocketknives to cut flowers and exotic animals out of the rug and the upholstery for trinkets—barbarisches Benehmen (barbarian behavior), some indignant Germans were calling it. Mutti said loudly that we had other things to worry about than keeping Hitler's rug intact. She was in great form that day.

When we got back home my good mood allowed me to realize that Haus Pfeilbrand, nestled at the foot of Obersalzberg and Kehlstein, actually had a particularly grand and open view in all directions. It was a handsome house, with wide balconies, green shutters, and strong, reddish wood planks covering the upper two

Kehlstein with the Eagle's Nest, summer 1946.

stories. A HAUS PFEILBRAND sign with a wreath of alpine flowers carved by Wasti hung from the balcony, now almost hidden by Frau Deil's still thriving begonias. No one would have suspected that Haus Pfeilbrand was teeming with refugees and evacuees.

On the ground floor, where we lived, there were only two bedrooms, a kitchen, and a living/dining room. Grandfather Muchei and Wasti occupied the bedroom that looked out on Untersberg and the motorcycle on the porch. Until the wedding Mutti had her own room, already furnished with the old flame-colored bedroom set from Haus Linden. She had succeeded in convincing the housing authorities that Ingrid and I needed our own bedroom on Frau Deil's second floor, which reduced that lady's quarters to one room. We approached our room via the balcony and out of politeness were very quiet when we used it, since only a locked connecting door separated us from Frau Deil. The other new tenants in Haus Pfeilbrand were two elderly couples bombed out in Munich, an unmarried couple from Breslau (now Wroclaw) in Silesia, and a young woman from somewhere in Pomerania. Some got along and some did not, causing Frau Deil, who bore the brunt of the invasion into her domain, endless heartaches. I did not feel sorry for her.

The harvest from unfertilized and destroyed fields was meager that fall of 1946, and there were not enough men, tractors, trucks, or fuel to bring it in. With mass starvation predicted, the U.S. Army made trucks and men available to help secure at least the crucial potato harvest. I read about it in the local paper and was so impressed, even moved, by the assistance that I wrote an essay about it in school. This essay became especially memorable because the *Studienrat* (title for a *Gymnasium* teacher) in response to my question as to how one spelled *Katastrophe* (catastrophe) recommended that I use the German word *Unglück* (bad luck) instead. Without defending my need to know, I accepted his advice even though it turned my sentence into nonsense. I was as stuck in my fear of opposing authority as he was in the Nazi dictum to use only words with German roots.

The Americans also provided children with a hot school meal every day, a much needed and appreciated act of charity. We called it *Schulspeisung* (school meal), but Mutti called it *Quäkerspeisung*, remembering post–World War I food assistance by U.S. Quakers. Army trucks delivered large containers of thick, hot soup or hot chocolate and white rolls to the centrally located *Hofbrauhaus* (court brewery). The bigger boys at the high school took turns wheeling the fragrant containers that looked like garbage cans up some steep steps to our school. They ladled out our portions too, which gave them power, and favoritism was not unheard-of. Max Sagaster, Rolf Weinberger, and a couple of other boys always filled my cup to the brim or even slipped me an extra roll. Max sat next to me in class and tended to invade my half of the desk space with his long arms and big elbows. Perhaps he tried to make up for this— and also stop my griping about it—with an extra spoonful of soup. So easy was corruption. After the meal we washed our enamel cups with cold water and hung them on hooks for the next day.

The only way to transform Wasti's hard-earned cigarettes into food was to take the early train out of the mountains into the farm-land for trading. Mutti, Ingrid, and I got off the train in villages like Dingolfing, retrieved our pull cart from the last wagon, and set off toward the farms, if possible in the opposite direction of the rest of the *Hamsterers* (literally, people behaving like hamsters). We kids, barefoot and in short summer dresses with let-out hems, walked gingerly behind my mother, for I was scared of the dogs that guarded most farms. They were not set upon us, but at their bark alone I became a complete coward, while Ingrid usually made friends with them and the assorted yard cats.

We would ask the farmer or his wife for a drink of water in hopes of being offered milk, and then Mutti would ask if they had butter, eggs, flour, or apples to exchange for cigarettes. Sometimes a farmer was already flush with cigarettes and told us to move on. One day at lunchtime a farm woman offered us a plate of soup in her kitchen. I saw Ingrid wrinkling her nose in disgust and no-ticed that an army of black kitchen flies had either drowned in the soup or were struggling to escape. "You can't be that hungry if you can't eat my soup," the woman said when she noticed our reluc-tance to eat. "You better get off my farm." We walked on, and I prayed that I would not eventually have to eat dead flies.

Further on we passed a beautiful, fenced apple orchard with hundreds of ripening apples beyond our reach. The only person coming our way on the rutted country road was a man in worn-out work clothes on an old bike. He got off his bike and said, "Would you like some apples? Come on, I'll open the fence for you and you may pick as many as you want." When Mutti asked if the apples were his, he assured us they were. We needed this good turn because Ingrid and I were getting very cranky and Mutti was dispirited by this particularly unprofitable day. The farmer opened a gap in the fence and helped us shake the branches of a tree. Suddenly he looked around and, swift as lightning, hopped on his bike and pedaled off at high speed. A very angry man came running through the orchard and demanded to know what the hell we were doing stealing his apples. Mutti, quite shaken, told him the truth about the man who had claimed to be the owner, and the rightful owner calmed down and even let us fill our small suitcase with the fruit. Then he took us home to his farm, and we ended the day with full rucksacks.

Train passengers' luggage had become the target of increased inspections designed to discourage the booming black market. If your luggage was searched, you could easily lose the entire treasure accumulated over a hard day. Indeed, that evening the inspector looked suspiciously at our suitcase and rucksacks and asked Mutti what was inside. Without missing a beat, displaying nothing of German honesty, she said, "The children's clothes." He looked at us, gave a knowing nod, and moved on. I was certain that I was on the verge of something akin to a nervous breakdown from all these humiliations and close calls. But when we got home, unpacked our loot, and regaled Wasti and Muchei with our adventures, we began to laugh at the absurdity and ironies of the day. It was the laughter that helped me face another *Hamster* trip.

Lack of food, lack of medical care, and our general anxiety had left us in an appalling state of health. Ingrid was thin, small, and afflicted with stomach trouble; Mutti had developed a life-threatening carbuncle on her leg; I had several boils on my head that were infected by lice and had been diagnosed with tuberculosis that summer. Each affliction was a small crisis, for we had no medication, most notably no penicillin yet. Dr. Oberndörfer, walking on foot from patient to patient, lanced Mutti's carbuncle in the nick of time. My head was half shaved and the crusty infections were opened and cleaned. I fainted during the procedure, not from pain but from the thought of the boils and the lice, which were finally brought under control. My case of tuberculosis was light, requiring rest and extra food. Like fools we rejoiced in the "good" fortune of a diagnosis that entitled me to small additional rations of white bread, milk, and butter. We thought that if the tuberculosis was curable it certainly would be cured here, where for years people from around the world had come to heal their lungs in the mountain air. A few years later, the doctors told me the infection had become encapsulated, remaining as a mere shadow on my lungs.

□   □

KRAETZE, A SEVERE SKIN RASH caused by malnutrition, had developed all over the scrawny bodies of the two men in the household. The itchy irritation plagued them all day long. Muchei, steeped in old Catholic traditions, insisted that Wasti pray with him in unison before and after every noon meal. After a number of rounds of Hail Mary and Our Father the *Kraetze* on their hands began to itch, and they would rub their hands and entwined fingers against each other to alleviate the agony. We sat still and waited while the men prayed, and I watched the daily battle of piety against *Kraetze* unfold. Muchei, more stoical and obviously with a higher tolerance for itching than Wasti, contained himself after a while and held still. Then, however, he became infuriated by his son's continuing, intense rubbing of his folded hands, and when gestures failed to stop him the old man would stomp his cane on the floor. All the while they continued to murmur their prayers. By the last amen the soup was cold and we sat down to eat.

Shortly before Mutti and Wasti were, after review of their questionnaires, judged to belong among the mere *Mitläufer,* indicating a low degree of Nazi involvement, an American soldier arrived at our door to verify some facts and signatures on one of the questionnaires. After he left we noticed that he had forgotten his beautiful Parker fountain pen. It was burgundy red with a gold cap and elegantly streamlined compared with our old fountain pens that no longer worked. We put the pen in safekeeping for a while, but when the soldier did not return for it I was allowed to use it in school. One sleety, icy day I sat on my school pack to slide down the unsanded, steep part of the Obersalzbergstrasse. I lost my pen out of the pack. I was certain that a young neighbor woman who came slipping down the mountain behind me must have found and kept it.

I will always remember that pen. It was the most beautiful thing I had ever owned. It seemed to have come from a country of unfathomable wealth, where the roads must indeed be paved with gold.

17 ESCAPE FROM DARKNESS

So wollen wir gemeinsam ans Werk gehen, gebeugt, tief gebeugt, aber—meine Damen und Herren—nicht gebrochen! (Let us now begin to work together, humbled, deeply humbled, but—ladies and gentlemen—not broken.)

—KONRAD ADENAUER, OCTOBER 1, 1945, BEFORE THE FIRST POSTWAR MEETING OF THE COLOGNE CITY COUNCIL APPOINTED BY THE BRITISH MILITARY GOVERNMENT

The old Pfnür farmer dealt quite calmly with the fact that his son was about to marry a Protestant widow with two children to boot. From the day in May 1946 on which we moved into Haus Pfeilbrand he seemed as kind and welcoming as could be expected of a mountain man of few words. For her part, my mother, probably not caring one way or another, committed to be married in a Catholic ceremony and promised to raise any child born to the union in the Catholic faith.

Deeply engaged in the Protestant youth movement and proud to be living in the diaspora, to be heir to Luther's Reformation, I, however, was doubly hurt by what I considered a defection from our original family religion. I firmly resolved not to attend the church wedding, to run away or otherwise hurt my mother, the traitor, the betrayer, and the unfaithful wife of my father. My mood darkened still more when Trudi became engaged to a young man who was recovering from a lung injury in Berchtesgaden and seemed to receive all of her attention. Visits to Tante Susi now re-

Onkel Peppi carving wooden sculptures to be paid for with American cigarettes, 1947.

quired a walk instead of a run upstairs, and with chores and school they became infrequent. When Onkel Peppi came back from Fürstenfeldbruck he had opened a wood-carving workshop in a tiny, unoccupied cottage, down where the Obersalzbergstrasse began to steepen at the first curve. Soon he sold as many sculptures as he could carve, sitting by the window for anyone, especially Americans, to watch. Naturally, Tante Susi no longer needed cigarette butts, making my early-morning dashes to gather them superfluous.

My friendship with Wiebke had also cooled since we moved to the other side of the road. Even before that I had felt slighted by her when she rode up the mountain in the convertible of a visiting uncle—the first privately owned car I knew about—and did not wave to me, much less have him stop to give me a ride. Wiebke was the first girl I knew who wore a pair of pale blue, long, silky-looking pants instead of a skirt for play one day. It had probably arrived in a care package, and I found myself critical of her switch to such outright American attire. The transition from German, Nazibred provincialism to a freer outlook on life, including fashion, hairdos, and cosmetics, was not automatic, even for a rebellious teenager like myself. I had, of course, gathered new best friends who brought fresh perspectives and interests to my present life, but I still missed Wiebke and the time with her in the Stadlerlehen park, our secret garden, our secrets themselves.

Ingrid seemed ready to make friends with our future stepfather and the old grandfather and ignored my coaching to maintain a cool distance. She was even ready to call Wasti, Vater (father), or rather its Bavarian version, Vata; I comforted myself that at least it was not Vati, which would have been the final straw.

A wedding was planned for November 1946, though the prospects of having a lavish feast in this time of extreme scarcity were not good. Cigarettes did not buy much in Berchtesgaden, and Wasti could only carve so many of his beautiful figures. Mutti had to carry her few last pieces of nice chinaware from shop to shop, pleading with shopkeepers in empty stores to save us tiny extra portions of butter and rendered fat, a piece of cheese, a little sugar, and some eggs for a cake. The only item that was not a problem was liquor. Mutti, of course, still had the bottles of champagne and wine that the S.S. had handed out through the barrack windows. The Berchtesgaden Hofbrauhaus was open and running, perhaps for the benefit of American soldiers, who greatly appreciated the fresh beer. The sickly sweet smell of hops and fermented grain filled the air on brewing days, signaling that I had to walk to town and fetch a pail of the grain wastes to feed our chickens.

For the wedding feast we planned to roast the fattest of our many rabbits. In the fall, after the last hay harvest, we let the rabbits out of their cages every morning to forage in the meadows and then rounded them up at night. Just before the wedding the biggest rabbit, slated for the wedding table, could not be found and Mutti was very upset at the prospect of having to kill two small ones instead. However, the day before the wedding Ingrid saw the rabbit moving in a bit of fresh snow under the lilac bush. Guided by her hungry stomach, she immediately told Mutti, only to weep when the animal was captured, killed, and served.

Onkel Hans and Tante Emma had arrived from Selb, having been granted a permit to travel beyond the imposed mileage limit for special family occasions. Onkel Hans had been released from his French prison camp in June, but we had not seen him since my grandmother died. We knew the two would arrive with a suitcase filled with discarded, cracked china from the dumps in back of the factories just so we could, even now, have a traditional Selb *Polterabend*. The night before the wedding Ingrid and I joined in the raucous custom of tossing and breaking china outside the kitchen door. The bride and groom then had to sweep the pieces up jointly, symbolizing cooperation and togetherness, even in messy situations, I guessed. Also, the shards would, according to old superstitions, bring the couple good luck.

Wasti's friends and relatives, most just back from the war, came to celebrate his belated betrothal. They showed up with bottles hidden under their jackets, one with a huge accordion, all fully intending to forget themselves in a drunken feast. No one mentioned the war or the present hardships, and no one left before the next morning's curfew was lifted at 6 A.M. On this night before the wedding Rottl Sepp, the accordion player, played anything he could think of, and Onkel Hans danced and flirted outrageously with the former housekeeper of Pfeilbrand, who had managed to come from Ludwigshafen.

I tried to sleep but again and again heard Onkel Hans singing his favorite drinking song, "Drum Brüder wir trinken noch eins, wir sind ja noch so jung" ("So, Brothers, Let Us Drink One More, for We Are Yet So Young"), and everyone falling in with voices heavy from wine. Finally the house went still except for the occasional sounds of retching and snoring coming from the guests laid out on sofas and pillows on the floor. I was disgusted and doubly bitter about my mother's marriage. It was clearly a sellout, not just of our religion but of our values.

A little after six in the morning loud explosions erupted in the raw November air. The comrades of my stepfather-to-be had assembled outside with their old, wooden *Böller* (pistols) that they had once again received permission to use, this time from the American authorities. They were bringing the traditional salute to the bride and groom on their wedding day, and someone rewarded them with morning schnapps. Wasti and others slept through the commotion. Muchei, the only one who had remained stone sober, lost his temper and beat his cane fiercely over his son's feather bed to wake him. Wasti came to with a jerk and began to dress. Mutti was already dressed in a black wedding gown that Wasti confessed he hated. She had made it from two of her mourning dresses— one of crepe de chine and one of shiny silk. Sadly beautiful, my mother's thin face was as white as a linen sheet. She wore a flower brooch of yellow amber that Vati had given her on the day of their engagement and the silver-fox stole from Norway.

The unaccustomed amount of alcohol accompanied by little food in malnourished bodies had taken its toll. Wasti was just barely ready when the black wedding carriage pulled by two skimpily decorated horses arrived. He looked ill and wan in his dark suit. It was about four sizes too big, but at least it was not my father's. I had sworn I would not attend the wedding, but in the morning I changed my mind after all and came along to the ceremony just to show that I did not care one way or the other.

The fog lay light gray and motionless over the valley, but the mountains were clear and winter white. Grandfather Muchei, Ingrid, and I rode the downhill stretches with the couple in the open carriage; even with the cover over our knees we were shivering. Tante Emma, Onkel Hans, and the Pfnür relatives from the farm in their best, festive national costumes had already set out to walk to church, and as we arrived on the castle square the bells in the towers of the *Stiftskirche* began to peal their announcement of the wedding mass. Mutti and Wasti went around to the sacristy to sign the church ledger. No booklet for family records was handed to them, and it did not matter what race they were. We had walked through the arches of the main gate into the tall, cold nave, our steps echoing on the red marble floor. A large crowd began to gather. I felt like crying and sat down in the back of the dark church to think my dark thoughts.

The high mass celebrated for my mother and stepfather's wedding seemed to go on forever. When the newly married couple finally turned away from the altar and began to walk down the marble steps to take their seats in the front row, my stepfather, obviously still under the influence, walked straight ahead into the air.

My mother marries Sebastian (Wasti) Pfnür on November 23, 1946.

Only thanks to my mother's fast grip and yank on his arm did he find his footing and avoid falling down the altar steps. I was mortified and hoped that no one else had noticed the incident.

On the way home only Grandfather Muchei was allowed to stay in the carriage on the steep parts of the road, while the coachman, newlyweds, Ingrid, and I walked and pushed to assist the skinny horses. A small group of lunch guests made their way back to Haus Pfeilbrand, and the women, including Mutti, rushed to cook the wedding meal of potato dumplings, sauerkraut, and roasted rabbit. Throughout the afternoon well-wishers dropped by and brought small gifts: myrrh and rosemary plants, a piece of shaped butter decorated with a sprig of green, a small envelope with black pepper or paprika, a side of bacon from Wasti's sister Lisi, and a pound of real coffee. The coffee was a sensation. It had been smuggled through the connecting salt-mine tunnels from Austria to Germany. Visitors toasted the couple with schnapps, and the day ended quietly and peacefully. Trudi brought out her zither and the women sang "Fein sein, beinander bleiben" ("Be Virtuous, Stay Together") and other old Bavarian wedding songs. Onkel Hans looked peevish. He didn't dare to start his drinking songs or, for that matter, his drinking. From what I could gather, he had been a little too flirtatious with his dance partner from Ludwigshafen and the women, firmly siding with an offended Tante Emma, were having no foolishness this evening.

On her wedding day Mutti had worn the brooch given to her by Vati. She had brought the flame-painted, ugly bedroom set from that first marriage, and a large photo portrait of Vati that had hung over their bed in Haus Linden now hung over the bed she shared with Wasti. He was too kindhearted a man to deny her wishes; still, after a few beers he would tell anyone who would listen that he and his wife had to sleep under his predecessor's picture. It was still there when he died of lung cancer in that very bed many years later. For Mutti this marriage was not so much a hopeful new beginning as an attempt to gain some kind of footing in a changed world. She must have felt lucky to have found a man who loved her deeply and was totally committed to her. She gave the marriage all she could, and that was enough to make it a solid and friendly partnership.

□ □

IN THE SUMMER OF 1947 I realized that Mutti was pregnant. She must have known how I would feel about it because for months she tried to hide her belly under the pinafores of her faded and worn dirndl dresses. At thirteen I was indeed embarrassed and unhappy about a new sibling for whom, in my opinion, she would have neither clothing nor food.

Tante Emilie came by train from Kassel to attend the birth of Mutti's third daughter. My mother's contractions began at around 2 A.M. on November 4, 1947. Vater—I too called him that by now— walked across the snowy field as fast as his bad leg allowed to reach the farm with the public phone. The midwife, Frau von Stetten, was attending a birth elsewhere, and no one was prepared to head into the curfew hours of this unfriendly night without proper credentials or at least some idea of birthing.

Distraught, Vater arrived home in time to help Tante Emilie light the iron stove in the living room for a little warmth and hot water. At this point the electricity went out. My mother tried to hold the baby back, even using her hand, and pleaded with it, "Wart halt noch ein bisserl mein Muckele" (Wait just a little, my Muckele). To no avail. My baby sister pushed forward and was born in spite of her mother's urging into the glow of a homemade candle's light. No owls had hooted. Perhaps that was a good sign.

Mutti, gravely ill after the delivery, recovered gradually, and her milk came in slowly. Vater and Grandfather Muchei were delighted with the new child. The day she was born Muchei added an extra set of Ave Maria and Our Father for the baby to the mealtime prayers and we waited still longer for our lunch.

The baby was, as Mutti had promised, baptized in the Catholic church and given the good old name Elisabeth, shortened by Grandfather Muchei to Lisl. I gave her the name Lumpenkind (rag

My mother with my half sister, Elisabeth, at about one year.

child), because of the ridiculous assortment of clothes that were put on her for lack of real baby clothes. Tante Emilie thought that Lumpenkind was very funny and appropriate for the times, but luckily it did not stick. (Elisabeth, however, never forgot the name I gave her.) Months later I finally agreed to hold Elisabeth and feed her a bottle. The event was so important to Mutti that she wrote a letter to Tante Emilie about it, saying how happy she was.

Aside from this moment of maternal happiness for Mutti, the winter of 1947–48 was one of survival at a minimal level, and we wondered how much longer we could live under such desperate conditions. The complexity of Allied power politics and strategies in dealing with postwar Germany and the other war-ravaged European countries largely escaped us. We welcomed the fact that in the fall of 1946 the United States and Britain had agreed to combine their zones into Bizonia, an economic entity that would allow Germany a better chance at becoming self-sufficient at some point in the future. The French and Russian zones, for different reasons, remained separate.

By the spring of 1948 rumors and radio reports began to mention the Marshall Plan but left us guessing what it would mean for us. We had no idea that this U.S.-financed plan would be the most comprehensive and costly reconstruction and aid program the world had ever seen, providing loans for rebuilding Europe's destroyed industrial capacity, including Germany's. Skeptics worried what it would cost us. We sensed that fundamental changes were in the air with events that became as dramatic and important for our future as the end of the war itself.

In May 1948 I celebrated my fourteenth birthday. By this time schoolwork had become quite peripheral to my life. Still in constant rebellion against my mother's control and influence, I admired the American women who smoked on the street and wore bright lipstick and nail varnish. Most of all I loved the American big-band music performed by U.S. Army bands on the castle square and played on the radio. One time I stole a pack of Lucky Strikes from my mother's stash and with some friends lit up in the woods behind Haus Pfeilbrand. My first attempt at smoking made me very sick to my stomach, and I decided not to try it again.

Beneath all the bravado I remained a committed Lutheran. My confirmation on Palm Sunday of that year in Berchtesgaden's Lutheran church had been a deeply religious experience for me. I wore a black dress sewn by Mutti from my Pöhlmann grandfather's wedding suit. Frieda, my godmother, had come from Selb, and since she could not give me the traditional present of a first wristwatch, she gave me a bright green, imitation-leather handbag that I found very ugly and never used. Trudi, Tante Susi, and a few other adults who had watched me grow up came to share in our *Kaffee und Kuchen* party at a table set with linen and what remained of Mutti's best porcelain.

A few months later the French finally agreed to fuse their zone with Bizonia, and on June 20, 1948, the momentous day arrived when the worthless reichsmark was devalued and the deutsche mark was introduced in the three western zones. The event deprived Stalin of his hope to keep Germany weak and neutral, prompting him to introduce a separate devaluation in the Russian Zone and blocking all land access to Berlin, the four-zonal city deep within East Germany. Mutti cried inconsolably when this part of Hitler's legacy for the country she so loved came to pass. The border of the Russian Zone that had until then allowed streams of desperate East Germans to flee west now became almost impermeable. Nevertheless, risking their lives, Mutti's old friend Ilse Höfig, widow of the porcelain painter Walter Höfig, fled from Dresden with her two girls, Inge and Ursel, to find a safe haven in Berchtesgaden. She told of people who disappeared overnight, of starvation and unspeakable living conditions there— far worse than they were under the Nazis during the war. And while we were ever more grateful to have fallen into American hands, we feared for our friends and relatives in the Soviet Zone.

On the day of the *Währungsreform* (currency reform) Mutti and Vater went downtown to receive brand-new, crisp bills in the amount of forty deutsche marks per person—no less, no more. The effect of the devaluation was stunning. Overnight boards that had covered display windows of the stores in town came down to expose an abundance of merchandise such as I had never seen before. My joy at this sudden plenty was mixed with anger that merchants had hoarded these desperately needed goods for months to benefit from a rumored new currency. However, our family had D.M. 240 to spend and make last until we could generate income and receive our orphans' pension in new money. An almost set order of purchase priorities prevailed, and not only within our family. First everybody dashed out to buy food—still rationed, of course, but suddenly available—then shoes, socks, underwear, and meters of different fabrics and wool for knitting. Ready-made was years off, but dressmakers and tailors, including Mutti, were overwhelmed with customers. The *Währungsreform* was truly the beginning of new hope and a new life, alas, without East Germany.

Political tension between East and West—soon to be called the cold war—did not let up. Defying Stalin's blockade of land access to Berlin, the United States faced down the Soviets with their unprecedented airlift of absolutely everything the western sector of this city needed to survive. No German would soon forget this determined action.

I was, of course, too young to vote, but as early as the fall of 1945 adults had been allowed by the military government to cast their vote in local elections. Turnout was high, and even Vater had limped down the mountain each time to cast his vote for mayor, town council, or county executive. Rebuilding democracy at the local level first made eminent sense and provided us with a small measure of local empowerment. However, it took until 1949 before the first federal elections were called in the united American, British, and French zones that from then on would be known as the Deutsche Bundesrepublic (German Federal Republic). The first contest for the chancellorship took place between Konrad Adenauer of the newly established Christian Democratic Union Party (CDU) and Kurt Schumacher, representing the Social Democratic Party of Germany (SPD). Konrad Adenauer narrowly won the election and became the first postwar chancellor of the new republic, West Germany. The newly elected government voted to make Bonn the capital. I was pleased that this small, unostentatious place without the reminders of recent history was to symbolize our new beginnings and democracy.

My mother in the Haus Pfeilbrand garden picking dahlias for guest rooms, summer 1948.

With new housing being built in cities and jobs in our recovering industries becoming available (mostly in northern Germany), the refugees began to move out of Haus Pfeilbrand to resettle. Mutti and Vater began taking in summer guests, many of them people who came to Berchtesgaden to reunite briefly with relatives in the Purtscheller Haus, the mountain house on Göll that straddled the German-Austrian border. We asked our visitors to write their names and comments on the blank parchment pages of the red leather book I had found in the Speer house on Obersalzberg, and I could think of no better use. From now on, instead of dedicating our vacation to the search for food, we were pulling our guests' suitcases up and down the mountain, helping to serve breakfasts, make up beds, and clean rooms.

The whole family worked very hard, but my spirits had begun to lift and I gladly arranged fresh summer flowers from my mother's garden in each guest room. During the second half of 1948, I began to feel that my Nazi girlhood had truly, finally, come to an end. With adolescent exuberance I rejoiced about my luck to be alive in a free and recovering country, filled with hopes and dreams. I could not know then of the lingering shadows, the everlasting legacy of the Third Reich that could not be expunged. I thought only of committing myself to building a democratic future, to assure that Germany would never again become a dictatorship, that we would never have war again, ever. We would make up for our guilt, and the world's people would be our friends again. At fourteen it seemed as simple as that. It had to be.

EPILOGUE

IN OCTOBER 1963, NINE MONTHS PREGNANT
with my second child, I stood among a mostly German-speaking
crowd at a pier in New York Harbor waiting to greet my mother,
who was about to arrive on the German ocean liner *Die Bremen* on
her first visit to the United States. I was living in Manhattan, settled comfortably in a very large, old apartment on Central Park
West with my husband, a Freudian psychoanalyst. As the ship
edged into its berth, my mind wandered back to my own arrival in
the United States only five years earlier.

A lumbering turbojet had brought me all the way from Munich
to San Francisco, where my husband-to-be was completing his
medical internship. I had met the young American doctor during
a springtime vacation in Rome, from where he had followed me
home to Berchtesgaden and proposed marriage after the briefest
of courtships. My ensuing emigration to the United States had
made my mother deeply unhappy and convinced my mountaineering friends that I was quite mad. For me the escape from
the shadows of my young life on the mountain, including my
mother's influence, seemed to promise wide-open horizons and
unknown freedom. Nonetheless, the long wait for my visa was
punctuated by anxiety about this unexplored future tempered by
the lure of adventure, the glamour of going to a foreign land, and
of course the conviction that I had found my perfect mate.

By the time I left Germany the *Wirtschaftswunder* (economic
miracle) under the free/social market economist Minister Ludwig
Erhard and Chancellor Konrad Adenauer was in full swing. Haus

Pfeilbrand had become the thriving *Pension* for which it had been intended, keeping my entire family in a flurry during the short but lucrative summer season. To Mutti's exasperation the house was ripped apart every few years for further adaptation to the modern world. Hot-water pipes were introduced, oil heaters replaced wood-burning stoves, and new wiring brought Mutti her first electrical appliances. Finally, an addition with more bedrooms and the incredible luxury of a full bathroom with a handheld shower replaced the woodshed that once housed the rabbit stalls and chicken coop.

My flight to the United States in 1958 stopped over in London, where I had previously spent a year as an au pair studying English. Two of my English friends from that time came to the airport to wish me well, reminding me that I had gone to England on a personal peace mission, namely, to forge friendships among people who had been enemies during World War II. When the Federal Republic of Germany under Konrad Adenauer agreed to join NATO that same year of 1955, I sided with the Social Democratic Party in strong opposition to German rearmament. It made me ill to think of young German men in uniform once again. Had the world not had enough of the German military? Had young men not had enough of playing soldier? Were they not still under the shadow of the horrible deeds that their elders had been used for or had committed? I was somewhat consoled by the fact that the German flag, now black, red, and gold striped, would fly among those of other nations, not alone as it had when the black swastika in the white circle on a fiery red background implied unlimited dominance and totalitarian power.

Here I stood now in my tentlike pregnancy dress waiting for the *Bremen* to disgorge its passengers. It occurred to me that I should warn my mother that many of my friends were Jewish and that she needed to guard against making an unthinking anti-Semitic remark. On my arrival in the United States my concerns about how Americans would receive a German immigrant were heightened when I discovered that most of my husband's friends and colleagues were Jewish. I was twenty-four then but had never knowingly met a Jew face-to-face. To my amazement most Jews, even if they had lost relatives in the Holocaust or were themselves refugees, showed generosity and acceptance toward me. A few, when they heard that I was from Berchtesgaden, became antagonistic, so that I learned to answer evasively questions about my hometown. For others I myself might be acceptable but Germany as a nation was not.

My first years in the States had not been easy. I was terribly homesick for the mountains and the familiar ways of Berchtesgaden. Peter, our son born in 1961, was a great joy, but as much as I was opposed to rigidity, how was I to reconcile my husband's latest child-rearing theories with traditional, German views on raising our little boy? I remained alone with my wartime memories and German suffering, as there was no one who would want to listen, not even my husband. No one understood that New York City fire sirens filled me with the terror of air-raid alarms or that I was paralyzed with fear during the Cuban missile crisis and could actually envision the nuclear missiles flying toward Manhattan destroying all I loved.

At last Mutti appeared, her graying braids pinned neatly around her head and her sun-wrinkled face immediately bringing a whiff of the old country and the mountain summer that had just passed. Tearfully we shook hands, and then I introduced her to her first American experience by hugging her and putting my face to hers. It took but a few days before she quite unexpectedly fell in love with the big city and its people. Aside from being an energetic, helpful grandmother to Peter and the brand-new baby girl, Karen Ingrid, born two weeks after her arrival, she became an eager explorer of the city. In her sensible brown walking shoes and tailored light gray tweed suit, she wandered through Manhattan's streets from Battery Park to the Cloisters. Soon she was pointing out to us, her supposed guides, a synagogue, a church, a fountain, a

My mother in New York City with grandson Peter and new granddaughter, Ingrid, on the way to a playground in Central Park, fall 1963.

small museum, or a pocket park that we had never noticed. "I wish I could have immigrated to this country when I was young," she said.

We talked about family and friends, cold war tensions and East German misery, but little about the war or the Nazi years. Elisabeth, by now a pretty sixteen-year-old attending the *Gymnasium*, was looking after Wasti during Mutti's absence. Ingrid, fluent in French and English, worked for Rosenthal Porcelain in Munich, dealing with its international customers. Sadly, my Pöhlmann grandfather had died when his bicycle collided with a delivery truck long before the worst times were over. We agreed that of all people he should have lived to put on a little weight and enjoy a peaceful old age. He would not know that the Marshall Fund loans and the Western Allies' need to create a strong buffer zone toward Stalin's East would save him from having to relive the frightful twenties. He did not witness the slow rebuilding, healing, and prospering of West Germany or the fact that his party, the Social

Democrats, would at last become a strong, major player in the new German democracy that emerged during the fifties.

I need not have worried about my mother making an anti-Semitic remark because she knew by now that racism, even of a verbal kind, was unacceptable. "We can't undo what happened," Mutti said during one of our rare, open talks about the issue. "All I can do is to pay my share of the financial reparation," which she pointed out, amounted to a total of ninety billion German marks. "I hope that it will reach the people who suffered and not those who just want to take advantage of us." Vestigial suspicion of the Jews remained. In fact, it seemed impossible for Mutti to feel personally responsible for the German crimes. But she accepted the collective guilt she shared with all Germans who had helped Hitler to power, paying no heed to his venomous intentions.

She believed that voting in local and national elections of the new German *Rechtsstaat* (constitutional state) was her solemn duty, also that her government would never let anything like the Holocaust happen again. I realized that she was still thoroughly conditioned to look to leadership, to the government, rather than to her own individual responsibility, let alone to personal activism, to guard the freedoms and guide the politics of the new republic. It was left to Ingrid, who, being of the next generation, would a few years later run for a Berchtesgaden town council seat under the banner of the Green Party, a brave minority stand in conservative Bavaria.

Mutti, now an average, elderly, and well-off German, did not hide her contempt for the German press with its sensational reporting of scandal and corruption and the public "washing of dirty linen" in political debate and controversy. She especially resented the vulgar commercialism of the advertising that paid for it all. "They should not allow that," she said, referring to some kind of authority that should have control over what was printed. Because of our difference in age and experience and my living in the United States, I, however, reveled in the many voices and choices, the freedom to speak out and the option to be actively engaged in environmental and other public causes at many different levels. I saw great fault in my mother's attitude and self-righteously told her so.

"Could the U.S. ever become a dictatorship?" my mother asked. "Never," I said, and tried to explain to her why. "This is the oldest democracy there is. Even in bad times there are open and fair elections and orderly transitions to any new government." I realized how thoroughly I enjoyed giving my mother a lecture. My categorical denial of possible threats to American democracy from within was leading me onto thin ice as I thought of the power of industry and the super-rich to influence the political process; of the McCarthy era, which I had just missed; and of racism. Mutti had listened. "If there were a bad economic downturn or perhaps a war with the Soviets, Americans too might accept a leader who promised to save them and the fatherland. We did not know how fast Hitler would change everything once he was chancellor. But he did." I told her as I had years ago in Berchtesgaden that nothing justified what Germany had done, and we ended our dialogue.

However, Mutti never failed to surprise me. She was with us in New York City the day President Kennedy was shot. Deeply shaken by the death of this young president who for her and many Germans stood for hope and strength at a time of cold war tension, she put on the darkest clothes she had brought and took a Greyhound bus to Washington to witness the funeral. Seeing Jackie Kennedy and her two small children follow the coffin must have reminded her of her own widowhood and deepened her sympathy.

In 1999, many years after Mutti's death, I visited Berchtesgaden with Mike Shor, my *Lebensgefährte* (life companion) of some twelve years. My life had again undergone many changes. Divorced, with grown children, a B.A. from Columbia University, and an M.P.A. from Harvard to my name, I wanted to show Mike, a Jew, where I had spent my childhood. Haus Pfeilbrand, which had become the summer home for Elisabeth and her family, who lived in Barcelona, still smelled of floor wax, damp loden coats, and decades of German cooking as it did when Mutti and my stepfather were alive. With Mike I walked once more up the Ober-salzbergstrasse to what had been Hitler's mountain. The physical evidence of the Nazi settlements was by now completely obliterated; even the presence of the U.S. Army had disappeared. Forests grew up where the Berghof had stood; a large golf course, a few guesthouses, and parking lots for tourists who took buses up to the Eagle's Nest had replaced the Nazi villas. Recently the Bavarian State had sold the Hotel Platterhof—Hotel General Walker under American operation—to private developers who planned to build a vast luxury hotel on the site. When we walked by the demolition site Mike noticed a sign forbidding the removal of even a stone or a brick, indicating the concern of German authorities that they might become Nazi memorabilia.

Mike Shor delighting in the Berchtesgaden mountains, summer 2000.

The question how to best remember Hitler's presence on the mountain had for many years rent the town. Many Berchtesgadeners would happily forget the notoriety the Third Reich had brought them. They were concerned that any marker would turn the mountain into a pilgrimage site frequented and revered by neo-Nazis from around the world.

If it had not been for signposts, I would not have found the new, small, and very modern information center that had recently been built near the site of the Berghof. The center, whose creation and content had once more stirred up emotions and debate, provides a photographic history of the mountain before and during the Nazi years, including photographs of Nazi victims and crimes not directly related to the mountain but planned and commanded from it. Large numbers of serious young Germans were slowly making their way through the exhibit, shaking their heads in disbelief as they entered into a small section of Hitler's bunker that was preserved as part of the exhibit.

Mike and I took a bus back into town for dinner with Ingrid, the only one of us three sisters who had remained in Berchtesgaden with her husband and two sons. Neither she nor my brother-in-law had been up to the visitors center, arguing that the benign beauty of the pre-Hitler years was receiving short shrift and that Hitler's twelve years on the mountain might better be forgotten. We also visited Trudi—the old Reitlechners were long dead—who in her seventies was not well but summed up her feelings about Nazi Germany the same way many others did: "Die Deutschen waren alle verrueckt damals" (The Germans were all mad at the time). The forms of denial or reconciliation with the past were manifold, always inadequate, and often pathetic.

□ □

IN DECEMBER OF THE FOLLOWING YEAR I visited with Tante Emilie, who had just turned ninety-three. Long since retired, she lived near the city of Kassel in a comfortable, light room with a sliding door that opened onto a small, carefully kept garden. She had access to a very cold kitchen and a bathroom down the hall where she sponged herself daily with cold water. There was room for me on her guest sofa. Since she walked poorly, a young German draftee who had elected to perform social services instead of military service came every morning to help her make up her bed, take care of chores, and do the shopping.

Tante Emilie still loved to laugh, tell old tales, and reveal my family's secrets, which she had, after all, observed and taken a part in over three generations. Since it was Christmastime, I had brought her an arrangement of evergreen branches with red candles that we lit and watched silently for a while. The two of us sang a few old carols before we began to talk about the past. Tante Emilie was proud that she had not been a Nazi, yet she too had had to come to terms with what had happened. She did not deny or make excuses about the *Konzentration* and death camps, but even for her it was difficult not to become defensive, seeking to stop and divert the conversation away from the painful topic. After a pause she told me of two horrendous weeks of almost continuous bombardment of Kassel, after which, when she surfaced from the shelter, most of the city had been leveled and burned. It was as if she hoped that her own suffering could somehow lighten the guilt she felt about the Nazi crimes. She still blamed herself for the time when she had raised her hand in the Hitler greeting as he drove past us on the Obersalzbergstrasse, and for joining the mandatory weekly political meetings to save her job at the institution that employed her at the time. I realized after a while that her search for answers had led her to God. She had become deeply religious, finding reconciliation, spiritual renewal, and hope for the future in her

Tante Emilie at age ninety-three talking about the past, December 2000.

Lutheran faith. She talked fondly of the Protestant nuns at the retreat center that she visited several weeks every year to gather strength and of the parson who came to talk and pray with her if she was too ill to go to church.

The Nazi years have left their mark on all who lived through them regardless which side they were on and how they came to terms with that past. Part of my Nazi legacy was that for the longest time I felt instinctively scared of authority figures—of teachers, policemen, anyone in uniform—and had to catch myself

My sister, Ingrid, and I revisiting childhood scenes. In the background are Kehlstein, Hoher Göll, and Hoher Brett.

from being unduly impressed by them. On the other hand I had resolved that what took place under Hitler could not be allowed ever to happen again. I promised myself that I would personally watch out for threats against the democracy I chose to live in. I would use and defend my right to march safely in protests against sexism and racism and for peace, speak openly with anyone about my views, and be critical of my chosen country and its government without fear. Over time I have altered my uncompromising pacifist position of the postwar years, recognizing that free countries need to be prepared to respond to aggression, but I firmly believe that unjust, unprovoked, aggressive wars can no longer be the way of civilized nations.

My adult life has afforded me the good fortune and the luxury to live freely both in Germany and in the United States, to raise my children well fed, well clothed, and well educated away from terror or war. I was able to work in an area that I care deeply about: the protection of our natural world, its precious balance and beauty in the United States and, in the past decade, even in Eastern Europe. Slowly the stigma of being German has receded, and I am coming to terms with the memories of my life as a girl on what for a short, dark time was Hitler's mountain.

ACKNOWLEDGMENTS

Throughout the writing of this memoir I was supported and encouraged by family and friends. The book, however, would not have become a reality had it not been for three very special women to whom I am deeply indebted. Joyce Seltzer first suggested years ago that I tell my story, and when I finally began, she generously and lovingly shared her clarity of vision, tremendous professional knowledge, and unerring advice. Susan Heath read, critiqued, and helped to refine the manuscript through many drafts with infinite patience, wisdom, and immense editorial skill. Susan Clampitt, always at my side, raised important questions about women in war, mother-daughter relationships under stress, and how children overcome the experience of violence.

While of course these are my own memories and I am fully responsible for the way I recount them and for changing some names, I am extremely grateful to members of my family whose goodwill and help were crucial for the project. Peter Hunt, my son, was always interested in the progress of my work and provided astute comments along with occasional admonitions for me to push harder. Daughter Ingrid forgave my preoccupation with writing even when I was officially baby-sitting for Leah and Jodi, my beloved new granddaughters. Very special thanks to my sister Ingrid Königer (née Paul) who wined and dined me during research visits in Berchtesgaden and who provided confirmation and additional information about our childhood. Spending days and weeks finding, copying, and mailing family photos and documents, she and Albrecht, her husband, contributed immeasurably to the book.

Thanks also to my sister Elisabeth Pfnür Herrero of Barcelona, for her steadfast support. My four Pöhlmann cousins in Selb graciously hosted me and submitted to taped interviews, and cousin Ingrid Hofmann (née Pöhlmann) kindly searched her attic for documents and photos and made them available.

Sadly my mother had died by the time I began to write. However, my thanks to Emilie Graupner (Tante Emilie), Mutti's childhood friend, who at her very old age was a cordial host and wonderful storyteller. She enlightened me on many points of my family history and provided vivid testimony about life in the 1920s and the Nazi dictatorship she had hated.

It is too late to thank Edeltraud Martin (née Trudi Reitlechner)—she died two years ago—for her willingness to talk to me about life in Haus Linden, my father, my mother's years as a widow, and her own journey through Hitler's war and the postwar period. I will never forget her or her contributions to the book. Among other friends from my youth who shared their recollections of the Nazi era with me were Gertraud Keyler (née Oberndörfer), Else Dehmel, Annemarie Richter, and Gerd Moors. Without the unwavering support and encouragement of many present-day friends I might have given up at various points along the way. I appreciated the thoughtful comments of and discussions with Maury Devine, Claudia Dissel, and Helen Nienhueser, my good friends from the Kennedy School for Government at Harvard (class of 1985); Marianne Ginsburg of the German Marshall Fund; Eliza Klose of ISAR (Initiative for Social Action and Renewal in Eurasia); Hilary Maddux; Gwen Moore; Isadore Seltzer; Terry Waltz; Robbie Ross Tisch; and Sigrid Thomas, herself a child of the Nazi era.

I am most grateful to my agent, Sarah Burnes, who believed in the book, helped shape it, and with immense enthusiasm and professionalism made sure that it would be published. Very special thanks to Jennifer Brehl, my wonderful editor at William Morrow, without whose fine perception, probing questions, and comments the manuscript would not have gone through the kind of thorough review it needed. In addition I much appreciated the caring assistance and vigilant attention to details given by Katherine Nintzel, also at William Morrow.

Several workshops at the Writer's Center in Bethesda, Maryland, were crucial to honing my writing skills, and Nan Heneson was tremendously helpful in her workshop as well as later, when she provided editorial comments and feedback during the final writing phase.

Finally, my boundless gratitude goes to Mike Shor, my companion of the past seventeen years. He never had any doubt about my endeavor, and while he did not get to read the story in progress—an agreement we made—he was willing to garden, to shop, to cook, to forgo hikes and walks, and stayed calm and optimistic throughout. His huge amount of work on the photo search in the collections of the National Archives was invaluable. His love and patience sustain me. Thank you, Mike.